CULTURES IN FLUX

LOWER–CLASS VALUES, PRACTICES, AND RESISTANCE IN LATE IMPERIAL RUSSIA

Edited by

Stephen P. Frank and Mark D. Steinberg

CULTURES IN FLUX

CULTURES IN FLUX

LOWER-CLASS VALUES, PRACTICES, AND RESISTANCE IN LATE IMPERIAL RUSSIA

*Edited by Stephen P. Frank and
Mark D. Steinberg*

PRINCETON UNIVERSITY PRESS

PRINCETON, NEW JERSEY

LIBRARY OF CONGRESS CATALOGING-IN-PUBLICATION DATA

CULTURES IN FLUX : LOWER-CLASS VALUES, PRACTICES, AND RESISTANCE
IN LATE IMPERIAL RUSSIA / STEPHEN P. FRANK AND
MARK D. STEINBERG, EDITORS
P. CM.
INCLUDES BIBLIOGRAPHICAL REFERENCES AND INDEX.
ISBN 0-691-03435-4 — ISBN 0-691-00106-5 (PBK.)
1. RUSSIA—SOCIAL LIFE AND CUSTOMS—1533–1917. 2. WORKING CLASS—
RUSSIA. 3. PEASANTRY—RUSSIA. 4. POPULAR CULTURE—RUSSIA—
HISTORY—19TH CENTURY. 5. FOLKLORE—RUSSIA. I. FRANK, STEPHEN,
1955–. II. STEINBERG, MARK D., 1958–.
DK222.C85 1994 306.4′0947—DC20 93-43708 CIP

THIS BOOK HAS BEEN COMPOSED IN ADOBE SABON

PRINCETON UNIVERSITY PRESS BOOKS ARE PRINTED
ON ACID-FREE PAPER AND MEET THE GUIDELINES
FOR PERMANENCE AND DURABILITY OF THE COMMITTEE
ON PRODUCTION GUIDELINES FOR BOOK LONGEVITY
OF THE COUNCIL ON LIBRARY RESOURCES

PRINTED IN THE UNITED STATES OF AMERICA

1 3 5 7 9 10 8 6 4 2

1 3 5 7 9 10 8 6 4 2
(PBK.)

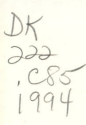

CONTENTS

CONTRIBUTORS

Daniel R. Brower (University of California, Davis) most recently published *The Russian City between Tradition and Modernity, 1850–1900* (1990).

Barbara Alpern Engel (University of Colorado, Boulder) has written, among other works, *Between the Fields and the City: Women, Work, and Family in Russia, 1861–1914* (1994).

Stephen P. Frank (University of California, Los Angeles) is author of the forthcoming *Cultural Conflict, Criminality, and Justice in Rural Russia, 1856–1914.*

Hubertus F. Jahn (Friedrich-Alexander Universität, Erlangen, Germany) has completed a forthcoming study of patriotic culture during World War I.

Al'bin M. Konechnyi works in St. Petersburg at the State Museum of the History of the City and has published articles on various aspects of life in St. Petersburg during the nineteenth century.

Boris N. Mironov (Institute of Russian History, Russian Academy of Sciences, St. Petersburg) has written widely on Russian social history; his most recent works are *Russkii gorod v 1740–1860-e gody* (1990) and *Istoriia v tsifrakh* (1991).

Joan Neuberger (University of Texas, Austin) is the author of *Hooliganism: Crime, Culture, and Power in St. Petersburg, 1900–1914* (1993).

Robert A. Rothstein (University of Massachusetts, Amherst) writes on Russian and Soviet popular song.

Mark D. Steinberg (Yale University) is the author of *Moral Communities: The Culture of Class Relations in the Russian Printing Industry, 1867–1907* (1992).

Christine D. Worobec (Kent State University) is the author of *Peasant Russia: Family and Community in the Post-Emancipation Period* (1991).

ACKNOWLEDGMENTS

MANY PEOPLE have contributed to the making of this book. The authors deserve greatest thanks for their thoughtful participation and their patience. They prove that intellectual individuality and scholarly community can indeed coexist.

Many others were also involved in this collaboration. The volume was conceived as a way to encourage more critical discussion and debate about lower-class cultures in Russia as well as to reflect work in this newly emerging field, most of which was still unpublished. We invited a number of people to propose essays that would reflect their research as well as grapple with problems of interpretation and theory. Most of the papers were first presented at several panels on popular culture at the 1990 and 1991 annual meetings of the American Association for the Advancement of Slavic Studies. Discussions continued among the contributors and editors as papers were revised. To facilitate revisions and help the editors select which works to include, each paper was critically reviewed by at least two other participants and an outside reader. All of these presentations, discussions, and evaluations have enhanced this collection—and, we hope, contributed to the development of informed and critical perspectives on the history of Russian popular culture generally.

We would like to express our appreciation and thanks to the many scholars who were involved in these discussions, in addition to those whose articles appear in this volume: Chris Chulos, Eugene Clay, Catherine Clay, Gregory Freeze, Abbott Gleason, Louise McReynolds, Roberta Manning, Brenda Meehan-Waters, Priscilla Roosevelt, Richard Stites, and William Mills Todd III. We are also grateful for the evaluations by the reviewers chosen by Princeton University Press. At the Press itself, Lauren Osborne did much to encourage and support the project. Nancy Trotic edited the manuscript with impressive care, thoughtfulness, and skill. Finally, the editors wish publicly to thank one another for their collegiality, friendship, tolerance, and good humor.

CULTURES IN FLUX

INTRODUCTION

Mark D. Steinberg and Stephen P. Frank

PARADOXICALLY, as our knowledge of postemancipation Russian society and culture has grown, we have produced a historical portrait that is increasingly rough, fractured, and blurred. The coexistence of the traditional and the new, of inertia and vibrancy, is increasingly familiar to students of late imperial Russia—and, indeed, of Soviet Russia as well. But these simple dichotomies only begin to convey the complex dynamism and fluidity of Russian society and culture as social relationships, values, and structures were battered and reconstructed. Russia's emerging public sphere—the civic space that, for many contemporaries and historians, constitutes the essential foundation for a democratic society—was a terrain in flux.

Our use of the seemingly archaic term *lower-class* in the title of this collection is meant to reflect this tenuous relativity and ambiguity of social boundaries and, thus, the inadequacy of simple and rigid categories such as *peasants* or *workers* to express the variety of situations, mentalities, and even identities among the urban and rural poor. Economic and demographic changes during the nineteenth and early twentieth centuries chipped away at an archaic, though still functional, paradigm of social estates. Social divisions deepened, but boundaries were also violated and renegotiated, and new actors appeared on the civic stage, often bearing new political and social claims. From Russia's rapidly growing and dynamic urban sector, for example, the emergence of professional and middle classes during the decades that followed the great reforms helped to reshape (and confuse) established identities as well as the country's social, intellectual, and cultural landscapes. The search for work and a better life saw thousands of peasant villagers journey to urban industrial centers and factory towns, swelling the ranks of the working class and creating a significant number of "worldly" peasants who served as cultural mediators between city and countryside while also increasing tensions and generational conflicts in their rural communities. Within the emerging proletariat, urbanized and literate workers grew steadily more conscious of their new working-class identity, but also increasingly distinct from the "dark masses," as they saw them, of workers and peasants. Groups as diverse as avant-garde artists and worker-intellectuals were among those standing astride both old and new class borders, at once alienated from their social milieux and claiming an influential voice. Meanwhile, philanthropic concerns among the educated elite led to diverse efforts to improve the condition of the lower classes, ranging from universal primary education to the dissemination of popular science, from soup kitchens to public-hygiene campaigns, from social insurance to rural cooperatives—all of which contributed to a greater mingling of classes and cultures. The aging autocracy contributed much to the unevenness of this development: with the one hand it encouraged economic modernization, while with the other it fought to maintain social order and guard its monopoly on power.

Cultural change was inseparably intertwined with this economic and social metamorphosis. Cultural boundaries blurred and were redefined as economic and social change stimulated a new dynamism in Russia's widening cultural arena. Consumer production and consumption, for instance, encouraged a transformation of material culture that altered the face of daily life and thought for many Russians. Changes in fashion, home decorating, diet, and tastes occurred not only among the gentry and urban middle classes but also in working-class communities and rural hamlets. Electricity and trams—to take but two late-nineteenth-century symbols of modernity and progress—spread to distant provincial capitals, creating at least a superficial presence of urban "civilization" outside Russia's major cities. Railroads (and even bicycles) moved former serfs, workers, and members of the educated elite around the country at distances and speeds unimaginable only a few decades earlier, inspiring new notions of time and space.

The rapid expansion of literacy among the lower classes (particularly from the 1890s) combined with a striking growth of print media to bring a wide range of impressions to lower-class readers. In cities and industrial towns, reading had become an integral part of working-class culture by the turn of the century. Rural areas, too, saw public reading rooms and free libraries open in large numbers starting in the late 1880s, initiated either by peasants themselves or by officials, clergy, or educated reformers. Advances in medicine and science were disseminated among the country's "dark masses" through various media—although propagandists of progress found their work difficult because, they complained, these new ideas frequently clashed with existing popular customs and worldviews.

Turn-of-the-century innovations in entertainment, such as popular theater, cabarets, magic-lantern shows, cinema, fêtes, People's Houses, workers' clubs, and tearooms, sprang up alongside more traditional forms of sociability and festivity (including the older tavern and pub, local festivals, and church processions) and played an important role in stretching the boundaries and repertoire of popular culture. Workers, peasants, and other groups navigated and appropriated these new media and arenas in a process that simultaneously served to reinforce and reinvent the culture of Russia's lower classes. As did midcentury western Europe and North America, late imperial Russia witnessed a transformation of the very concept of leisure, which became the subject of widespread public, clerical, and official debate between the 1880s and 1917. Classes, genders, generations, and cultures continually mingled—and sometimes collided—in a dynamic cultural space that the phrase *popular culture* only weakly represents.

Although recent scholarship on late imperial Russia has analyzed important aspects of this changing society (see the bibliography at the end of this volume), much remains unexamined or still superficially understood. Least of all do we understand how these processes functioned and acquired meaning at the lowest levels of society, in the minds and lives of individual peasants, workers, and others. Despite the virtual obsession of Russia's educated elite with culture, including popular culture, historians have only begun to explore the cultural context within which lower-class Russians experienced, interpreted, appropriated, and sometimes resisted change, and the complex intertwining of culture, class, economics, and politics.

This collection of essays examines the dynamic cultural world of Russia's lower classes during the last decades of the prerevolutionary order. The authors recall neglected or forgotten stories about popular life and culture. They recount diverse tales of peasant death rites and religious beliefs, family relationships and brutalities, defiant women in confrontations with social and political authorities, determined efforts by educated outsiders to control and transform popular festivities, folk songs and their creators, scenes from urban amusement parks, expressions of popular patriotism, scandals and dramas of everyday life as reported in the penny press, the creative encounters of worker-writers with notions of the self and the individual, and the insolent outrages of street hooligans.

Beyond this narrative and reconstructive purpose, the authors of these essays raise issues of methodology and interpretation, echoing and sometimes influenced by studies of the cultures and societies of other countries and times (see the bibliography). The differences among the authors in approach, emphasis, and argument will be clear. Influenced by different intellectual traditions and innovations, examining different evidence, and inclined to different interpretations of the dynamics of Russian history, they do not present a uniform answer to questions about the character and direction of the changes in Russian society and culture before the revolution. Indeed, one of the purposes of this collection is to provoke new and more critical questions. Still, as we emphasize in this introduction, these essays taken together suggest patterns and trends in the development of lower-class lives and mentalities that go well beyond the particular subjects discussed. There is also, it may be said, a unity in the diversity of evidence and argument presented, which reflects not only interpretive differences but also different facets of a popular culture that was itself richly varied and contradictory.

The interrelationship between popular culture and material conditions, social relations, and the exercise of power is an important theme in virtually all of the essays in this collection. These studies treat Russian popular culture not as a static, uniform, and separate world, but as the varied expressive practices of groups of people as they interacted with the material, social, and cultural worlds around them. As the peasants in chapter 1 viewed the apparent boundary between life and death to be porous, the authors view the culture of Russia's lower classes as inseparable from the whole of Russian life.

As studies from other societies similarly attest, lower-class culture often reflected images and experiences from that larger world. The popular penny press, discussed here by Daniel Brower, dwelled on the ordinary hardships of life among its less powerful and less moneyed readers. Popular prints, music, and even circuses during World War I, Hubertus Jahn shows, integrated entertainment with evaluations of national and international affairs. "Folk songs"—a genre that also reminds us of the blurred boundary between urban and rural cultures—were extremely sensitive in both form and content to changes in the daily lives of their singers, as Robert Rothstein demonstrates. Indeed, music provided an exceptionally useful medium for both peasants and workers, who, in their capacity as makers of culture, composed original songs that addressed a broad range of social and economic issues as well as national politics. Even those peasant rituals viewed by outsiders as "customary" or "traditional" spoke of social conditions, relationships, and ongoing changes. Christine Worobec argues that encounters with epidemics, storms, droughts, and other phenomena of the natural world shaped Russian and Ukrainian death rituals in conjunction with Christian rites, while Boris Mironov notes the influence of agrarian economic and social relationships on peasant institutions and mentalities that stood as powerful cultural barriers against the threat of fundamental change brought by capitalism and social reform. This evidence of the social rootedness of culture does not, however, necessarily demonstrate simple material or social determination. The structured conditions of everyday life and the judgments and beliefs that made these experiences meaningful in people's own minds are more often understood here as each giving shape to one another, as part of the common fabric of human experience, knowledge, and action.

Just as the idea of culture cannot be detached from the whole of people's lives, neither can the idea of "popular" culture be abstracted from
the culture of the rest of society. In facing death, Worobec argues, peasants interpreted the natural world with the help of Christian and other
ideas that mingled far more harmoniously than traditional (and still dominant) views of the peasantry's "dual faith" would have us believe. Folk
songs, as Rothstein describes, incorporated new ideas about the individual and about personal relationships, new stories from the popular press,
and new melodies and motifs from the repertoire of professional song.
Workers who took up the pen to voice publicly their views of themselves
and of the world around them, as seen in Mark Steinberg's essay, similarly drew upon and reworked ideas and images from the commercial and
radical press, the intelligentsia's social criticism, and both popular and
high literature, as well as from everyday experience. In the public amusement parks (*uveselitel'nye sady*) of St. Petersburg, described here by
Al'bin Konechnyi, scenes from operas and ballets were no less popular
than folk dances and Gypsy songs for an audience in which industrial
workers rubbed shoulders with shopkeepers. Classes and genres similarly
intermixed in the penny press and in popular theaters, where an emerging
"mass culture"—promoted by market-sensitive entrepreneurs—embraced
factory workers, migrant laborers, peasants, petty merchants, salesclerks,
and even the illiterate.

Perhaps the most striking indication of the blurred boundaries defining
the popular—and of the sheer diversity of lower-class cultures—was the
harassment of respectable pedestrians on city streets by hooligans, as discussed by Joan Neuberger. These petty outrages and crass behavior were
not simple reflections of the life of the poor. Setting hooligan behavior
beside the equally outrageous creations and public performances by futurist writers and artists, Neuberger encourages us to reconsider our understanding of both hooliganism and futurism. At issue is not only their
influence on each other, but a deep and widespread revulsion before
bourgeois propriety, order, and values. Here, as in the other essays, culture appears most often as an arena of conflict in which a broad range of
forces found expression: social hostilities, lower-class demands for respect, transformative visions, and, as Stephen Frank and Neuberger both
stress, bourgeois fears of a breakdown of moral authority, social discipline, deference, and public order.

Several of these essays challenge the long-standing paradigm within
Russian historical studies that posits a rigid dichotomy of tradition versus
change. The engagement between lower-class culture and the surrounding world cannot be adequately described as a simple confrontation between the traditional and the innovative or modern. Established cultural

forms often proved remarkably flexible and adaptable in the face of new circumstances and ideas or able to absorb new elements without being fundamentally transformed. By the same token, new experiences, expressions, and ideas were reworked against a body of older practices and thought. A new respect for the individual, for example, was increasingly evident among lower-class Russians, though, as Steinberg suggests, this idea was subjected to distinctive readings as workers refracted it through their particular social experiences and needs. Similarly, the "rational" recreations and invented traditions that middle- and upper-class moral reformers introduced, as Frank describes, to replace the perceived disorder of popular entertainment were themselves often appropriated and transformed by the very groups whose behavior they had been designed to alter. Villagers and urban dwellers alike maintained and reordered "traditional" practices and embraced and reworked new ones by rationally evaluating their utility—defining usefulness according to expectations, values, and desires, in response to pressures from within and outside their communities, and in accord with their understanding of the nature of the world around them.

Conventional assumptions about the separation of cultural creation and consumption are also treated critically in most of these essays. Brower, Jahn, and Konechnyi each show in different ways that we cannot understand culture produced "for" the people in isolation from its "implied" audience. Market-sensitive writers, editors, and cultural entrepreneurs shaped messages and forms not at will but as they imagined would best attract and retain a mass following. Popular artistic creativity—folk songs, stories, poetry, criticism—also had an intended audience in mind. Cultural production and consumption were parts of a common process in which both reader and author participated in shaping cultural forms and expressions.

Popular culture, like popular social life, was far from unified and harmonious, but reflected the fractures, estrangements, and conflicts within the lower classes. Indeed, though the cultural expressions described in these pages were most often collective practices and served ostensibly to strengthen and defend popular communities, they could not avoid reflecting the divisions within these aspiring or even well-established communities. In village rites and festivities we see divisions between generations, men and women, the strong and the weak, the rich and the poor, and the individual and the community, as well as between neighboring communities. The rural "cult of collectivity" itself, Mironov argues provocatively, disguised and promoted authoritarian domination of the old over the young, parents over children, men over women. Similarly, workers who fervently advocated class solidarity and struggle often felt deeply distant from the majority of workers, whom they ceaselessly berated for their appalling ignorance, drunkenness, and passivity. And in the countryside after 1905, peasants carried out violent assaults upon villagers who withdrew from the communes to live on independent farmsteads, while these "separators" sought out new and distinct identities. At the same time, fractures within social groups provided important sources of creativity and leadership. The separate roles of women in village life and the special license often accorded unruly women, in Russia as elsewhere, facilitated village solidarity and collective action. Similarly, culturally marginal workers out of step with the common laborer played an essential role in organizing workers, introducing them to subversive new ideas, and even promoting among them notions of class identity.

These studies also describe popular protest and defiance, especially practices not limited to moments of open rebellion. Resistance and challenge to subordination, powerlessness, and oppression appeared in folk songs and funeral laments; in the popularity of penny-press tales about abusive employers, greedy merchants, negligent landlords, rude sales-clerks, and cruel husbands; in the transgressions by worker-poets onto the stylistic terrain of high culture and in the uses to which received ideas were put; in the stubborn "vulgarity" of the poor; and in the more calcu-lated humiliations hooligans wreaked on respectable citizens in both town and country.

Critical voices such as these were not simply manifestations of social rebellion translated into the language of culture, however. Cultural con-formity and the sharing of values across class lines stood beside dissent and resistance. Among the urban poor, as Brower and Steinberg describe, notions of fairness, human dignity, and respect for the individual nur-tured feelings of moral outrage against oppression but were also part of a civic moral discourse that transcended class division. During the war, Jahn shows, many patriotic motifs were understood and appreciated by socially diverse audiences, although lower-class audiences were far more likely to jeer the kaiser than cheer the tsar—popular patriotism existed, but it was distinctive, adaptive, and relatively fragile. The same may be said of gender as of class. As Barbara Engel argues, even when village women momentarily stepped beyond their culturally imposed passivity and submissiveness amidst open rebellion, they acted mainly as wives and mothers to defend traditional structures of family and community. As in many societies, subordinate groups often sought simultaneously to be in-cluded in a larger polity and social community and to assert their own separate interests and collective power. Social resistance was as ambigu-ous as it was pervasive.

Subordinate classes were also often implicated in their own domina-tion, for the exercise of oppressive power was not limited to the ruling classes. The hooligan's uncultured behavior, after all, offended not only the bourgeoisie. "Respectable" peasants, until well into the Soviet period, punished village hooligans by violent mob justice, or *samosud*. Peasants maintained strict codes of morality and conformity by humiliating, beating, or banishing errant individuals. An oppressive patriarchy reigned within peasant families—indeed, throughout much of lower-class social life—while village elders and officials struggled to maintain control over a younger generation corrupted by urban ways. Similarly, "cultured" and "conscious" workers not only criticized the heavy drinking, slovenly habits, and common cultural tastes of the majority of workers, but sought to impose on them their own standards of cultivation, morality, and, eventually, political radicalism—goals that, apart from the politics, were strikingly similar to those propounded in temperance societies controlled by the Orthodox church or by middle-class moral reformers. In the view of Mironov—who is thinking also of Soviet times—much of Russia's traditional culture was stifling and oppressive, especially toward the individual.

These essays describe a variety of popular cultural expressions, suggest patterns, challenge certain established paradigms, and consider methods for study. But they do not propose a finished portrait. The collection offers an admittedly motley picture, plentifully decorated with overlapping categories and ambiguous meanings as well as conflicting interpretations. This seems appropriate, after all, since our knowledge and understanding of lower-class culture in imperial Russia is still fragmentary. But it may also be that this picture of variety, disorder, and ambiguity is the most plausible representation of a vital and changing culture.

1

DEATH RITUAL AMONG RUSSIAN AND UKRAINIAN PEASANTS: LINKAGES BETWEEN THE LIVING AND THE DEAD

Christine D. Worobec

IN THE PREINDUSTRIAL and early industrial worlds, people had to confront death frequently. The average life expectancy was much lower than it is today in developed countries, and sudden death, brought on by epidemics or famine, was a regular phenomenon. Individuals had to deal with the loss of not only the elderly, but also wives, husbands, sisters, brothers, and other adults in the prime of life—as well as children, many of whom died before the age of ten.[1]

Religious beliefs and the enactment of elaborate death rituals that provided linkages between the living and the dead helped the bereaved cope with the continual loss of relatives, helpmates, and actual or potential laborers for the family economy. Belief and ritual also provided the hope and strength to continue with life's struggles: "It is religion, with its attendant beliefs and practices, which legitimates death and enables the individual 'to go on living in society after the death of significant others and to anticipate his own death with, at the very least, terror sufficiently miti-

An earlier version of this essay was presented at the annual meeting of the American Association for the Advancement of Slavic Studies in Washington, D.C., in October 1990. The comments of J. Eugene Clay, Chris Chulos, Barbara Evans Clements, Stephen Frank, and Gregory Freeze were invaluable in helping me make substantial revisions, as was a National Endowment for the Humanities 1992 Summer Stipend, which permitted me to do research in Helsinki.

[1] The mortality rate in imperial Russia declined steadily, from 36.9 per thousand in 1861–70 to 34.2 per thousand in 1892–1900 and 31.0 per thousand in 1901–5. A. G. Rashin, *Naselenie Rossii za 100 let (1811–1913 gg.): Statisticheskie ocherki* (Moscow: Gosudarstvennoe statisticheskoe izdatel'stvo, 1956), 5. Nevertheless, these rates were extremely high and reflective of a premodern society. More than 25 percent of infants died within the first year of life; an additional 20 percent did not reach adulthood. See Peter Gatrell, *The Tsarist Economy, 1850–1917* (London: B. T. Batsford, 1986), 31–37; and V. O. Demich, "Pediatriia u russkago naroda," *Vestnik obshchestvennoi gigieny, sudebnoi i prakticheskoi meditsiny* 11, no. 2 (August 1891), pt. 2:128.

gated so as not to paralyze the continued performance of the routines of everyday life.'"[2] As conditions for life improved and life expectancy grew significantly, and as death became more remote from the experience of the living—today, people generally die in hospitals rather than at home, and morticians instead of relatives prepare the body for burial—many of the traditional death rituals disappeared, leaving only a shell of beliefs to help (often inadequately) the living cope with the loss of a loved one.

Death ritual is normally a subject of inquiry for anthropologists. Only recently have historians of European societies turned their attention to this intriguing subject, asking many of the questions that anthropologists have devised for their field studies and posing new ones that provide a historical framework for the study of societies.[3] Death rituals reveal a great deal about past societies, including their mores and worldviews, the power relationships between the elderly and the young as well as between men and women, the individual's relationship to the community, and the interchange and tensions between clerical and popular or unlearned religion. The examination of death ritual among Russian and Ukrainian peasants in imperial Russia in the last decades of the nineteenth century attempts to elucidate these variables. These two peasant societies, despite variations among regions and even villages, shared a subsistence economy and common cultural patterns, particularly in the belief structure of the Orthodox religion.

The sources documenting death ritual among postemancipation Russian and Ukrainian peasants are largely from nineteenth-century ethnographers intent on preserving the lore of the traditional village, which they worried would disappear once urbanization and a cash economy captured the imagination of the peasantry. The sources are problematic in that they describe only practices that occurred outside the institutional church. They tend to be silent on Orthodox ritual and only mention in passing the priest's role in the funeral and subsequent commemorative services. This lack of interest in the official ritual may be explained in part by the familiarity of the authors and their educated readers with Orthodox practices, which they felt did not need further comment, and in part by the authors' disdain for the Orthodox church—a sentiment shared by a significant segment of educated Russian society. They considered the church unresponsive to the needs of society at large. For them, it had become a bulwark of the autocracy, beginning in the early eighteenth century with Peter the Great's abolition of the Moscow Patriarchate and

[2] Loring M. Danforth and Alexander Tsiaras, *The Death Rituals of Rural Greece* (Princeton: Princeton University Press, 1982), 31.

[3] The pioneering effort in this regard is Philippe Ariès, *The Hour of Our Death*, trans. Helen Weaver (New York: Alfred A. Knopf, 1981).

relegation of the church to the status of a bureaucratic wing of the government. The ethnographers' search for pagan remnants in peasant religious beliefs testified to the institutional church's ineffectiveness. Indeed, these observers in the field sometimes took an ahistorical approach, assuming that religious practices and their meanings were immutable and that nineteenth-century peasant beliefs were indicative of the medieval worldview.[4]

Russian Orthodox ecclesiastics and clergy added to the perception of the peasant as heathen. In his memoir, four years before the emancipation, the parish priest I. S. Belliustin bemoaned the fact that

> out of one hundred male peasants, a maximum of ten can read the creed and two or three short prayers (naturally, without the slightest idea or comprehension of what they have read). Out of one thousand men, at most two or three know the Ten Commandments; so far as the women are concerned, nothing even needs to be said here. And this is Orthodox Rus'! What a shame and disgrace! And our pharisees dare to shout for everyone to hear that only in Russia has the faith been preserved undefiled, in Rus', where two-thirds of the people have not the slightest conception of the faith![5]

Belliustin went on to characterize Russian peasants as not having "the remotest conception of anything spiritual."[6] He sought to awaken his ecclesiastical superiors to the problems plaguing the institutional church, particularly the unsatisfactory education and untenable economic position of parish priests, who were dependent on the good graces of their parishioners. In his opinion, it was no wonder that with ill-prepared, alcoholic priests and nonordained servitors, the church failed miserably in its mission to reach the masses. While Belliustin was correct in pointing out the church's failure to move beyond the liturgical framework and teach peasants the catechism, he took his denial of the faith of illiterate peasants too far. Faith cannot be reduced to the reading of the Creed and a few prayers and the recitation of the Ten Commandments. The judgment of the Orthodox church, with its increasingly rationalist views from the mid-eighteenth century onward, denied popular beliefs any validity, wishing to assert a monopoly over mediation with supernatural forces.

---

[4] The notable exceptions are D. K. Zelenin, *Ocherki Russkoi mifologii*, vol. 1, *Umershie neestestvennoiu smert'iu i rusalki* (Petrograd: Tip. A. V. Orlova, 1916); and P. V. Ivanov, "Ocherk vozzrenii krest'ianskago naseleniia Kupianskago uezda na dushu i na zagrobnuiu zhizni," *Sbornik Khar'kovskago istoriko-filologicheskago obshchestva* 18 (1909): 244–55.

[5] I. S. Belliustin, *Description of the Clergy in Rural Russia: The Memoir of a Nineteenth-Century Parish Priest*, trans. Gregory L. Freeze (Ithaca, N.Y.: Cornell University Press, 1985), 35.

[6] Ibid., 125.

Scholars of the Orthodox church and religious practices of the Russian and Ukrainian masses have tended to agree with nineteenth-century observers of the peasantry, stressing the dual nature of Orthodoxy as a syncretic amalgam of Christian and pagan beliefs. They continue to present nineteenth-century peasant beliefs as having been strongly influenced by the pagan past and at times insist that these beliefs mirrored the thought pattern of the masses throughout the centuries. According to the preeminent scholar of Russian Orthodoxy, G. P. Fedotov, "the Russian peasant has been living in the Middle Ages through the nineteenth century."[7] One literary scholar more recently expressed astonishment "at the degree to which the Russian peasant succeeded in preserving his ancient, pre-Christian customs and worldview."[8]

It is time for historians of the Russian Empire to follow the lead of social historians of western Europe by critically approaching ethnographic and religious sources and examining the belief systems of the masses on their merits, heavily influenced as they were by the doctrines of the official church.[9] This means going beyond the binary model of paganism and Orthodoxy, or *dvoeverie*, and rejecting the assumption that nineteenth-century beliefs and rituals among Russian and Ukrainian peasants mirrored those of the ancient past until those beliefs and rituals can be systematically compared with medieval texts. That is not to deny the flexibility of Christianity in both western and eastern Europe to incorporate pagan elements during the conversion process, but to shift the focus away from the early history of the Orthodox church to the living practices of the faithful in the nineteenth century, when distinguishing between Christian and pagan elements was no longer relevant. Otherwise, the label

[7] *The Russian Religious Mind: Kievan Christianity, the Tenth to the Thirteenth Centuries* (New York: Harper Torchbooks, 1960), 3.

[8] Linda J. Ivanits, *Russian Folk Belief* (Armonk, N.Y.: M. E. Sharpe, 1989), 3. For another recent ahistorical approach to popular religion, see Joanna Hubbs, *Mother Russia: The Feminine Myth in Russian Culture* (Bloomington: Indiana University Press, 1988).

[9] See, for example, Ellen Badone, ed., *Religious Orthodoxy and Popular Faith in European Society* (Princeton: Princeton University Press, 1990); William Christian, Jr., *Apparitions in Late Medieval and Renaissance Spain* (Princeton: Princeton University Press, 1981); idem, *Local Religion in Sixteenth Century Spain* (Princeton: Princeton University Press, 1981); Natalie Zemon Davis, "From 'Popular Religion' to Religious Cultures," in *Reformation Europe: A Guide to Research*, ed. Steven Ozment (St. Louis, Mo.: Center for Reformation Research, 1982), 321–42; Charles Stewart, *Demons and the Devil: Moral Imagination in Modern Greek Society* (Princeton: Princeton University Press, 1991); and Keith Thomas, *Religion and the Decline of Magic* (New York: Charles Scribner's Sons, 1971). Among historians of Russia, Gregory Freeze has taken the lead in challenging the notion that popular Orthodoxy in Russia was a static belief structure by looking at the ways in which the church tried to raise the level of "spiritual literacy" among the masses between 1750 and 1850. See "The Rechristianization of Russia: The Church and Popular Religion, 1750–1850," *Studia Slavica Finlandensia* 7 (1990): 101–36, esp. 102.

"Christian" becomes meaningless, referring only to a tiny spiritual and educated elite that knew how to interpret evangelical texts and church dogma correctly.[10] Russian and Ukrainian peasants believed themselves to be practitioners of Orthodoxy, drawing upon Christian symbols and magical rites to guard against the vagaries of everyday life. Such an approach does not ignore the Orthodox church's censure of some peasant practices, but pinpoints the reality that in all cultures "religion as practiced" does not always meet the ideal of prescribed religion.[11] It also underscores the fact that clerical beliefs and what the church termed superstitious beliefs stemmed from the same worldview.[12]

Certainly, to the nineteenth- and twentieth-century scientific mind, the popular belief system was riddled with superstition revolving around apparitions, fairies, magical healing, and the fantastic. But the very word *superstition* is a value judgment of a largely secular world. Such condescension ignores the fact that peasants took these beliefs seriously, confident that they were complementary to the magical rituals of the Orthodox church. Christianity, after all, stressed such things as the immortality of the soul, linkages between the living and dead through prayer and memorial services, the purification of holy water, healing through prayer, and the power of the cross, all of which the peasants absorbed and elaborated upon in making their world intelligible and manageable. According to anthropologist Clifford Geertz, "For those able to embrace them, and for so long as they are able to embrace them, religious symbols provide a cosmic guarantee not only for their ability to comprehend the world, but also, comprehending it, to give a precision to their feeling, a definition to their emotions which enables them, morosely or joyfully, grimly or cavalierly, to endure it."[13] This study looks at the ways in which late-nineteenth-century Russian and Ukrainian peasants, largely in conformity with Orthodox practice, coped with the world around them and healed the rift created by the loss of individuals from the community and family. In examining the Ukrainian peasants' understanding of life after death in Khar'kov province, an ethnographer of that time rejected the opinions of

[10] Mary R. O'Neill makes this point in a review essay in response to Jean Delumeau's conclusion that the European masses were never fully Christianized. See "From 'Popular' to 'Local' Religion: Issues in Early Modern European Religious History," *Religious Studies Review* 12, nos. 3–4 (July–October 1986): 222–23.

[11] Ellen Badone, introduction to Badone, *Religious Orthodoxy*, 6.

[12] Mary R. O'Neill reaches a similar conclusion in her examination of clerical culture and folkloric or popular culture in sixteenth-century Italy. See "*Sacerdote ovvero strione*: Ecclesiastical and Superstitious Remedies in Sixteenth-Century Italy," in *Understanding Popular Culture: Europe from the Middle Ages to the Nineteenth Century*, ed. Steven L. Kaplan (Berlin: Mouton Publishers, 1984), 75.

[13] "Religion as a Cultural System," in *The Interpretation of Cultures: Selected Essays* (New York: Basic Books, 1973), 104.

many of his contemporaries, concluding that "it is . . . necessary to remember that neither dual faith nor superstition and prognostications
constitute the basic foundation of the people's philosophy; rather, a deep,
heartfelt religious feeling" undergirds that philosophy.[14]

Death ritual and popular beliefs about death during the period from
1870 to 1917 serve as a microcosm of the Russian and Ukrainian peasant
universe, in which there existed a strong linkage between the world of the
living and the world of the dead—a linkage predicated on the Christian
concept of the soul's immortality. The deceased were not divorced from
the living but continued to play an active role in society, communicating
with the living in a variety of ways. At times they were benevolent and at
other times dangerous to the well-being of the community. To facilitate
their benevolence, family and community observed numerous customs to
ease the passage of the dead from this world to the next. The care with
which they prepared the deceased for the afterlife also reinforced the community's unity and the respect accorded the elderly. The active participation of community members in the services and rituals that honored and
bade farewell to the dead served both to placate the dead and to ensure
that similar care would be taken when they died.[15] The dead, in turn,
were expected to intercede with God in behalf of the living.

The world of nineteenth-century Russian and Ukrainian peasants was
inhabited by a host of spirits and demons who were believed responsible
for such recurring calamities as drought, freak storms, illness, and even
death. The peasants ultimately feared the dead and interpreted some of
these disasters as their vengeful acts. Death was understood as the will of
God, and the extent to which the deceased had sinned during their lifetime determined whether they experienced a peaceful or torturous afterlife. Peasants viewed an unexpected death as divine punishment of sins.[16]
Deaths inflicted by the human hand, whether suicide or murder, were
unnatural and against God's will. Denied a Christian burial, the souls of
the victims were destined to wander the earth and avenge their sufferings
by inflicting problems on the living.

Russian and Ukrainian peasants did not take death lightly. The elderly
and the seriously ill, who knew that death was imminent, had to make
preparations to ease their transition from this world to the next. This
meant cleansing the conscience and taking steps to ensure that the living
carried out their Christian obligation to remember the dead through
prayer. In the Orthodox funeral service, the dead ask the living to say

[14] Ivanov, "Ocherk vozzrenii," 245.
[15] Arthur C. Lehmann and James E. Myers, *Magic, Witchcraft, and Religion: An Anthropological Study of the Supernatural* (Palo Alto, Calif.: Mayfield, 1985), 286.
[16] A. Balov, S. Ia. Derunov, and Ia. Il'inskii, "Ocherki Poshekhon'ia," *Etnograficheskoe
obozrenie* 10, no. 4 (1894): 88.

prayers for them: "Therefore I beg you all, and implore you, to offer prayers unceasingly for me to Christ our God, that I be not assigned for my sins to the place of torment; but that He assign me to the place where this is Light of Life."[17]

Signs portending the imminence of death aided individuals in their preparation for it. The fourteenth-century icon of Saints Boris and Gleb in Kolomna includes an image of Boris dreaming about his impending death, depicted here as a black dog.[18] Death imagery in dreams was also strong among peasants. For example, the inhabitants of the Ukrainian village of Shebekino, Kursk province, put a good deal of stock in dreams and the actions of birds as messengers of death. An individual who dreamt about a deceased father or grandfather building a house (in this case signifying a grave) and inviting the dreamer to live with him was destined to die shortly. If in a dream a person lost a tooth without experiencing pain, the person's spouse, brother, or sister would soon die. If, on the other hand, losing that tooth involved a great deal of pain and the appearance of blood, death would claim a child, mother, or father. Death might also be heralded by a screeching owl, a bird beating at a window at midnight, or a bird trapped in the hut.[19] In the Russian province of Riazan', death might appear as a skeleton or old woman when the individual looked in a mirror at night; as white flowers in a dream; or as a bird darting in and out a window. Death was also likely when a person's hair and nails grew quickly.[20] Unusual occurrences in dreams and reality thus confirmed the foreboding of death that elderly or gravely ill individuals had.[21] Such premonitions of death were characteristic of premodern societies in which "there was no clear boundary between the natural and the supernatural."[22]

---

[17] Quoted and translated in Danforth and Tsiaras, *Death Rituals*, 48.

[18] M. V. Alpatov, *Drevnerusskaia ikonopis'* (Moscow: Iskusstvo, 1978), icon 52–53.

[19] Volodymyr Hnatiuk, comp., "Pokhoronni zvychai i obriady," *Etnografichnyi zbirnyk* 31–32 (1912): 403–4. In Starokonstantinov and Zaslavl' districts, Volynia province, several old women specialized in the interpretation of dreams. Iv. Ben'kovskii, "Smert', pogrebenie i zagrobnaia zhizn' po poniatiiam i verovaniiu naroda," *Kievskaia starina*, September 1896, 231.

[20] O. P. Semenov, "Smert' i dusha v pover'iakh i v razskazakh krest'ian i meshchan Riazanskago, Ranenburgskago i Dankovskago uezdov Riazanskoi gubernii," *Zhivaia starina* 8, no. 2 (1898): 228–29.

[21] Judith Devlin makes this point about omens in general: "The girl who wanted to daydream about a future husband, a man who wanted to avoid going on a journey, a woman who was anxious about the welfare of her children or about the family fortunes, all could draw on a rich set of images with which to confirm their feelings—rather in the way the ancient Greeks had procured the kind of dreams they wanted." *The Superstitious Mind: French Peasants and the Supernatural in the Nineteenth Century* (New Haven, Conn.: Yale University Press, 1987), 97.

[22] Ariès, *Hour of Our Death*, 8.

With death looming, peasants made arrangements concerning the state of their soul. Confessing sins to a priest and taking the Sacrament eased their conscience.[23] In isolated Russian villages of Vladimir province, the elderly sometimes also asked the ground for forgiveness, invoking the biblical reference to the body's being made out of earth. In the village of Golovina, Grigorev canton, an old man had his family carry him out to the fields so that he could get down on his knees and bow to the ground in all four directions. With each genuflection he crossed himself and said, "Damp Mother Earth, forgive me and accept me!"[24] In Poshekhon'e district, Iaroslavl' province, Russian peasants believed that a few days prior to death the body emitted a smell of earth and developed black spots, suggesting that "the earth is coming out."[25]

Dying peasants also generally made arrangements concerning the devolution of their property to relatives in mainly oral, but sometimes written, testaments. Fortunately, a few of the written testaments have survived. They reveal the peasants' concerns about death. One childless widow of Podcherkov canton, Dmitrov district, Moscow province, left an extraordinary testament dated August 22, 1871. She expressed gratitude to a large circle of kin, settling property on a brother, two nieces, a sister-in-law, two nephews, and an adopted son. She also made the following stipulations:

> I am asking my executors, named at the end of this testament, upon my death, to sell my home and yard with one cow, located in the village of Ochevo, Podcherkov canton. The net capital is to be placed in one of the credit institutions in the name of the holy Church servants of the parish Chernogriazh for the eternal memory of my and my husband's souls. . . . I am bequeathing two pieces of linen to the poor and miserable. . . . I am leaving ten measures of rye to the Nikolopestush monastery for the remembrance of my and my husband's souls.[26]

The importance of the living praying for the souls of the dead is evident from the testament. Having no children of her own and with relatives inhabiting other villages, the widow left money to servants of the church and a monastery to ensure that someone would pray for her and her husband's souls. By dispensing Christian charity and giving alms to the

[23] Balov, Derunov, and Il'inskii, "Ocherki Poshekhon'ia," 87.

[24] G. K. Zavoiko, "Verovaniia, obriady i obychai velikorossov Vladimirskoi gubernii," *Etnograficheskoe obozrenie* 26, nos. 3–4 (1914): 88.

[25] Balov, Derunov, and Il'inskii, "Ocherki Poshekhon'ia," 86.

[26] *Trudy Kommisii po preobrazovaniiu volostnykh sudov: Slovesnye oprosy krest'ian, pis'mennye otzyvy razlichnykh mest i lits i resheniia: volostnykh sudov, s"ezdov mirovykh posrednikov i gubernskikh po krest'ianskim delam prisutstvii,* 7 vols. (St. Petersburg, 1873–74), 2:525–26; translated in Christine D. Worobec, *Peasant Russia: Family and Community in the Post-Emancipation Period* (Princeton: Princeton University Press, 1991), 67.

poor, she helped pave her way to a peaceful death.[27] In another testament of March 17, 1869, Dmitrii Andreev Skachkov, of the village of Petrov in Usman' district, Tambov province (Russia), referred to his wife's responsibility for caring for his soul: "If there remains money after my death it is to go to my wife Mariia Ivanova on condition that she bury me and have memorial services said for me in the Christian manner."[28] Once again the testator stressed the importance of memorial services. In a spiritual testament from a Ukrainian province, a parent warned his children that unless they lived in harmony, they would destroy his eternal peace and sully his memory. If, on the other hand, they lived according to God's commandment, "I will pray from the grave to Our Lord on High for your happiness."[29]

These testaments attest to a strong linkage between the living and the dead. The living were obliged to bury their deceased relatives in a Christian fashion. This involved arranging for a *chernichka* (a spinster who devoted her life to the work of Christ without, however, taking the vows of a nun) or literate male peasant to read the Psalter over the deceased, as well as arranging for a funeral mass before the interment.[30] Family and community members also had to bid farewell to the deceased, absolving him or her of past sins. According to Ukrainian peasants in Starokonstantinov district, Volynia province, "To be afraid of, to shun the dead is a sin; we will all die, . . . [we] will not get to heaven alive. Who knows . . . what kind of death God sends each one of us."[31] In other words, mortals were not to judge and torment the dead. God would make the final judgment.[32] After the funeral, family members were expected to arrange for the continued reading of the Psalter, sometimes until the fortieth day, as well as for several memorial services.

In both the Russian and Ukrainian provinces, memorial services and repasts involving the entire community were held to honor the dead on the third, ninth (sometimes twentieth), and fortieth days after death.[33]

[27] Worobec, *Peasant Russia*, 68.

[28] *Trudy Kommisii* 1:609–10; Worobec, *Peasant Russia*, 68.

[29] P. P. Chubinskii, *Trudy etnografichesko-statisticheskoi ekspeditsii v zapadno-russkii krai*, 7 vols. (St. Petersburg, 1872–77), 6:310–11.

[30] G. A. Kalashnikov and A. M. Kalashnikov, "S. Nikol'skoe," in "Materialy dlia etnograficheskago izucheniia Khar'kovskoi gubernii," part 1, "Starobel'skii uezd," *Khar'kovskii sbornik* 8 (1894): 234; Ben'kovskii, "Smert'," 243.

[31] Quoted in Ben'kovskii, "Smert'," 247.

[32] Ukrainian peasants believed that for forty days after death, when the deceased's soul wandered the earth, the deceased would come back at night to haunt and chase with a stick anyone who refused to forgive the dead person of a major sin. Hnatiuk, "Pokhoronni zvychai," 413.

[33] In the village of Nikol'skoe, Starobel' district, Khar'kov province, memorial services were also held on the twentieth day. Kalashnikov and Kalashnikov, "S. Nikol'skoe," 236.

They commemorated the resurrection of Christ on the third day, his reappearance to his disciples on the ninth day, and his wandering in the wilderness for forty days. Absorbing the church's practices, Russian and Ukrainian peasants believed that the soul wandered the earth for forty days. During that time, according to Russian peasants of Vladimir province, angels of the Lord took the soul to places where the deceased person had committed sins during his or her lifetime. On the third, ninth, twentieth, and fortieth days, the soul returned home, where it could drink from the glass of water and eat the bread left out for it. In the village of Mostki, Khar'kov province, Ukrainian peasants ascribed purificatory powers to the water left on the windowsill closest to the icon corner, believing that the deceased's soul cleansed itself of its sins by bathing in the water. On the fortieth day, the priest officiating at the memorial service released the soul from this earth and sent it on its way to "the dark place to await Christ's judgment."[34]

Russian and Ukrainian peasants' belief in the continued materialism of the human body after death was also expressed by the practice of burying the deceased with food as well as, in some cases, household tools and other items. While the custom began to die out by the end of the nineteenth century, it did not contradict church teachings or practices.[35] According to the Gospel of St. Luke, Jesus ate grilled fish upon his resurrection.[36] On the fortieth day, a bereaved family may even today bring food—bread and fruit—into the church and place it on the side altar used for the postliturgy memorial service.[37]

Peasants understood the importance of prayers for the welfare of the deceased, in keeping with the teachings of the Orthodox church. Marva Romanova of the village of Mar'ino, Riazan' province, explained to an observer that the souls of deceased adults, both the righteous and sinners,

---

[34] Zavoiko, "Verovaniia," 87–89; S. A. Khotiaintseva and A. A. Usikova, "Sl. Mostki," in "Materialy dlia etnograficheskago izucheniia Khar'kovskoi gubernii," part 1, "Starobel'skii uezd," *Khar'kovskii sbornik* 8 (1894): 63–84; Kh. Iashchurzhinskii, "Ostatki iazychestva v pogrebal'nykh obriadakh Malorossii," *Etnograficheskoe obozrenie* 10, no. 3 (1898): 93–95. Nineteenth-century French peasants also believed in the efficacy of water for guaranteeing a person's salvation. Devlin, *Superstitious Mind*, 50.

[35] By the late nineteenth century, the practice of burying the dead with food and drink was dying out in Ukrainian areas. An elderly Ukrainian peasant noted that the practice had been popular under serfdom. In Obonezhskii krai, on the other hand, it was still common to bury the deceased with food, household tools, or other household items. See Ben'kovskii, "Smert'," 255; Iashchurzhinskii, "Ostatki iazychestva," 93; and G. I. Kulikovskii, "Pokhoronnye obriady Obonezhskago kraia," *Etnograficheskoe obozrenie* 2, no. 1 (1890): 50–52.

[36] Luke 24:41–43.

[37] Fedotov, *The Russian Religious Mind*, 16–17. This practice is widespread today in the Ukrainian Orthodox Church in Canada.

awaited the Last Judgment in a dark, empty place. The purpose of memorial services after the fortieth day was to provide the souls with light so
that they could determine whether they would live out their eternal life in
heaven or hell. Relatives and close friends on earth could, however, save
a soul destined for hell through their prayers, a concept that reflected
Orthodox belief.[38] In the words of the Orthodox scholar Sergei Bulgakov, prayers "can ameliorate the state of the soul of sinners, and liber-
ate them from the place of distress, and snatch them from hell. This action
of prayer, of course, supposes not only intercession before the Creator,
but a direct action on the soul, an awakening of the powers of the soul,
capable of making it worthy of pardon."[39] The church's belief in the efficacy of prayer was also demonstrated in a practice during the funeral: the
officiating priest placed in the hands of the deceased a letter with a prayer
asking God for forgiveness for past sins.[40] According to the peasant
woman Romanova, souls could not pray for themselves, but prayed for
the living when the latter held commemorative services for them: "We
pray for them, and they for us—they can't be without us, we can't be
without them." Arina Domozhilova of the village of Muraevo, Dankov
district, Riazan' province, advised that memorial services for the dead
should be held four times a year—on the Saturday before *maslenitsa*
(Shrovetide), the Tuesday of Fomina week, the Saturday of Troitsa (Trin-
ity), and October 26, St. Dimitrii Day, all important days in the Orthodox calendar.[41] The Orthodox church set aside the first two dates as well
as the Saturday before Troitsa and the Saturday of the first week of Lent
for remembering the dead. Of these, the Tuesday of Fomina week was the
most important because the Orthodox believe that during Easter week
the souls of the dead are relieved of suffering, a belief to which the peasants subscribed.[42]

In addition to saying prayers for the dead, the living eased the deceased's journey to the other world and removed the threat of death from
their own lives through a series of rituals. Russian and Ukrainian peas-

[38] Semenov, "Smert' i dusha," 230.

[39] Sergius Bulgakov, *The Orthodox Church*, revised translation by Lydia Kesich
(Crestwood, N.Y.: St. Vladimir's Seminary Press, 1988), 182.

[40] Hnatiuk, "Pokhoronni zvychai," 413.

[41] Semenov, "Smert' i dusha," 230–31. In some areas, a memorial service was held every
Sunday. Kulikovskii, "Pokhoronnye obriady," 56. In Kostroma province, a memorial
luncheon occurred also on the deceased's name day. V. Smirnov, "Narodnye pokhorony i
prichitaniia v Kostromskom krae," *Trudy Kostromskago nauchnogo obshchestva po izuch-
eniiu mestnogo kraia* 15 (1920): 41.

[42] A. N. Minkh, *Narodnye obychai, obriady, sueveriia i predrazsudki krest'ian Saratovskoi gubernii, sobrany v 1861–1888 godakh*, Zapiski Imperatorskago russkago geo-
graficheskago obshchestva po otdeleniiu etnografii, vol. 19, no. 2 (St. Petersburg: Tip. V.
Bezobrazova, 1890), 132.

ants believed that bodies continued to act after death.[43] They ascribed to the deceased's body the power to take lives in the transitional period between life on earth and life in the next world. Anthropologists classify this time as one of liminality, when "the participants in rites of passage are neither in one state nor the other; they are 'betwixt and between.' . . . The liminal period epitomizes that which is ambiguous, paradoxical, and anomalous. As a result, things associated with it are often considered unclean, polluting, and dangerous."[44] Thus, among Russian and Ukrainian peasants only the elderly (usually women), who were close to death themselves, were permitted to wash the dead.[45] Precautions against death's claiming someone else in the household were taken with the items—comb, soapy water, and earthenware containers for the water—used to prepare the body. They had to be disposed of in a place where people did not walk, preferably a river.[46] To prevent another death in the family, the preparers of the body also closed the deceased's eyes and mouth, placing coins on the eyes and sometimes tying the head with a cloth to keep the mouth shut.[47] On the day of the funeral, a number of rituals had to be observed to ensure that the soul left the place of death and did not reanimate the body or remain in the hut to plague the living. Pallbearers carried the body out of the house feet first, in some places out of the window rather than the door. Once the funeral procession was out of the yard, a family member closed the gates and tied them with a belt. The hut was swept clean of any traces of death and holy water sprinkled along the path of the procession to neutralize the power of the dead.[48]

Through ritualized mourning, nineteenth-century Russian and Ukrainian peasants honored and placated the dead. Grieving did not, however, allow uncontrolled passions. The peasants of Vladimir province considered it a great sin to grieve uncontrollably for the dead. God had willed the death of a loved one; it was not for mortals to question his will. Indeed, the Orthodox church, stressing the glorious resurrection of Christ and eternal life, encouraged its followers to view death as a new birth.[49]

---

[43] Such a belief was common among peasants across premodern Europe. See Paul Barber, *Vampires, Burial, and Death: Folklore and Reality* (New Haven, Conn.: Yale University Press, 1988), 178.

[44] Danforth and Tsiaras, *Death Rituals*, 36–37.

[45] In Poshekhon'e district, Iaroslavl' province, the elderly women who prepared the body of the deceased were *keleinitsy*, or lay sisters. In Vladimir province it was usual for an old man, serving two or three villages, to carry out this task. Chubinskii, *Trudy etnografichesko-statisticheskoi ekspeditsii* 4:699–700; A. Balov, "Ocherki Poshekhon'ia: Verovaniia," *Etnograficheskoe obozrenie* 13, no. 4 (1901): 88; Zavoiko, "Verovaniia," 90.

[46] Semenov, "Smert' i dusha," 228; Zavoiko, "Verovaniia," 92.

[47] Ben'kovskii, "Smert'," 244.

[48] Balov, "Ocherki Poshekhon'ia," 89; Kulikovskii, "Pokhoronnye obriady," 53; Kalashnikov and Kalashnikov, "S. Nikol'skoe," 235.

[49] The same was true of the Catholic church. Ariès, *Hour of Our Death*, 13.

Ukrainian peasants accordingly greeted death with the saying "Praise be to God that he died" (*Slava Bohu, shcho vmer*).[50] An ethnographer, clearly offended by the joy that peasants expressed through song and dance at a grave site after a memorial service, was reminded by an elderly woman, "What do you mean? We had a memorial service, remembered the deceased; now it is time to cheer them up or they will be offended if we leave sad."[51] For a mother to mourn the death of baptized children under the age of seven was particularly egregious. Peasants believed that these sinless children were destined to go straight to heaven and become angels. If a mother cried for such a child, her tears would drown or burn the child.[52] Instead, emotions were to be released through laments, sung in a recitative style by the deceased's close female relatives. In some Russian villages, relatives hired professional mourners.

Through laments, wailers communicated between the worlds of the living and the dead in a public setting, before and after the church-officiated funeral. They addressed deceased persons as if they were alive, asking them for forgiveness, praising them with tender words, and identifying them with diminutives. The mourners also described the sufferings of bereaved relatives. A mother from Kamenets district in the Ukrainian province of Podol'ia addressed her deceased daughter directly and asked, "My daughter, my dissatisfied [daughter]! Did you fear that [by living] you would deprive me of years?! Were you afraid that I would lose days?! Did you worry about interfering in my work?! Where are you going, my child? I rejoiced in you and looked after you. What will happen to you now? Why aren't you laughing . . . ? Why aren't you stretching out your small arms?"[53] Clearly, the mother was trying to absolve herself of guilt over the death of her daughter, pointing out to her daughter and her neighbors that she had loved and cared for her. There is also an insinuation here that children were a burden on women, who had strenuous tasks to fulfill in the home and fields in addition to looking after children. In a similar lament from the Russian province of Kaluga, the guilt of a neglectful mother is far more pronounced; the mother actually blamed herself for her children's death, agreeing with them that she had not fed them properly.[54] A daughter from Skvirsk district in the Ukrainian province of Kiev bemoaned the death of her father, noting that the entire family had depended upon his labors and guidance: "Our father, dearest,

[50] Zavoiko, "Verovaniia," 97; Chubinskii, *Trudy etnografichesko-statisticheskoi ekspeditsii* 4:699.

[51] N. Ivanenko, "Etnograficheskie materialy iz Orlovskoi gubernii," *Zhivaia starina* 19, no. 4 (1910), pt. 2:326.

[52] Zavoiko, "Verovaniia," 97; Smirnov, "Narodnye pokhorony," 54.

[53] Recorded in Hnatiuk, "Pokhoronni zvychai," 388.

[54] Quoted in V. N. Dobrovol'skii, "Smert', pokhorony i prichitaniia (Etnograficheskii material Kaluzhskoi gubernii)," *Zhivaia starina* 10, nos. 1–2 (1900): 292–95.

why did you abandon us little ones? Who will look after us, who will plow for us, who will grind [the grain] for us, who will mow for us, who will give us away in marriage, and who will guide us along the path?"[55] Similarly, in Tula province (Russia), a father was described in laments as the provider of the family and head of the household. Without him, those left were destined to walk around naked, cold, and hungry. In Vladimir province, a young widow bemoaned the fact that her husband's death left her an orphan, underscoring the unenviable position of a widow in the community.[56]

While laments placated the dead and helped overcome guilt, their descriptions of the burdens carried by the living were a form of protest that women utilized to express their "social isolation and ambiguous status" in a patriarchal society.[57] They pinpointed the stark reality of a subsistence economy and the precarious balance between survival and destitution. The loss of a laborer, particularly an adult male, could result in economic disaster for the remaining family members. Widows without adult male children to support them had to depend on the benevolence of in-laws and the commune. When that aid was insufficient or not forthcoming, they were forced out of the village to seek a living as wage laborers. The fact that only women served as wailers among Russian and Ukrainian peasants attests to the greater economic and social hardships that women suffered as a result of the loss of able-bodied family members.[58]

Complex laments, however, were on the wane in many parts of rural Russia by the late nineteenth and early twentieth centuries. They had disappeared from Dmitrovsk district, Orel province, and were fading from the popular memory in Ustiuzhna district, Novgorod province, by 1910.[59] In 1920 the ethnographer V. Smirnov noted that there were still some professional mourners in Varnavin and Chukhloma districts of Kostroma province, but in general they were rare in the Kostroma region. Wailers remembered only a few phrases of the stylized laments and tended to substitute hysterical sobs for songs. The disappearance of com-

[55] Quoted in Hnatiuk, "Pokhoronni zvychai," 391.

[56] Quoted in A. Sobelev, "Prichitaniia nad umershimi Vladimirskoi gubernii," *Etnograficheskoe obozrenie* 23, nos. 3–4 (1911): 194.

[57] Anna Caraveli makes a similar point about Greek peasant women in "The Bitter Wounding: The Lament as Social Protest in Rural Greece," in *Gender and Power in Rural Greece*, ed. Jill Dubisch (Princeton: Princeton University Press, 1986), 181.

[58] V. M. Sokolov, *Russian Folklore*, trans. Catherine Ruth Smith (New York: Macmillan, 1950), 226.

[59] Ivanenko, "Etnograficheskie materialy," 326; A. Malinovskii, "Pokhoronnye prichety v Perskoi volosti Ustiuzhenskago uezda, Novgorodskoi gubernii," *Zhivaia starina* 18, no. 1 (1909): 70–79.

plex laments may be explained in part by the clergy's sustained attacks on the wailers.[60] Priests clearly viewed these women as a threat to their power. Simplified urban funeral rites may also have had an effect on rural practices, especially in the industrial belt of central Russia.[61] That women expressed public grief over death despite modern influences penetrating the countryside demonstrated their continuing vulnerability in a patriarchal society.

Through their mourning for the dead, women also underlined the pivotal role they played in death ritual as a whole. As givers of life, they had the added responsibility of conducting the dead along the path to the other world. Indeed, *smert'*, the word for death in Russian and Ukrainian, is feminine. In the popular mind, death could take the form of a human skeleton, a young woman, a beautiful maiden, a cripple, or an old woman carrying a scythe and sometimes a torch. The woman with a scythe symbolized an inversion of traditional agricultural practices, in which men wielded scythes and women sickles.[62] The identification of death as a woman represented the real world turned upside down. While on earth the patriarchy controlled and subordinated women, in the world beyond women were in control and took their revenge on the patriarchy by snuffing out life. As anthropologist Gail Kligman put it, "Death does what she wants, to whom and when she pleases."[63] Given the feminization of death, it was natural that women were the intercessors between the dead and the living. The lament was the medium through which they communicated with the dead. While they bemoaned the fact that the dead refused to awaken from their deep sleep, they asked them for other signs that they were well, beseeching them to send a bird from heaven down to earth with a message for them.[64] Ukrainian peasants believed that if women mourners spent the night at the grave site after memorial services, they could communicate directly with the dead, who would visit them in their sleep and thank them for their prayers.[65]

[60] Smirnov, "Narodnye pokhorony," 55.

[61] Malinovskii, "Pokhoronnye prichety," 71.

[62] Ia. Generozov, *Russkie narodnye predstavleniia o zagrobnoi zhizni na osnovanii zaplachek, prichitanii, dukhovnykh stikhov, i t. p.* (Saratov: Kimmel, 1883), 17; L. Lenchevskii, "Pokhoronnye obriady i pover'ia v Starokonstantinovskom u., Volynskoi gub.," *Kievskaia starina*, July 1899, 70. Death also appears to Romanian peasants as a woman with a scythe. See Gail Kligman, *The Wedding of the Dead: Ritual, Poetics, and Popular Culture in Transylvania* (Berkeley: University of California Press, 1988), 64. In Kostroma province, peasants often described death as a long-haired woman holding a cup of green liquor, presumably poison. Smirnov, "Narodnye pokhorony," 50.

[63] *Wedding of the Dead*, 176.

[64] S. Brailovskii, "Malorusskaia pokhoronnaia prichet' i mificheskoe eia znachenie," *Kievskaia starina*, September 1885, 76–77.

[65] Chubinskii, *Trudy etnografichesko-statisticheskoi ekspeditsii* 4:711–12.

In spite of the various precautions and rituals to placate the dead and ease their journey to the other world, the dead sometimes remained in the world of the living, haunting them and causing calamities to befall them—a belief the Orthodox church censured as superstitious. Ukrainian and Russian peasants believed in the existence of the walking dead, those souls who had died unnaturally and were therefore usually denied or deprived of a Christian burial as a sign of God's wrath. Until laid to rest, they would be tormented and seek revenge on the living. The so-called unclean dead were either victims of suicide or murder, or witches and sorcerers who during their lifetime communicated with demons and dabbled in black magic. Alcoholics were also prime candidates for revenants or ghosts, because of a belief that alcoholism was the work of the devil.[66] The *rusalki*, or water nymphs, were common to the pantheon of spirits inhabiting the worlds of Russian and Ukrainian peasants. They were believed to be the souls of unbaptized babies and young unmarried women—many of them spurned by their lovers—who ended their lives tragically by drowning.[67] Ukrainians had a special word for the walking

---

[66] A Ukrainian legend provides an explanation for the connection between alcoholics and evil. According to the tale, the devil first introduced liquor by treating the Apostles Peter and Paul to several glasses when they and Christ wandered the earth. When St. Paul asked for a third glass and had no money to compensate the devil, Christ announced to the devil that his payment would come in the form of deceased alcoholics. Recorded in D. Zelenin, "K voprosu o rusalkakh (Kul't pokoinikov, umershikh neestvestvennoiu smert'iu, u russkikh i u finnov)," *Kievskaia starina*, nos. 3–4 (1911): 365. The story is a fascinating illustration of the way in which peasants used Christian characters to help explain life's realities. Their worldview was permeated with Christian symbols and personages, if not always doctrine. David Christian points out that alcoholics "who died in a tavern could be denied Christian burial." *"Living Water": Vodka and Russian Society on the Eve of Emancipation* (Oxford: Clarendon Press, 1990), 106.

[67] Ukrainian peasants viewed the death of young men and women of marriageable age as particularly tragic. If the individuals died of natural causes, they were not unclean. Nevertheless, their souls had to be placated by combining wedding with funeral ritual and creating the illusion that they had married in the world beyond. The deceased were dressed in their wedding finery, while their friends stood vigil over the bodies as bridesmaids and attendants. A wedding bread was baked and distributed among the mourners at the grave site after the funeral. These measures were to prevent the deceased from returning to earth and seeking to avenge their unfulfillment of life's responsibilities. Iashchurzhinskii, "Ostatki iazychestva," 94; Ben'kovskii, "Smert'," 249–50; Chubinskii, *Trudy etnografichesko-statisticheskoi ekspeditsii* 4:708–9. The mixing of marriage and funeral customs was common among other eastern European peasant societies, including those of Romania, Greece, Bulgaria, and Hungary. See Kligman, *Wedding of the Dead*; and Margaret Alexiou, *The Ritual Lament in Greek Tradition* (Cambridge: Cambridge University Press, 1974), 230 n. 64. I have not come across accounts of any similar practices among Russian peasants. According to D. I. Uspenskii, mothers in Tula and Venev districts, Tula province, did not lament the death of unmarried daughters, especially if the family had several daughters. D. I. Uspenskii, "Pokhoronnyia prichitaniia," *Etnograficheskoe obozrenie* 4, nos. 2–3 (1892): 102. Russian

dead—*upiry*, who were akin to bloodsucking vampires.[68] Russian and Ukrainian peasants believed that unclean bodies did not decompose and that ultimately the earth refused to accept them.[69]

It was natural for the peasants to believe that the dissatisfied dead roamed the world at night. The dead, both good and evil, were thought to communicate with the living in their sleep, when they were most vulnerable.[70] Indeed, death itself often warned people of their impending death through dreams.[71] The countryside's physical environment also played havoc with peasant imaginations. "Forests, misty bogs and nights unilluminated by electricity were conducive to strange visions. . . . Furthermore, the greater prevalence of illness and delirium meant that hallucinations were probably more common in the last century than now, and they furnished people with a range of disconcerting images which seemed to corroborate the authenticity of traditional beliefs."[72] While the belief in revenants was anathema to the Orthodox church, peasants must nonetheless have been influenced by the important Christian concept of the resurrection of the dead. When they heard the reference in the Gospels to demoniacs emerging from a tomb, their suspicions about the power of the dead were confirmed.[73]

At the same time, not every unusual manifestation was a hallucination or apparition. As Paul Barber demonstrated in his recent study of vampires in European societies, unembalmed corpses undergo a great deal of physical change. Microorganisms in the intestines produce gases that

---

peasants viewed daughters as a drain on the household economy; no sooner did they grow up and start contributing their labors to the household than they married and departed the parental home with dowry in hand.

[68] For an excellent discussion of the unclean dead and popular beliefs about them, see Zelenin, "K voprosu o rusalkakh," 357–424.

[69] Balov, "Ocherki Poshekhon'ia," 91.

[70] Marva Romanova of the village of Mar'ino, Riazan' district, told the story of a merchant who had committed suicide. The merchant appeared before his wife every night with a noose around his neck. The wife, being a very pious woman, prayed to God day and night and went on several pilgrimages, but the husband kept appearing. Finally, an elderly monk with one foot in the grave advised her to have a bell cast. The monk told her that every time the bell rang, thousands of Christians would cross themselves and appeal to God. With each ring of the bell, it would become easier for her deceased husband's soul. The wife did what the monk told her, and as a result the nightly visits stopped four years later. A half year later, the husband again appeared before his wife, but this time without the noose around his neck and with a joyous face. Now she knew that her husband's sins had been forgiven. The story is recorded in Semenov, "Smert' i dusha," 233. In Poshekhon'e district, Iaroslavl' province, the ringing of bells was also thought to rescue souls from hell. Balov, "Ocherki Poshekhon'ia," 92.

[71] Hnatiuk, "Pokhoronni zvychai," 403.

[72] Devlin, *Superstitious Mind*, 80.

[73] Matt. 3:28–34.

cause a corpse to bloat to twice its original size. "Eventually the abdominal cavity bursts from the pressure, like an overinflated balloon, unless the pressure is relieved." Corpses also change color and continue to bleed. Russian and Ukrainian peasants, like their European counterparts, were not imagining the sounds they heard from the graves. Nor were they imagining the bodies they saw uncovered by animals digging at shallow graves or the corpses that resurfaced after being buried in a swamp or drowned in water. And when they saw these bodies or heard movement in the earth, they assumed that the corpses were active, doing some harm to the living.[74]

The harm that the unclean dead visited on the living sometimes came in the form of sudden, unexplained deaths. A Ukrainian tale from Khar'kov province relates how a rusalka tickled a small boy to death because his father had been digging trenches on the Thursday of Troitsa week, the day set aside for the festival of the rusalki. The water nymph was also taking revenge on the family because she had been their stillborn child whom they had buried unbaptized under the threshold of their hut.[75] The tale helped explain the high mortality of children and advised peasants to refrain from work on the Thursday of Troitsa week as a way of placating the rusalki.

The walking dead could also harm the living by bringing upon them epidemics or weather disturbances, such as droughts and hailstorms. Peasants could explain these visitations as manifestations of the deceased's jealousy, anger at a living relative for not fulfilling his or her last wishes, or longing for the world of the living. Illnesses were traditionally considered to be the work of witches and sorcerers; it was only a short extension for peasants to assume that the corpses of evil-minded persons were sometimes responsible for cholera or smallpox epidemics.

During the cholera epidemics of the mid-nineteenth century, Russian peasants in some places believed that the first cholera victim was a vampire. To placate the deceased and end the epidemic, the unclean dead had to be disinterred, an act censured by both church and state. According to article 234 of the Russian Criminal Code, exhumation of bodies was a

[74] Barber, *Vampires, Burial, and Death*, 90–91, 141, 165, 169. Russian and Ukrainian peasants usually buried suicides in unconsecrated ground, often at crossroads. Murderers out of haste often left their victims in fairly shallow ground; and it was not uncommon for peasants to throw the bodies of the unclean dead into water, believing that it served as an obstacle to their roaming the earth. Zelenin, "K voprosu o rusalkakh," 394–95.

[75] Translated in Ivanits, *Russian Folk Belief*, 186. Burial of unbaptized children under the threshold of a hut was a common practice among Ukrainian peasants. Persons entering the hut normally made a sign of the cross, which had the added benefit of speeding up the time when the soul would be freed from its state as a rusalka. Ivanov, "Ocherk vozzrenii," 247.

serious crime.[76] That law, however, was insufficient to deter peasants from acting on their impulses when cholera raised its ugly head:

> On the seventeenth of August 1848, the pastor of the Veliko-Shukhovits church informed the local district judge that the peasants, against his will, had disinterred the deceased peasant girl Iustina Iushkov, had taken her out of the coffin, and had performed on her a "bestial operation;" and they had done this in order to end the reign of cholera among them. When an investigation was opened in this matter, the peasants admitted everything and recounted the following: Iushkov had been the first to die of cholera, but in August, when the epidemic grew in strength, the medical officer Rubtsov, who lived among them, had assured all the peasants that a dissolute girl who had died in a condition of pregnancy was the cause of the sickness. In order to drive away the cholera, it was necessary to open the grave and see what was the situation of the unborn child and whether or not the girl Iushkov's mouth was open. If the mouth was open, then a stake must be driven into it. At first the peasants had not listened to the medical officer, but when the cholera continued to increase, they had decided to take refuge in the suggested method. They had opened the grave, taken out the corpse, and cut it open. But an unborn child was not to be found in the mother's body, and so they had looked through the coffin and had found the body of a baby. Then they had thrown Iushkov back into the grave, but had first driven an ashen stake into her, since they had found her mouth open. After the peasants had done all this, they had covered up the grave and gone home in the complete expectation that the cholera had been disposed of.[77]

During another cholera epidemic in 1851, Russian peasants dug up the corpses of a couple, decapitated them, cremated the heads, and then drove ashen stakes through the bodies.[78] Before 1871, Ukrainian peasants reportedly would sometimes "cut off the head of the corpse and place it at its feet."[79]

As late as 1893, an entire village in Sterlitamaksk district in the Russian province of Ufa responded to a raging epidemic by participating in the unearthing of a woman they believed to have been a sorceress. Peasants had reported that at night they saw a ball of fire emanating from the woman's grave; it broke into smaller fires that carried the disease to vari-

---

[76] Stephen P. Frank, "Cultural Conflict and Criminality in Rural Russia, 1861–1900" (Ph.D. diss., Brown University, 1987), 339. Many thanks to Professor Frank for providing me with a copy of the relevant chapter.

[77] Aug. Lowenstimm, *Aberglaube und Strafrecht* (Berlin, 1897), 98–100, translated in Barber, *Vampires, Burial, and Death*, 35–36.

[78] Barber, *Vampires, Burial, and Death*, 75.

[79] Frank, "Cultural Conflict," 340.

ous peasant huts. When the villagers dug up the unfortunate woman's grave, they drove an aspen stake into her back.[80] The Christian symbolism of the aspen stake—invoking Judas's suicide by hanging himself from an aspen tree—is evident here.

There are several reports from New Russia and the Volga provinces in the last three decades of the nineteenth century about exhumation of bodies felt to be responsible for unnatural frosts or drought. According to A. A. Levenstim, a nineteenth-century observer of rural practices, peasants believed that unconfessed persons became vampires upon their death and that they had the power to "milk the clouds and steal the dew from the ground of the village in whose cemetery they are buried."[81] In some cases, villagers made a connection between environmental disasters and God's ire over undeserved Christian burials. Here peasants were invoking traditional rights to bury alcoholics, murder victims, and witches and sorcerers outside the boundaries of the cemetery—rights that contravened contemporary secular law, which had overturned late-seventeenth-century regulations.[82] For example, in 1890, in the midst of a drought, the Russian villagers of Usovka in Saratov district and province dug up the corpse of an alcoholic and threw it into the river Tereshka. The peasants rationalized their action by claiming, "God is punishing [us] with drought because we buried a drunk in the cemetery." Similar incidents were reported in May 1889 in the village of Kuromoch, Samara province, and in the village of Elshanka, Saratov province. In 1887, a correspondent from the newspaper *Khar'kovskiia gubernskiia vedomosti* related an incident in which a rumor circulated around the village of Ivanovka, Pavlograd district, Ekaterinoslav province, that their recently deceased *znakhar'* (healer) and church elder had not died naturally, but had committed suicide. If this was true, a Christian mass should not have been said over him and he should not have been buried in consecrated ground. In 1886, a lengthy drought visited the peasants of Ivanovka, and they connected the lack of rain with the tormented soul of the *znakhar'*. They opened his grave and poured four barrels of water into it. As they went to fill the fifth barrel, the rains began. This measure, however, had only a temporary effect. In 1887, with drought in their midst, the peasants removed the stone cross from the healer's grave, broke it into several pieces, and buried the fragments out in the wild steppe. They also disinterred

---

[80] A. A. Levenstim, "Sueverie i ego otnoshenie k ugolovnomu pravu," *Zhurnal Ministerstva iustitsii*, no. 1 (January 1897): 215; also cited in Frank, "Cultural Conflict," 340.

[81] "Sueverie," 216; also cited in Frank, "Cultural Conflict," 341.

[82] The ethnographer D. K. Zelenin cites a ruling of December 26, 1697, by the Moscow Patriarch Adrian whereby suicides, persons murdered or drowned, and those who died from alcohol poisoning were denied a Christian funeral and were to be buried in forests or in fields outside the boundaries of cemeteries. *Ocherki russkoi mifologii*, 56.

the *znakhar*'s body and threw it into a deep ravine far away from the village.[83]

It is difficult to estimate the number of times peasants exhumed the bodies of individuals believed responsible for natural disasters. However, it happened frequently enough for the bishop of Podol'ia and Bratslava in 1892 to admonish priests not to encourage peasants in their popular beliefs. Responding to an incident in which a priest had cooperated with his parishioners in digging up the body of a suicide victim, one Vasilii Shupakov, and throwing it into the forest, Bishop Dimitrii ordered the priest to serve penance at the St. Troitskii monastery in Kamenets for a month. Further, he wrote,

> It has come to the attention of the eparchial clergy that some priests, despite the archbishop's admonition, are indifferent to the popular superstition that God punishes suicide with drought and other misfortunes until the bodies of the unfortunate are unearthed from the cemetery graves and thrown in either the forest or field, after which water is poured over the bodies; and not only do they not use their pastor's influence to put a stop to this superstition, which they are obliged to do by their position and in carrying out eparchial instructions, but they also do not report such disgraceful actions (disinterring bodies, desecrating them, etc.) to their eparchial authorities.[84]

While peasants believed it necessary to unearth the bodies of the unclean and to act contrary to the church and state injunctions, they accepted the Orthodox church's prohibition against disturbing the bodies of absolved Christians. In the early twentieth century, a priest and his parishioners, numbering almost fifteen hundred, tried to prevent legal and medical authorities from exhuming a body for an autopsy. They explained to the court investigator and feldsher "that once the burial service (*otpevanie*) had been performed by the priest, a body could not be dug up. 'It is illegal!' claimed the priest, while the crowd shouted 'Why dig him up? Why disturb him? It's not allowed, *batiushka*! We also won't permit it.'"[85]

The walking dead served an important function in nineteenth-century Russian and Ukrainian peasant life. Their very existence and the elaborate stories about their revenge on the living provided a mechanism of

---

[83] Zelenin cites several examples in the second half of the nineteenth century of peasants in the Volga region and New Russia opening graves and pouring water on the corpses. In Sergach district, Nizhnii Novgorod province, peasants normally poured water into fresh graves before and after bodies were laid in them as a precaution against summer droughts. Zelenin, "K voprosu o rusalkakh," 383–86, 390–91; *Ocherki russkoi mifologii*, 66–73, 81–82.

[84] The bishop's admonition first appeared in *Podol'skie eparkhial'nye vedomosti* and was reprinted in *Smolenskii vestnik* 15, no. 115 (October 2, 1892).

[85] Frank, "Cultural Conflict," 352.

control for the elderly, who had to contend with the challenges and disrespect of the younger generation. The fear of revenants among the living provided a measure of security for the elderly when they prepared their testaments and requested that the living bury them in a Christian fashion and have commemorative services. Invoking the wrath of the deceased was also a deterrent to disobeying the other provisions of a testament. Rebellious youths, who might scoff at some of the beliefs of their parents and grandparents, became believers when disaster struck those around them.

In conclusion, death rituals among nineteenth-century Russian and Ukrainian peasants reveal a great deal about these societies. They were not as cut off from prescribed religion as contemporaries and historians have assumed. Peasants had absorbed the teachings of the Orthodox church, interpreting them to fit their life's circumstances in an attempt to cope with the loss of relatives and community members. Their beliefs were complementary rather than antagonistic to Orthodoxy's conception of the universe. Easing the burdens of the soul on its journey to eternity through prayer and remembrance services was an important responsibility of the Christian community. The soul's struggle to fend off demons and cleanse itself of sin created an image in the mind of these Orthodox peasants of an earthly world inhabited by demons and unclean spirits, who periodically visited upon them epidemics and weather that harmed the agricultural economy. As a result, the dead needed to be placated, and intercessors were necessary to carry out that responsibility. It was not sufficient to read the Psalter and hold funeral and memorial services. Women of the community, whether the elderly who helped prepare the deceased's body or the relatives who recited lamentations, supplemented the services of the male priesthood. Their laments and dreams in which they communicated with the dead may have taken place outside the church, but they were no less important in mediating between the worlds of the living and the dead.

Not all mediations were successful. Individuals who suffered unnatural deaths were among the restless dead, existing in limbo between the other world and the world of the living. Suffering for their unchristian actions, they tormented the living by visiting plagues and storms upon them. As peasants began to understand their universe in educated terms and embalming practices were introduced, belief in the walking dead gradually disappeared. The point at which that belief began to erode must still be determined. Ethnographers observing the peasants in the first two decades of the twentieth century noted that the belief in the unclean dead was still very strong.

Death rituals among Russian and Ukrainian peasants of the late imperial period expressed the peasants' view of the world as an unpredictable and often hostile place. To combat that world and find the strength to go on living after a death, they embraced Christian beliefs and interwove them with their other survival strategies. Community participation was as important in the mourning and honoring of the dead as in the other dramatic events of life (such as birth and marriage) and in agricultural tasks. Social relationships and community unity were solidified in the face of death, which disrupted the family and community by removing a loved one. The careful observance of Christian memorial rites comforted the living: they, too, would be remembered when they died. The linkage between the worlds of the living and the dead also provided some safeguards against God's wrath. The deceased joined the ranks of ancestors in heaven, who with their prayers could intercede with God in behalf of the living—as long as the living fulfilled their part of the bargain by remembering the dead. Calamities brought on by God's wrath or by the revenge of the unclean dead could not be prevented but could, nevertheless, be mitigated by human action. Even the damned could ultimately be saved by constant prayers. The living could also take action to ease the suffering of the unclean dead and neutralize their evil—a responsibility peasants felt so strongly that they broke the law to exhume and mutilate bodies. If such action protected the living against further harm, the peasants at least gained some psychological comfort in their hostile world.

2

WOMEN, MEN, AND THE LANGUAGES OF

PEASANT RESISTANCE, 1870–1907

Barbara Alpern Engel

ON SEPTEMBER 16, 1872, the former state peasants of Zhilomostnoe and Pravorot' villages in Kursk province confronted the official who had come to survey their land at the governor's orders. The entire population of the villages stood facing the surveyor, the women with babies at their breast in the forefront. Shouting "We don't agree, we'll force you to stop; you won't get away with this robbery!" the women placed their children on the ground in front of them and blocked the surveyor's path. Each time he tried to proceed in a different direction, the women threw their infants under a bush directly in his way, then screened the bush with their bodies. The police proved unable to disperse the women or to remove the children. Undeterred by the presence of the police, the women tore the surveyor's stake out of the ground and broke it, to the men's shouts of encouragement. The surveying party was forced to withdraw, overcome by the women's defiance, reinforced as it was by over four hundred peasants who had congregated on the spot.[1]

This incident combined most of the elements that characterized Russian peasant women's resistance in the decades between the emancipation of the serfs and the outbreak of World War I. In published accounts of peasant unrest, there is abundant evidence of women's activism: police intending to confiscate village property are attacked by women brandishing hoes and pitchforks; efforts to survey disputed land are blocked by women with their bodies; men cutting trees in noblemen's forests are joined by axe-wielding women. During the revolutionary upheavals of 1905–6, women figured prominently in collective seizures of food or fodder. These by no means exhaustive examples of women's resistance are

I would like to thank Christine Worobec for her thoughtful reading of an earlier draft of this article.
[1] N. M. Druzhinin, ed., *Krest'ianskoe dvizhenie v Rossii v 1870–1880 gg.: Sbornik dokumentov* (Moscow, 1968), 114–16 (hereafter *KD, 1870–1880*).

difficult to reconcile with the common portrayal of the peasant woman as passive, subordinated, and oppressed.[2] They provide a rare glimpse into peasant women's mentality. Deciphering the language of women's resistance sheds light on the sources of their strength and the aspects of their society and culture that empowered them.

Economic need and the struggle for subsistence invariably provided the backdrop. The source of women's strength was their need to ensure the survival of their family under exceedingly difficult circumstances. The emancipation of the serfs in 1861 did not favor the Russian peasantry. It allotted peasants less land than they had tilled as serf, and the land was of poorer quality because noble landlords kept the best land for themselves. Peasants also lost access to forest and meadowlands that they had freely used in the days of serfdom. And they had to pay for the land they received at prices often far beyond its market value. They also paid taxes to the state and dues to support the work of the local elective government, the *zemstvo*. In most of rural Russia, the land did not yield enough to feed the peasants year-round, let alone to pay the burden of dues and fiscal obligations laid upon it. To feed themselves and pay their taxes, peasants often had to rent land from a neighboring landowner, or work for wages in agriculture or industry. The debate continues over the extent of peasant poverty in the decades following the emancipation.[3] However, no one seriously doubts that peasants had to struggle for survival.

In that struggle, peasants could rely only upon themselves. Tsarist officials, rural police, and virtually everyone from outside the village were likely to be enemies, bent on depriving the peasants of the little they had. Census takers counting heads and assessing property might find reasons to raise peasants' taxes. Land surveys might deprive them of land they considered theirs. Tsarist officials and rural police came to the village to punish peasants who failed to pay their taxes, arresting the debtor (or his village elder) or seizing household property.[4]

The threats outsiders posed to the peasants' survival prompted peasants to engage in overt and collective conflict with these enemies, despite

---

[2] See, for example, Rose L. Glickman, *Russian Factory Women: Workplace and Society, 1880–1914* (Berkeley, 1984), chap. 2.

[3] For two of the latest sallies, see Elvira M. Wilbur, "Peasant Poverty in Theory and Practice: A View from Russia's 'Impoverished Center' at the End of the Nineteenth Century"; and Stephen G. Wheatcroft, "Crises and the Condition of the Peasantry in Late Imperial Russia," in *Peasant Economy, Culture, and Politics of European Russia, 1800–1921*, ed. Esther Kingston-Mann and Timothy Mixter (Princeton, 1991), 101–27, 128–72.

[4] Wheatcroft, "Crises," 169–70; Jeffrey Burds, "The Social Control of Peasant Labor in Russia: The Response of Village Communities to Labor Migration in the Central Industrial Region," in Kingston-Mann and Mixter, *Peasant Economy*, 75–76.

the risks involved. For example, in 1890 the entire village of Arkhangel'skaia, Viatka province, mobilized to prevent the authorities from inventorying and confiscating the moveable property of villagers in arrears on their tax payments. The women were among the more aggressive. Varvara Stepanova threw mud at one policeman and threatened another with her stick; Stepanida Tot'meninova struck a policeman. Evdokiia Rezvykh and Efrosiniia Evstigneeva pushed another in the chest, and Irina Kozhevnikova tore the scarf from yet another policeman's neck as the crowd of peasants surrounded the intruders, calling them thieves and brigands. The police were forced to beat a hasty, if temporary, retreat.[5] In June 1880, police came to confiscate the sheep and pigs belonging to the villagers of Shchetinino, Pskov province, in payment of a disputed debt to their former owner. The police chose a day when the men were all in court, contesting the confiscation. Finding all the houses locked, the police headed straight for the fields, where they rounded up the sheep and pigs and started to drive them down the road to the landlord's estate. But five or six peasant women stopped them. Led by Efrosiniia Nikandrova, who hit a policeman with a stick, and Pelageia Efimova, who bit another on the finger, the women overcame the policemen's resistance and "did their business," as the reporting officer put it, and drove the confiscated livestock back to their village.[6] In another incident that took place in 1883, officials came to confiscate property from the household of Nikolai Komoropov, who was in arrears on his taxes. His wife held them off with a crowbar, while he shouted insults and attempted to tear the badge from around the *volost'* (township) elder's neck.[7]

James Scott has argued that in fact, the most common acts of peasant resistance are those that occur in everyday forms and often elude detection. They represent the "prosaic but constant struggle between the peasantry and those who seek to extract food, labor, taxes, rents and interest from them." Peasants ordinarily choose forms of struggle that do not eventuate in collective action. "In place of land invasion, they prefer piecemeal squatting; in place of open mutiny, they prefer desertion; in place of attacks on public or private grain stores, they prefer pilfering. When such stratagems are abandoned in favor of collective action, it is usually a sign of great desperation."[8]

[5] N. M. Druzhinin, ed., *Krest'ianskoe dvizhenie v Rossii v 1890–1900 gg.: Sbornik dokumentov* (Moscow, 1959), 33–34 (hereafter *KD, 1890–1900*).

[6] *KD, 1870–1880*, 390–400.

[7] N. M. Druzhinin, ed., *Krest'ianskoe dvizhenie v Rossii v 1881–1889 gg.: Sbornik dokumentov* (Moscow, 1960), 284 (hereafter *KD, 1881–1889*). A similar case can be found on 373–74.

[8] *Weapons of the Weak: Everyday Forms of Peasant Resistance* (New Haven, Conn., 1985), xvi.

The desperate need to defend their fragile family economy mobilized Russian peasant women to engage in the vast majority of the actions that became part of the written record—actions sufficiently unsettling to attract the attention of policemen, officials, governors, and other representatives of the educated classes, who described them for their superiors. These accounts were deposited in archives and would be published by Soviet historians after the revolution. Although they are more confrontational than the everyday forms of resistance that Scott describes, none of the acts in which Russian peasant women participated before 1905 really deserves to be characterized as part of a "peasant movement." They were localized and spontaneous, temporary and comparatively short-lived responses to particular circumstances, and they lacked the coordination and purposefulness that the word "movement" usually implies. They represent skirmishes, rather than full-scale battles, between Russian peasants and the forces with which they struggled.

When peasant women engaged in skirmishes with representatives of official Russia, they acted as members of their family and their community. The family was the "most significant and indispensible condition of life for every peasant," and its well-being was crucial to the well-being of its individual members.[9] The peasant household was a production unit and the holder (although not the owner) of allotment land. In the Russian village, private ownership of land was rare. Instead, land was communally owned and administered by the *mir* (commune); it was allocated to households according to the number of male workers (in some areas according to the number of consumers, or "eaters") and periodically reapportioned to reflect changes in household composition and need. Similarly, tax burdens were allocated by ability to pay. Peasants saw the interdependence this system fostered as a key to their survival. Thus, both family and community served as the basis for women's resistance, rather than its target. In this, women seem indistinguishable from their fathers, husbands, and brothers, who also defended their interests by indicating their need to maintain and provide for the family. Likewise, both women and men acted collectively rather than individually, "together with the mir and in the name of the mir."[10]

Yet given women's subordinate status in the Russian peasant family and community, this mode of action appears paradoxical. Women's relation to the larger peasant community was in many respects mediated by

---

[9] M. M. Gromyko, *Traditsionnye normy povedeniia i formy obshcheniia russkikh krest'ian XIX v.* (Moscow, 1986), 261.

[10] M. M. Gromyko, "Sem'ia i obshchina v traditsionnoi dukhovnoi kul'ture russkikh krest'ian XVIII–XIX vv.," in *Russkie: Semeinyi i obshchestvennyi byt*, ed. M. M. Gromyko and T. A. Listova (Moscow, 1989), 7–9.

their husbands and fathers. Only under unusual circumstances did women serve as heads of households, and never did they serve as village elders. In the overwhelming majority of villages, women were barred from participating in the assembly (*skhod*) that governed community affairs such as the allocation of land and taxes. Moreover, women lacked direct access to the land that was so often the cause of confrontations with outside authorities. However, women's absence from positions that conferred formal authority in village life evidently did not preclude their direct involvement in village affairs. Therefore, in addition to shedding light on neglected aspects of women's lives, examining women's participation in peasant unrest may prompt us to rethink some of our assumptions about gender and the allocation of power in Russian peasant culture.

My periodization of Russian peasant women's activism is no different from the periodization of men's. The first section of this article will treat women's participation in peasant resistance from 1861 to 1905; the second will deal with the revolutionary period from 1905 to 1907. As I will argue in the following pages, while the intensity and focus of peasant women's engagement may have varied according to this periodization, its essential character remained remarkably consistent, except in a few areas where activists succeeded in winning some peasant women over to a different comprehension of their interests. But everywhere else, women acted collectively to preserve the family and the community throughout this period.

The characteristics of women's resistance emerge clearly in the decades before the revolution of 1905, when peasant women acted in their roles as wives, mothers, and daughters to defend the family economy against destitution or destruction—just as lower-class women did elsewhere in Europe.[11] Women's resistance was selective: they stayed at home when their menfolk attacked the estates of local landlords, and they stood apart from local power struggles such as attempts to oust *volost'* officials.[12] But when outsiders threatened the subsistence of the household or the community, women often rose to the defense. They fought against officials who tried to confiscate their property to pay off arrears. To surrender

[11] Olwen Hufton, "Women and the Family Economy in Eighteenth-Century France," *French Historical Studies* 9, no. 1 (Spring 1975): 1–22; Cynthia Bouton, "Gendered Behavior in Subsistence Riots: The French Flour War of 1775," *Journal of Social History* 23, no. 4 (Summer 1990): 741; Malcolm Thomis and Jennifer Grimmett, *Women in Protest, 1800–1850* (New York, 1982), 51–58.

[12] Between 1890 and 1900, such attacks constituted 3 percent of a total of 627 peasant actions; the power struggles, 12.4 percent. A. M. Anfimov, *Ekonomicheskoe polozhenie i klassovaia bor'ba krest'ian evropeiskoi Rossii, 1881–1904 gg.* (Moscow, 1984), 202.

sheep, pigs, cows, or other farm animals meant to lose a source of manure as well as animal by-products, like wool or milk, that could be sold to supplement household income. Confiscation of animals also affected the food supply, although to a lesser degree; peasants consumed meat very rarely, but when they did it most often came from pigs, sheep, or domestic fowl.[13] Women seem to have been particularly ardent when they defended their own turf from the encroachments of outsiders, protecting property that belonged to their customary sphere of household and barnyard.

But Russian peasant women also mobilized when the threat involved turf that lay outside of their sphere. In these cases, the enemy might as often be a local noble landowner as a genuine outsider. Decades after the emancipation, landlords and peasants continued to contest boundaries and lay claim to lands that the other considered theirs. Land was at stake in 46.4 percent of the documented instances of peasant resistance between 1890 and 1900, as it was in the vast majority of cases between 1861 and 1905 for which documents have been preserved and published.[14] In these incidents, Russian peasants rarely attempted to extend their holdings; rather, they defended long-standing rights against the encroachments of local landowners, as they did in the incident that introduced this article. And women often played a prominent role in these engagements. For example, in the spring of 1883 in Orel province, the court ordered a survey of land that the peasants had already sowed with grain. Believing that the court's decision in favor of the landlord was unjust and fearing that the survey work would damage their crop, the peasants requested the authorities postpone the work. The authorities refused. The day of the survey, a crowd composed primarily of peasant women and children blocked the path of the surveyor and then broke his cart when he tried to circumvent them. Hurling stones, shrieking and shouting threats, the crowd finally succeeded in driving him away.[15] By default, women in a Samara village led the resistance to a land survey, after soldiers prevented the men from going to the fields to work. Making their way to the disputed terrain, the peasant women drove off the village elder who was assisting the surveyor, cursed the peace mediator, broke the landmarks, tore the shovels from the laborers' hands, and brought the entire operation to a halt.[16] It is impossible to calculate the frequency of women's participation in such actions, because when women did not fig-

---

[13] R. E. F. Smith and David Christian, *Bread and Salt: A Social and Economic History of Food and Drink in Russia* (Cambridge, 1984), 265–66.

[14] Anfimov, *Ekonomicheskoe polozhenie*, 202.

[15] *KD, 1881–1889*, 209–11.

[16] Ibid., 434–35; see also *KD, 1870–1880*, 308–9.

ure prominently, police or government officials did not bother to note their presence among the nameless, faceless mass of peasants who defended collective rights.[17]

These confrontations can serve to remind us of the complexity of the Russian peasants' relationship to land. Although land was allocated by men in the *skhod* to men in the household and was in that sense a "male attribute," to borrow Rose Glickman's phrase,[18] the women who engaged in these acts of resistance clearly felt that the land was "theirs" as well.[19] It was "theirs" because land produced the grain that women transformed into bread to feed their families, and because women's labor was as essential to reaping that harvest as men's was. Moreover, to the extent that the land really belonged to anyone, it belonged to the community as a whole. Women were very much part of that community, despite their exclusion from the formal aspects of village power and their subordination to husbands and fathers. Women played a vital role in community life and exercised informal power through their control of the domestic sphere and their role as mothers. Peasant women's networks served as a source of women's power. As a group, women participated in a wide variety of community events, and they enforced community standards by shaming individuals who transgressed them. The peasant custom of mutual aid (*pomoshchi*) mobilized village women to do exclusively women's work. These networks, which maintained and perpetuated the community, could be marshaled to defend it when it seemed threatened.[20] As the community's future, children were important, too; but they were not powerful, as their mothers were, so small children usually remained in the background when peasants confronted outsiders.

Membership in the community made it imperative that Russian peasant women participate in community action to defend the community's property. In several instances, peasants actively resisted the authorities' attempts to divide villagers by sex and age when disputes over community property arose. In 1890, for example, the vice-governor of Saratov province ordered only male householders to appear at the *volost'* administration to negotiate a property dispute that involved the lands of two villages. Despite his insistence that "under no circumstances should women and children appear," women and children came nonetheless, and in-

[17] For circumstances where officials did note their presence, see *KD, 1881–1889,* 716–18; and *KD, 1890–1900,* 280–88.

[18] *Russian Factory Women,* 17.

[19] This sense that the land was "theirs" was made explicit in a village in Podol'ia province. See *KD, 1881–1889,* 338–41.

[20] For a discussion of women's informal power, see Christine D. Worobec, *Peasant Russia: Family and Community in the Post-Emancipation Period* (Princeton, 1991), 177–82, 204–6, 215–16. On *pomoshchi,* see Gromyko, *Traditsionnye normy,* 53, 61.

sisted on remaining there in defiance of soldiers who ordered them to withdraw.[21] In Orel province, the authorities proved equally unsuccessful in separating women and children from a crowd of peasants resisting a land survey.[22] The presence of all community members, irrespective of age or sex, underscored peasants' claims to be acting as a community and in the community's name.

Yet even as Russian peasant women joined other members of the community in defense of the community's rights, they often adopted a language of resistance that differed from that of peasant men. In some ways, women's resistance during the last decades of the nineteenth century resembles the *bab'i bunty* that Lynne Viola has described for the period of collectivization. As Viola defines them, *bab'i bunty* were women's riots, characterized by "irrational behavior, unorganized and inarticulate protest, and violent actions."[23] For Viola as well as others, tactical considerations best explain women's visibility: women tended to lead because "they were less vulnerable to repression than peasant men."[24] The wording of many prerevolutionary accounts of resistance supports this interpretation. In Orel in 1885, villagers claiming the right to work disputed land declared that if they were prevented from harvesting the hay and grain, "their wives would take their place and, using their scythes and knives, would cut anyone who tried to stop them."[25] In 1886, peasant men from a village in Riazan' province, instead of acting themselves, "sent" the women and youths out to defend a disputed peat bog and prevent hired workers from cutting peat.[26] In July 1892, in Obolesheva village, Orel province, the men stood back and cheered while their wives, sisters, and daughters attacked the local land captain and tried to stop him from rebuilding a dam on disputed land.[27] While the men stood aside, peasant women in Zubovskii village, Voronezh province, in 1889 prevented the police from removing the fence around a garden that the court had just transferred to a local landowner. One woman gave the signal that mobilized a whole crowd of women armed with sticks, rakes,

[21] *KD, 1890–1900*, 84–85. See also *KD, 1881–1889*, 211.

[22] *KD, 1881–1889*, 210–11.

[23] "*Bab'i bunty* and Peasant Women's Protest during Collectivization," *Russian Review* 45, no. 1 (January, 1986): 23.

[24] Ibid., 37. See also Roberta Manning, *The Crisis of the Old Order in Russia: Gentry and Government* (Princeton, 1982), 153; and Maureen Perrie, "The Russian Peasant Movement of 1905–7: Its Social Composition and Revolutionary Significance," in *The World of the Russian Peasant: Post-Emancipation Culture and Society*, ed. Ben Eklof and Stephen P. Frank (Boston, 1990), 208.

[25] *KD, 1881–1889*, 429–30.

[26] Ibid., 490–91.

[27] *KD, 1890–1900*, 180–84.

pokers, and other implements. The women raced to the garden, shouting "Don't come near, we won't let you," and refused to retreat. The men, "those responsible for the women," initially played no role, because they "were convinced that the police would not touch their wives"—or so Vice-Governor Karnovich believed.[28]

But how much weight should we give such explanations? The authorities in Russia, like authorities elsewhere in Europe, had a tendency to assume that the inspiration for resistance inevitably derived from men, even when women were in the forefront of it. It is precisely because of this assumption that they were more reluctant to resort to violence when women were in a crowd.[29] Even when tactical considerations encouraged women's visibility, other factors were often at work as well: women were not mere pawns in a confrontation staged by men. The language of women's resistance provides evidence that women's customary roles could empower them as well as limit them.

Under certain circumstances, women's very subordination to men in Russian peasant culture freed them from responsibility for their actions. Like the riotous women whom Natalie Davis describes, Russian peasant women took advantage of "the complex license accorded the unruly woman," which held a woman under the sway of her emotions unaccountable for what she did.[30] As in early modern France, that license in peasant Russia derived from ideas about womanhood. A Russian male peasant would have put it this way: "A woman's hair is long but her brains are short." According to peasant men, women needed to be controlled because they were so susceptible to their own emotions. In addition to being the natural guardians and protectors of their wives and daughters, men were responsible for women's behavior. They were supposed to instruct their wives as to how to conduct themselves properly, by beating them if necessary.[31] Village men collectively administered justice to male villagers, but usually left the disciplining of women to their husbands.[32] Women could take advantage of this belief in their irresponsibility, which was shared by the authorities as well as by village men.

But custom also granted the unruly Russian peasant woman a more positive license: she had the right "as subject and as mother to rise up and tell the truth."[33] Women large with child or holding babies to their breast

[28] *KD, 1881–1889,* 679–80.

[29] See the discussion in Thomis and Grimmett, *Women in Protest,* 54.

[30] Natalie Zemon Davis, *Society and Culture in Early Modern France* (Stanford, 1975), 146. The following discussion draws heavily on Davis's insights.

[31] Worobec, *Peasant Russia,* 188.

[32] Stephen P. Frank, "Popular Justice, Community, and Culture among the Russian Peasantry, 1870–1900," *Russian Review* 46, no. 3 (July 1987): 251–55.

[33] Davis, *Society and Culture,* 147.

might confront the authorities with hunger in the village or articulate the community's collective rights, as they did in the incident that introduced this article. Of the three women who tried to prevent the police from entering a barn to confiscate peasant property in Shchetinino village, Pskov province, in May 1880, two were pregnant.[34] Several of the women from Tugovishcha village, Smolensk province, held nursing infants in their arms when they stood atop a dike to save it from destruction at the hands of the police.[35] In 1892, in Riabov village, Novgorod, male peasants halted their efforts to stop laborers from cutting wood on disputed land, only to return several hours later accompanied by their wives. The women carried infants and were armed with sticks. Together, the men and women attacked the carts on which wood had been stacked, and confiscated axes from the workers.[36] Peasant women also employed the symbolism of motherhood to evoke sympathy from officials, who might be expected to respect mothers and to spare their children.[37] The fact that women sometimes employed their infants with apparent disregard for the child's well-being, as in the incident with which this essay began, underscores the strategic nature of the symbolism of motherhood. This apparent carelessness is also a reminder that desperate women might sometimes neglect the youngest, weakest members of the household to ensure the survival of the rest.[38]

When Russian peasant women took advantage of their complex license to resist outsiders, their menfolk usually cast themselves as the women's protectors. For that reason, women's supposedly greater immunity from repression could cut two ways. Men became enraged when the authorities arrested or hurt women, and on occasion this served to escalate the level of violence. For example, when the police tried to remove three women who blocked the door of a barn in Pskov in June 1880, the women created an uproar. "They're murdering us!" they screamed. One of the women fell to the ground, galvanizing the peasants who had gathered from neighboring villages. They surrounded the police and assaulted them with sticks and fists.[39] In the 1889 confrontation in Zubovskii

---

[34] *KD, 1870–1880*, 398.

[35] *KD, 1890–1900*, 339–41.

[36] Ibid., 175–77.

[37] These expectations were sometimes appropriate. For example, police in Orel were advised to avoid arresting pregnant women or women with nursing infants. *KD, 1890–1900*, 185.

[38] On peasant women's attitudes toward their children, see David Ransel, "Infant-Care Cultures in the Russian Empire," in *Russia's Women: Accommodation, Resistance, Transformation*, ed. Barbara Evans Clements, Barbara Alpern Engel, and Christine D. Worobec (Berkeley, 1991), 113–32.

[39] *KD, 1870–1880*, 398.

village, peasant men had stood aside to let the women protect a garden. The women even attacked a small police detachment. But as soon as the women were threatened physically, the men took the offensive. Seeing that one woman's face had become bloodied, they rushed to beat the policemen.[40] Much the same thing happened in the 1892 incident in Obolesheva village, when the authorities came to arrest one woman per household after the women attacked the local land captain and prevented him from rebuilding a dam on disputed property. The men "noisily and heatedly" refused to surrender the women, insisting that they preferred to go to Siberia themselves. When the police proceeded to seize the women anyhow, the women fought back as fiercely as the men. Evdokiia Komiagina and Nastasiia Poliakova beat the two policemen who detained them, while other women threw their nursing infants beneath the feet of the arresting officers. Ivan Artamanov struck a policeman with a rake, declaring that anyone who went near the women would not remain alive. The other men attacked the police with their fists, forcing them to retreat without arresting the women. For this resistance, only the men were punished, three of them sentenced to one hundred or more blows with the rod.[41]

In the decades after the emancipation, peasants who engaged in acts of resistance generally acted as a community and in the name of the community to defend what they believed to be theirs by long-standing right. Drawing upon their informal power within the community and on the networks they had generated, women joined and sometimes led these acts of resistance. Often, they exercised the license granted the unruly woman to act on her emotions and to speak the truth as she saw it. Even as they spoke for their family and community, women employed symbols—the symbol of motherhood in particular—that were likely to evoke sympathy from an audience of outsiders.

In the turbulent years between 1905 and 1907, Russian peasant resistance became more common, and it often turned from defense into aggression. The term "peasant movement" is surely merited for this period. Although peasants resisted representatives of officialdom by refusing to pay taxes or send recruits for the army, in these years the local landowner was most commonly the target. Peasants had accumulated new grievances against him (or, quite often, her) in the decades following the emancipation, especially after Russia's spurt of industrialization in the 1890s. Rapid population growth in the villages intensified peasants' need to rent land from the landlord or to earn wages to feed additional mouths. But real wages for agricultural labor declined after the mid-1890s, and op-

[40] *KD, 1881–1889,* 679–80.
[41] *KD, 1890–1900,* 177–80, 182.

portunities for renting land had diminished by the early twentieth century because some landlords had switched to capitalist methods of farming; instead of renting out the land, they worked it for profit themselves. Sometimes these landlords restricted peasants' access to forests and pasturelands, too.[42] As a result, between 1905 and 1907, peasants engaged in unprecedented assaults on landlords' property: burning or destroying estates and outbuildings, illegally cutting wood, seizing meadows and pasture and arable land, engaging in agricultural strikes, and raiding barns and granaries.

The sheer quantity of published documentation on peasant activity in 1905 casts the patterns of women's resistance into sharper focus, but it does not alter the picture very much. To be sure, peasant women, like their husbands, fathers, and brothers, often became more aggressive in 1905. But with the exception of a comparative handful of women (of whom more will be said later), peasant women acted, as before, to defend their family and community. Far more than women's "generally subordinate position," this helps to explain women's uneven role—sometimes active and at other times passive—during those years.[43] The documentary record indicates more clearly than in the earlier period that Russian peasant women's involvement was not only prompted by their role in household and village; it was circumscribed by it as well. Women participated in resistance selectively, and according to a gender-related system of values that led them to refrain from some activities while plunging into others. Women were most visible and most likely to lead when peasants acted collectively to seize food or fodder, although such actions constituted only a tiny fraction (5.8 percent) of recorded acts of resistance.[44]

[42] Wheatcroft, "Crises," 148–49; Perrie, "Russian Peasant Movement," 194–95.

[43] Perrie, "Russian Peasant Movement," 208. In exploring the role of women in the 1905 events, aggregate records such as those left by the correspondents for the Free Economic Society are often of little help. What are we to make of statements such as "women do not take active part, but are more bitter than the men" and "women, along with old men, restrained the movement," or, conversely, "women took active part" and "encouraged and incited action"? *Agrarnoe dvizhenie v Rossii v 1905–1906 gg.*, Trudy Imperatorskago vol'nago ekonomicheskago obshchestva, vol. 1, no. 3 (St. Petersburg, 1908), 66, 78, 93. Such accounts often tell us nothing about the actions that women led, joined, or restrained. For this kind of detail, published documentary collections are far more useful, and it is primarily on them that the following discussion will rely.

[44] Perrie, "Russian Peasant Movement," 196. It is impossible to provide comparable statistics for women's participation because the documents do not always tell us when women took part in collective acts of resistance. For example, it is likely that they were present among crowds that illegally cut hay, harvested orchards, and stole grain, but the sources do not always say so explicitly. There would have been no way of knowing that women as well as men were illegally harvesting Prince Shcherbakov's grain in Voronezh province had not two women been wounded when troops fired on the peasants. S. M. Dubrovskii and B. Grave, eds., *Agrarnoe dvizhenie v 1905–1907 gg.* (Moscow, 1925), 318; see also 444.

Some examples illustrate the point. In Orel province, Olimpiada Sotskaia was one of four peasants detained as ringleaders in an attack by about two hundred peasants on a landowner's estate in the late fall of 1905. Before the arrests had been made, the peasants had managed to steal 4,800 rubles' worth of grain, 111 sheep, and all the chickens.[45] In Liapunovka village, Riazan' province, ten women and twenty men broke into the granary of two wealthy fellow villagers in June 1905 to seize the grain and distribute it among themselves.[46] Seizures of grain in particular displayed characteristics of protest against the growing market system, in which grain was treated as a commodity to be stored and sold even when neighboring peasants went hungry. As custodians of family well-being, women played a prominent role in such actions, too. Among the fifty peasants from the village of Solovykh, Riazan' province, who demanded the keys to the granary from the steward of a local estate in June 1905 were half a dozen women. When the steward refused them, the peasants broke the lock on one of the doors, then loaded and carried off rye on the carts they had brought with them. Every one of the thirty-four men and six women who later admitted the theft to the police officer refused to relinquish the grain. They insisted that they had taken another's property only because they were desperate and had nothing to eat, and that they would prefer going to prison to giving back the grain. That way, at least their family would have something to eat.[47] The women of Bunin village, Orel province, invoked a mother's right to speak the truth when the land captain attempted to confiscate grain the peasants had stolen from a local landowner in July 1906. Pushing their children before them, the women got down on their knees, beat their breasts, and shouted, "There is nothing to eat and he [the landowner] has a fortune. . . . The mir decided to take the grain so we wouldn't die of hunger. Take us all, beat us, murder us and our children." The women refused to budge or to cease shouting until the troops that had been called in finally left the village.[48] In at least one instance, peasants explicitly defended (or perhaps invented?) a paternalistic tradition that, unlike the market, sought to meet human needs. The peasants believed that landlords were obliged to feed "their peas-

[45] Dubrovskii and Grave, *Agrarnoe dvizhenie*, 191.

[46] *Krest'ianskoe dvizhenie v Riazanskoi gubernii v gody pervoi Russkoi revoliutsii* (Riazan, 1960), 55–56.

[47] *Agrarnoe dvizhenie 1905–1907 godov v Moskovskoi oblasti: Sbornik dokumentov* (Moscow, 1936), 102–5; *Krest'ianskoe dvizhenie v Riazanskoi gubernii*, 51–52.

[48] Dubrovskii and Grave, *Agrarnoe dvizhenie*, 216–17. See also *Revoliutsionnoe dvizhenie v N. Novgorod i Nizhegorodskoi gubernii v gody pervoi Russkoi revoliutsii* (Gorki, 1955), 400; and *Revoliutsionnoe dvizhenie v Voronezhskoi gubernii v 1905–1907 gg.* (Voronezh, 1955), 163.

ants" in hungry years and to provide the grain for free, a police chief reported to the governor of Riazan' province.[49]

Evoking the "complex license accorded the unruly woman" to defend her family and community, women sometimes took advantage of gender-related conventions that allowed them greater immunity from repression by outside authorities.[50] The women (and occasionally children) might test the waters before the men plunged into illicit actions themselves—as happened in Voronezh, where women and children were the first to pick fruit in other people's orchards. The adult men joined in later, when it became clear that the peasants could get away with the pilfering.[51] Or women might stand in the forefront of resistance when authorities came to confiscate property, as in the earlier period. Encouraged by the men, the women of Gaponov village, Orel province, dragged away logs that the police had already piled on their carts and forced them to abandon their efforts to confiscate stolen wood.[52] When in August 1905 the police arrived in Berezovo village, Riazan', with a court order to confiscate the hut of the peasant woman Lisichina, it was the women of the village who defended her. Having armed themselves with stakes or stones and surrounded the house, the women launched their offensive as soon as the police showed up, bombarding them with stones and shouting, "We won't let you ruin Lisichina! We'll kill you!" One of Lisichina's daughters stood on the roof throwing stones, and another threw them from inside the house. Lisichina herself sat in her garret armed with a pitchfork and heaved bricks at the police. The men sat quietly at home during the defense of Lisichina's property. Nevertheless, the police chief believed that the men had put the women up to it and were merely "waiting for someone to touch the women so they would have a reason to attack and to create a disorder." But, perhaps precisely to avoid this outcome, no one touched the women. Bombarded by stones, the policemen instead beat a hasty retreat.[53]

On the other hand, women were far less likely to participate—even as "an advance party composed of the weakest elements of the community," to borrow Maureen Perrie's words[54]—in peasant disturbances that brought little direct benefit to household or village. This helps to explain

[49] *Krest'ianskoe dvizhenie v Riazanskoi gubernii*, 100.

[50] Viola, in "*Bab'i bunty*," reports much the same behavior in the early 1930s.

[51] Perrie, "Russian Peasant Movement," 209.

[52] Dubrovskii and Grave, *Agrarnoe dvizhenie*, 194. See also *Krest'ianskoe dvizhenie v Riazanskoi gubernii*, 605–6.

[53] *Krest'ianskoe dvizhenie v Riazanskoi gubernii*, 65–66.

[54] "Russian Peasant Movement," 208.

their very low visibility in acts of arson or destruction against landlords' estates. Such acts were far more frequent (constituting 18.1 percent and 15.7 percent respectively of the total number of actions) than any other collective peasant actions during 1905–6.[55] But only a few documents mention women engaging in arson, and those women never played a leadership role.[56] Women are mentioned somewhat more often, but similarly never as leaders, when peasants destroyed landlords' estates.

Women's comparative passivity here is understandable. The risk of retribution for engaging in arson and destruction was enormous, and it directly threatened the household and community that were women's primary concern. Moreover, in terms of women's paramount interests, there was little to be gained from these actions. It may also be that the landlord's estate represented truly alien territory, by contrast with the arable land, forest, and meadowlands that nominally belonged to the landowner. During the days of serfdom, the peasants had worked that land, cut wood in that forest and hay in those meadows, so that when they "illegally" did the same during this revolutionary period, they were from their own perspective merely reclaiming what was in fact "theirs."[57] The estate of a noble landlord was a different matter. To attack it meant to venture outside the peasants' domain, in addition to inviting the most severe repression.[58] For their effrontery, peasants were flogged, their houses sometimes burned, and their leaders subjected to summary execution. The character of the action, at least as much as women's "lack of development" and their failure to "understand the meaning and significance of the movement"—the analyses offered by correspondents for the Free Economic Society in its study of the agrarian revolution—accounts for why women often opposed attacks on landlords' houses, despite their manifest hostility to the landowner.[59]

It was young peasant men, not women, who most often took the lead when peasants encroached on the landlord's terrain.[60] Young men were more likely to be literate and to have some experience of the larger world as a result of having served in the armed forces or worked for wages outside their village; some may have become acquainted with socialist thought. Equally important, young men had much less to lose. Still single

[55] Ibid., 209.

[56] See, for example, *Revoliutsionnoe dvizhenie v Voronezhskoi gubernii*, 434.

[57] Manning, 154; in a different way, Gromyko also makes this point in "Sem'ia i obshchina," 7–8.

[58] Manning discusses this hesitancy (*Crisis of the Old Order*, 153–54).

[59] *Agrarnoe dvizhenie v Rossii v 1905–1906 gg.* 1:119; also 49, 93, 139.

[60] Very young women may have shared some of their male counterparts' recklessness. In Serdobskii district, Saratov province, in October 1905, four underage girls were tried with six other peasants for arson against a noble's estate. Ibid., 1:136.

and free from responsibility for women and children, they were more prepared than their mothers and fathers to take risks and to act on their anger and defiance.[61]

In the few recorded instances where women did figure in attacks on landlords' property, they are usually to be found dragging things home for their family or village. When one man and several women representing the entire village of Berezovo, Tula province, revenged themselves in July 1905 on a local landowner who refused to rent land to them, they went to his estate, destroyed part of a snow fence, and cut down two dead aspens. They then chopped these up for firewood, brought them back to the village, and distributed them among the households.[62] In November 1905, women and men from a couple of villages in Orel province stole four ricks of hay and forty-five stacks of peat from Prince Kurakin before arming themselves with axes, shovels, and pitchforks in order to overcome the police and break into his barn. By sunset, they had pillaged and burned the entire estate.[63] In early December 1905, in Kaluga province, men and women actually came into conflict because the men wanted to complete their destruction of a landlord's house while the women took a more practical approach, insisting that they should first break into his granary and take grain for their families.[64]

The way that pillagers treated nobles' personal property suggests a shift in peasant mentality. During the Pugachev uprising over a century earlier, peasants had destroyed the modern features of nobles' estates as symbols of an alien civilization.[65] In 1905, instead of rejecting the nobles' material culture as alien, peasants appropriated pieces of it for themselves. For example, a crowd of two hundred peasants, including women and children, attacked the estate of the landowner Ershov in Kaluga province and stole nine hundred rubles, four silk dresses, one wool dress, two jackets, two sheets, and two pairs of curtains, as well as edibles of various sorts.[66] In Voronezh province, women completed a theft that their men had initiated a day and a half earlier by dragging home the estate's wallpaper, blinds, and upholstery from the furniture.[67] Although it is doubt-

---

[61] Perrie, "Russian Peasant Movement," 209.

[62] Dubrovskii and Grave, *Agrarnoe dvizhenie*, 129–32.

[63] Ibid., 171–72. See also *Agrarnoe dvizhenie v Rossii v 1905–1906 gg.*, 78; and *Revoliutsiia 1905–1907 v g. Samare i Samarskoi gubernii: Dokumenty i materialy* (Kuibyshev, 1955), 254–56.

[64] *Revoliutsionnoe dvizhenie v Kaluzhskoi gubernii v period pervoi Russkoi revoliutsii 1905–1907 godov: Sbornik dokumentov* (Kaluga, 1955), 104.

[65] Marc Raeff, "Pugachev's Rebellion," in *Preconditions of Revolution in Early Modern Europe*, ed. Robert Forster and Jack Greene (Baltimore, 1975), 198.

[66] *Revoliutsionnoe dvizhenie v Kaluzhskoi gubernii*, 49–51.

[67] Dubrovskii and Grave, *Agrarnoe dvizhenie*, 290.

ful that the peasants hung the wallpaper or used the curtains and blinds as window coverings, the women could utilize the fabrics to make clothing, and they may well have worn the wool or silk dresses on special occasions. Increasing numbers of peasant women had adopted this sort of attire by the early twentieth century. This was evidence of their desire to "move up in the world" that a century earlier they had tried to eradicate.[68]

Some documents suggest other changes in women's aspirations. They offer evidence that in at least a few regions, especially those with substantial levels of urban-rural contact as a result of out-migration for wages, peasant women could be responsive to the political appeals of people more educated than themselves. During the years of upheaval, school-teachers and other educated rural people engaged in political activity and propaganda, stimulating some peasant women as well as men to formulate ideas about their political rights. Thus, in June 1905, women from a village in Novotorzhok district, Tver' province, joined with men to sign a petition that called for popular control of government by an electoral system that enfranchised all adults, women included.[69] A correspondent for the Free Economic Society reported that the women of seven villages in Kashin district, Tver' province, took active part in the local branch of the Peasant Union and "even convened [their own] assemblies [skhodki]."[70]

In a very few cases, women expressed explicitly their aspirations to a more formal political role. When political power became institutionalized in a new way through elections to the Duma, the status of women became a question, as it had not been when women's informal power in the household and community more or less counterbalanced men's formal authority over community affairs. As peasant women from several Tver' villages expressed it in a letter to a Duma deputy, "Before, although men might sometimes beat us, still we resolved matters together. Now, by contrast, they say, 'You are not our comrades,' because only men can vote and be elected to the Duma. . . . Before, we and the men had one authority, but now the men will be writing the laws for us." Apologizing for the ignorance that led them to express themselves so poorly, the women nev-

[68] On moving up in the world, see Eugen Weber, *Peasants into Frenchmen: The Modernization of Rural France, 1870–1914* (Stanford, 1976), 230. On the spread of urban dress among rural women, see T. A. Bernshtam, *Molodezh'v obriadnoi zhizni russkoi obshchiny XIX–nachala XX v.* (Leningrad, 1988), 77; John Bushnell, *Mutiny amid Repression: Russian Soldiers in the Revolution of 1905* (Bloomington, Ind., 1985), 5; and Barbara Engel, "The Woman's Side: Male Out-migration and the Family Economy in Kostroma Province," *Slavic Review* 45, no. 2 (Summer 1986): 265.

[69] A copy of the petition is reproduced in Dubrovskii and Grave, *Agrarnoe dvizhenie*, 85–86.

[70] *Agrarnoe dvizhenie v Rossii v 1905–1906 gg.* 1:26–27.

ertheless asserted their right to a share of political power: "Our affairs are mutual, so let them also ask us women how to resolve them." Fearful that their husbands and the authorities might make their lives even harder, the women did not sign their names or name their villages. According to the letter, the writing had been done by a young girl.[71]

Women from a few other villages also claimed the vote for women. Responding to a Duma deputy's assertion that women had no desire for political rights, fifty-five women from Voronezh signed a letter insisting that the deputy did not speak for them. "There are no women deputies in the Duma who could represent all women, so how does he know? He is wrong to say that the peasant woman doesn't want rights. Did he ask us? We, the *baby* [women] of Voronezh district, Voronezh province, understand that we need rights and land just as men do."[72] Peasant women from Samara province gave similar reasons for protesting the same speech. Calling on the Duma to remember "the half of the human race that is struggling to escape humiliating slavery and to become citizens with equal rights," they declared their support for those Duma deputies who supported women's suffrage.[73]

It is quite likely that these letters were influenced (and in the case of the Samara letter, even written) by members of the Union for Women's Equality, whose demands for women's suffrage and peasant women's right to land and education they reflect. The letters from Tver' and Voronezh were published in the Union's newsletter; the language of the letter from Samara is suspiciously high-flown. But feminist influence does not mean that the letters lacked peasant women's genuine endorsement. As Scott Seregny has remarked about outsiders' influence on peasant petitions, if peasants were not already receptive to ideas, propaganda would have little effect on them. "No 'agitator' can force a peasant to sign an address not corresponding to his [sic] own wishes and needs."[74] Some women were evidently receptive to feminist concepts. So were some men: influenced no doubt by the Peasant Union or a local schoolteacher, a handful of peasant petitions called for women's suffrage, among other political demands.[75]

---

[71] Tsentral'nyi gosudarstvennyi istoricheskii arkhiv g. Moskvy, f. 516 (Russkii soiuz ravnopravii zhenshchin), op. 1, ed. khr. 4, l. 42.

[72] Ibid.

[73] *Revoliutsiia 1905–1907 v g. Samare i Samarskoi gubernii*, 323–24.

[74] *Russian Teachers and Peasant Revolution* (Bloomington, Ind., 1989), 157.

[75] See, for example, Dubrovskii and Grave, *Agrarnoe dvizhenie*, 8 (Arkhangel), 38 (Viatka), 85–86 (Tver'); *Agrarnoe dvizhenie v Rossii v 1905–1906 gg.* 1:26–27 (Tver'); *Agrarnoe dvizhenie 1905–1907 godov v Moskovskoi oblasti*, 105 (Riazan'); *Revoliutsionnoe dvizhenie v Kaluzhskoi gubernii*, 106; and *Vserossiiskaia politicheskaia stachka v Oktiabre 1905 goda* (Moscow and Leningrad, 1955), chap. 2, 374 (Novgorod).

Yet even as some women exchanged their sarafans for silk dresses or—in a handful of cases—expressed aspirations to a more formal political role, thereby embracing certain cultural or political elements of the modern world, in 1905–6 most peasant women, like their menfolk, resisted many of its economic dimensions. Most notably, they rejected those aspects of the expanding market system that had had a negative impact on their lives. To the practice of storing grain for sale even when peasants went hungry, they reacted by breaking into granaries and seizing the grain for themselves. Peasants invaded and tilled fields that capitalist-minded landlords had set aside for their own use instead of renting them to the peasantry. Peasants also acted on other grievances, cutting wood in forests and pasturing cattle in meadows that noble landlords had reserved for themselves.

Nevertheless, even when peasants were righting old wrongs, the character of their resistance differed from that of the earlier period. Between 1861 and 1905, resistance was primarily defensive, aimed at outsiders who tried to take from peasants what they considered "theirs." In 1905–7, the peasants' target was most often the local landowner, and women as well as men were far more aggressive. However, women's aggression remained essentially linked to their role as custodians of family and community well-being. Women figured prominently when peasants confiscated grain from landlords' granaries or cut wood in landlords' forests to distribute among themselves. They labored alongside their menfolk to till illegally a landlord's fields. But when peasants engaged in arson or acts of destruction for which the risks outweighed the benefits, women were rarely to be found.

While the target and the intensity of peasant resistance might change, women's role in it throughout both periods was in the vast majority of cases conservative: they struggled to preserve what they had in the name of family and community. Even their demands for political rights were often couched in terms of women's family roles. If they possessed political rights and land, the peasant women from Voronezh wrote, they would "be able to intercede in behalf of their husbands and children." "Slaves can only nurture a servile spirit in their children," argued the women from Samara province. So long as women lacked the vote, there would be no harmony (*lad*) in the family, wrote the women from Tver'.[76]

---

[76] It is illuminating to compare this language to that employed by some working women in 1905 protesting their exclusion from the workings of the Shidlovskii commission. There, the appeal is to the unity of the working class; family references are completely lacking. See Glickman, *Russian Factory Women*, 106. Then again, we do not know who chose the language and framed the petitions, nor whether what we read reflects the mentality of workers and peasants or the preconceptions of intellectuals who sought to organize and speak for them.

Women would act this way again during the period of the Stolypin reforms (1906–14), which were aimed at breaking up the mir and creating a strong, independent, capitalist peasantry that would serve as a source of stability in the countryside. Women figured in virtually every attempt to prevent individual households from separating from the village community.[77] And women would emerge prominently yet again to resist collectivization in the early 1930s.[78] In their efforts to preserve family and community, the women were not very different from their menfolk. But they sometimes drew on their own, women's networks when they engaged in acts of defiance. And when they took advantage of the license granted the unruly woman, they spoke their own language of resistance. To disarm the authorities, women clasped nursing infants to their breasts or thrust children before them. Men of all classes shared assumptions about women's emotionality and irresponsibility, and women turned those assumptions to the advantage of the peasantry. Before 1905, they bit, hit, pushed, and in other ways physically attacked representatives of officialdom who threatened their family or village; after 1905, they led selected assaults against neighboring landowners.

Almost invariably, these Russian peasant women acted as wives and mothers, as well as members of the community. If there were tensions within the family between mothers-in-law and daughters-in-law, or between husbands and wives, they became submerged in the face of a larger threat to the peasants' way of life. In the relatively few cases where peasant women raised political demands on their own behalf, they employed the language of the family rather than the individual. Even in situations where the peasant woman behaved neither passively nor submissively, the family was a source of resistance instead of an institution to be resisted. After the revolution, the Bolsheviks would only slowly learn this lesson.

[77] See S. M. Dubrovskii, *Stolypinskaia zemel'naia reforma* (Moscow, 1963), 556; and A. V. Shapkarin, ed., *Krest'ianskoe dvizhenie v Rossii v 1907–1914 gg.* (Moscow and Leningrad, 1966), 218–21, 285–87, 301–2, 344–46, 387–88, 415, 422–23.
[78] Viola, *"Bab'i bunty."*

3

PEASANT POPULAR CULTURE AND THE

ORIGINS OF SOVIET AUTHORITARIANISM

Boris N. Mironov

THIS ARTICLE OFFERS several preliminary views on the sources of Soviet authoritarianism, which I seek to locate within the popular culture of the prerevolutionary peasantry. The essence of my hypothesis rests on a fundamental reality of life in the prerevolutionary Russian countryside: authoritarian relations served as the basic model for all interpersonal relations among peasants, including social relations. This was a result of the fact that the peasantry's primary social institutions—the family and the commune—were authoritarian, cultivating, through socialization, authoritarian personalities. The Russian peasantry (which accounted for more than 80 percent of Russia's population in 1917) and Russian workers (the overwhelming majority being of peasant background)—in fact, virtually the entire Russian people, since half of the urban population consisted of peasants—were permeated with an authoritarian spirit. One could thus argue that Russians were an authoritarian people. The revolutions that liberated them from the fetters of the old state, with its law and order, were able to build a new society even more authoritarian than under the tsars. This was not only because nonauthoritarian relations were unknown, but also because the construction of the "Future City" (*Grad Griadushchego*) was accomplished through authoritarian methods and under the leadership of people armed with an authoritarian doctrine.

Before turning to an elaboration of this argument, we will examine briefly the keys to understanding the research at hand—definitions drawn from sociological and sociopsychological literature regarding the authoritarian personality, the authoritarian style of rule, authoritarian relations, and authoritarian and totalitarian societies.

The traits most characteristic of the authoritarian personality are emotionality, irrationality of behavior, and, closely tied to these, a readiness

Research for this article has been supported by the Kennan Institute for Advanced Russian Studies.

to rely on any kind of superior force (which might appear in the form of a god, fate, or a leader) on the one hand and, on the other, constant revolt in relation to a weak authority. Other traits of the authoritarian personality include an inability to cooperate; an inclination towards anarchy, destructiveness, cynicism, and hostility and enmity toward people; painstaking observance of accepted norms of behavior; aggression against those who violate these norms; faith in superstitions and in mythical predestination of the material world; and a preconceived notion that the outside world is filled with savage and terrible things.[1] Under the influence of such traits, the authoritarian personality is distinguished by conservatism, aggression, contempt both for the intelligentsia and for different ethnic groups, and conformity and stereotypy of thought or dogmatism.

The authoritarian style of government is characterized by a maximum of centralization and a minimum of democracy, concentration of power in the hands of one person, elimination of others from decisions on the most important issues of collective activity, suppression of popular initiatives, and the predominance of coercion as a means to influence people.[2] The supremacy of authoritarian relations in society, then, along with the authoritarian personality type, are characteristic of an authoritarian style of rule and are founded on domination and subjugation, forming the basis of authoritarian regimes and sociopolitical systems. The totalitarian regime or system is a combination of these. In both authoritarian and totalitarian societies, there is a cult of the strong leader. In the first case, this cult is combined with passive obedience on the part of the masses, but in the second case it is linked with the active participation of citizens in the political arena under principles established by those in power.[3]

The identity of Russian peasant culture found its sharpest expression in the patriarchal family and the repartitional rural commune. These were the basic institutions of the peasantry throughout the prerevolutionary period, and we now turn to them in order to determine the prevailing pattern in their relations.

Before 1917, the patriarchal family structure, consisting of two or three generations, predominated among the Great Russian peasantry.[4]

---

[1] T. W. Adorno et al., *The Authoritarian Personality* (New York, 1950); H. Marcuse, *One-Dimensional Man* (Boston, 1964).

[2] *Rukovodstvo i liderstvo* (Leningrad, 1973); R. Stogdill, *Handbook of Leadership* (New York, 1974).

[3] J. J. Wiafr, *Socjologia stosunkow politycznych* (Warsaw, 1977); E. Vitr, *Sotsiologiia politicheskikh otnoshenii* (Moscow, 1979), 269.

[4] All references to the peasantry in this article are limited to the Great Russian peasantry.

This type of family organization involved not only blood relations but, no less important, a household union. It was founded on the division of labor according to age and gender, in which the dominant position belonged to the household head—the *bol'shak*. Family property was owned collectively. For those observing the surface of peasant life, the large family seemed ideal (as it does to some even now), for the interests of each member were protected while order, peace, and well-being reigned. In reality, such was not the case. The patriarchal peasant family was akin to an absolute government, only with a smaller constituency. The bol'shak (usually the oldest and most experienced male) distributed labor among family members; he allocated, directed, and supervised all of their work. He resolved internal arguments and punished the guilty. His responsibilities included maintaining morality, making purchases, concluding transactions, and paying taxes. His role was further strengthened by the fact that family members could enter into a transaction only through the head of the household. Similarly, the bol'shak was able to delegate work to his son or younger brother against their will. He represented the family at all times and in all places. Thus, the bol'shak was the leader of a familial cult, and he was accountable before the village, society, and state for managing the family.

Under this patriarchal yoke, the position of family members proved difficult at times. Custom did not recognize the rights of children to demand a division of resources among themselves. The operating principle was "Children do not divide the spoils during the lifetime of their fathers." Likewise, the bol'shak could (and often did) squander family property. Since custom allowed him to engage in transactions with several shares of the landed property under his control, communal relations greatly affected family relations.[5]

---

[5] On family life, see A. Vesin, "Sovremennyi velikoruss v ego svadebnykh obychaiakh i semeinoi zhizni," *Russkaia mysl'*, no. 9–10 (1891); A. Zhelobovskii, *Sem'ia po vozzreniiam russkogo naroda* (Voronezh, 1892), 1–63; Ia. Kuznetsov, *Polozhenie chlenov krest'ianskoi sem'i po narodnym poslovitsam i pogovorkam* (St. Petersburg, 1904); M. Sinozerskii, "Domashnii byt krest'ian," *Zhivaia starina* 9, no. 1 (1899): 403–35; A. Smirnov, *Ocherki semeinykh otnoshenii po obychnomu pravu russkogo naroda* (Moscow, 1877); G. I. Uspenskii, "Krest'ianskie zhenshchiny," in *Polnoe sobranie sochinenii*, vol. 12 (Moscow, 1952); E. P. Busygin, N. V. Zorin, and E. V. Mikhailichenko, *Obshchestvennyi i semeinyi byt russkogo sel'skogo naseleniia srednego Povolzh'ia: Istoriko-etnograficheskoe issledovanie (seredina XIX-nachalo XX v.)* (Kazan', 1963), 91–103; O. I. Zotova, V. V. Novikov, and E. V. Shorokhova, *Osobennosti psikhologii krest'ianstva* (Moscow, 1983), 139–40; I. N. Milogolova, "Sem'ia i semeinyi byt russkoi poreformennoi derevni, 1861-1900 gg." (dissertation, Moscow, 1988); N. A. Minenko, *Russkaia krest'ianskaia sem'ia v Zapadnoi Sibiri (XVIII-pervoi poloviny XIX v.)* (Novosibirsk, 1979); A. V. Saf'ianova, "Vnutrennii stroi russkoi sel'skoi sem'i Altaiskogo kraia vo vtoroi polovine XIX–nachale XX v. (Vnutrisemeinye otnosheniia, domashnii uklad, dosug)," in *Russkie: Semeinyi i obshchestvennyi byt*, ed. M. M. Gromyko and T. A. Listova (Moscow, 1989), 91–110; and *Selo Viriatino v proshlom i nastoiashchem* (Moscow, 1958).

Let us try to enrich the distinctive features of internal family relations with the principles on which they rested. The first principle was the hierarchy within the family and the resulting inequality among family members. All were subjugated: women before men, youth before their elders, children before adults, and daughters-in-law before the *bol'shukha* (wife of the household head). "The old man [bol'shak] is the despot, to whom all should be subordinate," R. Ia. Vnukov attested.[6] Under the rule of the bol'shak, one might love and truly care about other household members, but family members believed that strictness and a firm hand in internal matters were sincerely for the good of all. "The woman stands in the background," noted A. N. Minkh, a well-known ethnographer from the end of the nineteenth century. "She does not possess a voice. She must blindly obey her elders and her husband. Her relations with the latter are like those of a worker with an employer. It often happens that she catches hell from him. Beatings by the husband are customarily showered on an unfortunate woman for any sort of little misdeed, and, moreover, they occur with drunken fists when she is completely blameless. The husband is not subject to any reproach."[7]

The obligation of children to obey the will of their parents without question acquired the force of law as early as the seventeenth century. The 1649 Code of Law forbade children from reporting their parents for imposing corporal punishment on them. In the nineteenth and early twentieth centuries, the Fifth Commandment was strictly enforced throughout the countryside. "In the peasant's view, parental responsibility before their children is lacking. However, the children's responsibility before their parents exists in an exaggerated manner. The Fifth Commandment is a special favorite. 'Disrespectful' was the most offensive of epithets for children," wrote a former peasant in 1929.[8] As the ethnographer P. S. Efimenko noted in his detailed study of Arkhangel province, "the fathers' obligation for raising the children is relinquished to the mothers, but fathers still establish a pattern with their children. They raise them in a lackadaisical manner, incorrectly, rudely, and roughly. There is no other care for them. From a very early age, from eight years old onward, they force their children to work."[9]

Violence was recognized as a completely normal and important form of interaction. Children were punished physically—the younger ones with particular frequency, although the rod was not spared with the older children. Women suffered terribly if they betrayed their husbands.

[6] *Protivorechiia staroi krest'ianskoi sem'i* (Orel, 1929), 18.

[7] *Narodnye obychai, obriady, sueveriia i predrassudki krest'ian Saratovskoi gubernii* (St. Petersburg, 1890), 7.

[8] Vnukov, *Protivorechiia*, 17–18.

[9] *Materialy po etnografii russkogo naseleniia Arkhangel'skoi gubernii* (Moscow, 1877), 2:162.

Maksim Gorky personally observed on July 15, 1891, in the village of Kanybovok, Nikolaevsk district, Kherson province, how the husband of an adulterous woman bound his naked wife in a cart, climbed into the cart himself, and flogged her with a whip. Accompanied by a howling crowd, the cart made its way along the village street. In other places, according to Gorky, cases of "betrayal" were dealt with "more humanely": "They strip their wives, smear them with tar, strew chicken feathers over them, and lead them through the street. In summertime, they smear such women with molasses and tie them to a tree, where they are at the mercy of insects."[10]

Forced collectivism and centralism, or democratic centralism with the emphasis on centralism, predominated in the peasant family. The individual interests of particular family members were not taken into account. This was displayed graphically during betrothal agreements; young peasants usually married according to the will of their parents, whether or not the arrangements concurred with their own desires. Parental authority in this case did not reflect the caprice of the elders, but rather the interests of the family as a whole. Marriage was viewed as nothing more than a transaction involving property—a transaction that should be advantageous for the family as an economic unit.

These points are sufficient to allow us to view the peasant patriarchal family (or matriarchal family, which could result if the bol'shak died or for other reasons) as an authoritarian type. Its foundation was the collective family property and the immense power of the bol'shak, while cooperation among its members was achieved by using coercion and by muting those with less power. One could find traces of democracy within the family only in the rarest cases. It must be noted, of course, that outwork and labor migration, which were closely linked with the city, industry, and commerce, greatly affected a number of villages and regions during the late nineteenth and early twentieth centuries. Some of the resultant changes regarding the "democratization" of internal family relations have been noted by historians.[11] Yet it is difficult to agree with those scholars who exaggerate the level of such changes and who view them as having affected the entire peasantry.[12]

[10] M. Gor'kii, *Sobranie sochinenii* (Moscow, 1949), 2:5–7, 569. On the role of this type of punishment (*vozhdeniia*) in the system of measures for social control, see S. P. Frank, "Popular Justice, Community, and Culture among the Russian Peasantry, 1870–1900," *Russian Review* 46, no. 3 (1987): 239–65.

[11] See, for example, F. Pokrovskii, "O semeinom polozhenii krest'ianskoi zhenshchiny v odnoi iz mestnostei Kostromskoi gubernii po dannym volostnogo suda," *Zhivaia starina* 6, no. 1 (1896): 459–60.

[12] I. V. Vlasova, "Russkie: Sel'skaia sem'ia," in *Semeinyi byt narodov SSSR* (Moscow, 1990), 26–27.

By contemporary standards, the large patriarchal peasant family may seem like an irrational and ineffective organization. Why, then, did it exist for so long? The authoritarian style of rule provided a sufficiently high level of worker productivity among family members on the basis of a division of labor and the ever-present threat of physical force. The patriarchal family provided shelter for the old and the weak. It provided insurance-type benefits to the sick. Most important, neither serious spiritual interests nor the personality were awakened to a meaningful degree. Life was so difficult and basic that the goal of everyday life was reduced to mere survival. According to the zemstvo doctor A. I. Shingarev, "the most terrible thing is the ignorance, the lack of understanding and knowledge of almost everything that lies outside the narrow range of vision of life on the farm. A degree of prejudice and superstition has existed from time immemorial." Naturally, it would follow that "the all-powerful knout seemed necessary to empower both the employer and the pedagogue."[13]

The Russian peasant family lived within the framework of and under the tutelage of the rural agricultural commune, or *mir*, as the peasants called it. This social organization, according to the opinions of such experts on Russian life as Konstantin Aksakov, Lev Tolstoy, Gleb Uspensky, V. I. Semevsky, and many others, was the peasants' hearth and home and determined all tenors of life. And for investigators of rural life, the commune was, like Rome, where all roads inevitably led. It was along these roads that they wandered in search of a Russian truth and the foundations of Russian life. What did the village commune actually represent?

The commune had a broad range of responsibilities—or, in the terminology of sociologists, fulfilled a multitude of functions: it was responsible for production (the distribution of land, which was not private but communal property, and the organization of production); financial matters (the apportionment and collection of taxes); legal affairs (civil and petty criminal matters among commune members); religion; administrative law enforcement; protection of members (defense of the interests of the peasantry before the state, landowners, and others); education; philanthropy; and social control. As a result, the peasantry was united in the commune by economic interest, social struggle, the administration of justice, religious life, the organization of leisure, and mutual aid. The state did not conduct its relations with individual peasants, but with the commune. The commune in its entirety was responsible for fulfilling obligations to the state. In practically all areas of his or her existence, the peasant was a member of the commune, and all of the member's social relations existed either within the framework of the commune or by means of the commune. The commue also served as a conduit for official ideas—

[13] *Vymiraiushchaia derevnia* (St. Petersburg, 1907), 169, 174.

for the directives and norms that the government maintained. It did not serve blindly, but flexibly and selectively. The commune accepted instructions from above, but if such instructions ran counter to its interests or traditions, they were distorted, either consciously or unconsciously.

On the one hand, the commune governed the lives of its members. It was responsible for their vital needs and stood as the defender of their interests before the government. On the other hand, it was an administrative and law-enforcing organ, through which the state expropriated taxes, took recruits, and held the peasant in obedience. Therefore, the commune had the characteristics of an unofficial democratic organization; it served to strengthen and pool the resources of neighbors while overseeing the necessities of life for the peasants. But it was simultaneously an officially recognized organization used by the ruling class and the state for their own goals.

In sociological terms, the commune was a small social group although its membership was comparatively large, containing from twenty to five hundred people of both sexes. Its members were in frequent, direct, and informal contact, and thus found themselves to be greatly interdependent.

The commune played an enormous role in societal opinion and constituted an effective system of unofficial control. It regulated the behavior of its members primarily through absorption of the peasant's personality—enslavement or domination, one might say—and through control of the member's economic and other activities. These features developed because the commune was a small social group and because they were the logical consequences of the centralism inherent in communal organization and communal land tenure. Let us elaborate on this connection.

Decisions of the supreme organ of the commune, the village assembly, by law had to be accepted by a two-thirds vote. The dissenting minority was obligated to yield to the majority, and thus individual peasants could be denied the opportunity to lead their life according to their own opinion.

The communal form of property combined aspects of both collective and private ownership. Land belonging to the commune was apportioned by the village assembly among all peasants who worked it (or according to some other principle), but peasants did not own the land individually. The commune also controlled the lease, sale, security, and inheritance of the land. Through its assembly, it worked out a system of crop rotation, divided land into plots, decided what would be sown on them, determined the precise time for agricultural work, and so on. But all peasants worked their portion of the land independently. Communal land ownership and distribution dictated crop rotation, and collective responsibility created a system of production relations under which commune members, in all of their activities, were interrelated and interdependent. Production proceeded according to the commune's general plan. Economic activity was thus the most important type of relation between peasant and commune, having a decisive influence on the peasant's interrelations with the commune as well as in all other spheres of his or her life. Relations of production within the commune created a type of social interaction under which the peasant was absorbed by the commune.

Like serfdom, the commune could not, of course, completely restrain the peasant. But in the areas of peasant life under consideration here, obedience was the norm, and deviations from the norm proved minimal. The possibilities for a peasant to act as an individual within the commune were insignificant. At the same time, opportunities for the commune to act on behalf of the peasant were limitless. For example, while young peasants with able-bodied fathers (or brothers) could demand and obtain a division of family land against their fathers' wishes, they did so only with significant concessions in their elders' favor. Such concessions, as well as the property division itself, would be decided not by the family, but by the mir. Thus, to a significant degree, the peasant was consumed by the communality of interests of the majority. Such communality dictated that property differentiation must not take on destructive proportions. Yet absorption by the commune did not produce traumatic effects on the peasant's psyche. For that reason, it did not seem to the majority of peasants that the commune was enslaving them. Individuality—the conscious sense of "I"—was still so underdeveloped among the rural population that the "I" harmoniously and fundamentally combined with the "we," that is, with the commune.

Another important feature of the commune was its great seclusion and isolation from the outside world—from other social groups, the city, etc. In other words, the commune had a low level of social mobility, which impeded social change within the village and helped preserve the communal order.

Like the patriarchal family, the commune was not, of course, an ideal institution. It embodied contradictions that made it far from suitable for eternal existence. However, over the course of several hundred years, it did serve the needs of the time. It was a completely acceptable form, perhaps even the best of all possible forms, both for the control of property and for peasant life in general. The drawbacks of the commune as a social organization—its repression of initiative, absorption of the individual personality, traditionalism, collective responsibility, and so on—were, from the peasants' point of view, its benefits. The commune furthered consolidation among the peasantry by protecting it from the ruling class and the state. It impeded development of property inequality and guaranteed peasant ownership of land, thus offering social security as well as protection from the outside world. The commune's shortcomings, from the perspective of those in power, were its low level of and slow development of productive capabilities and its role as an obstacle to raising taxes and penalizing tax evaders. In compensation for these shortcomings, however, the commune prevented the peasantry from taking greater power into its hands. It also succeeded (most of the time) in keeping peasants obedient and collecting rents. The economic interests of society and state were thus victimized by the political interests of the ruling class.[14]

In comparing the commune with the peasant family, we find so many similarities that the family might be considered a commune in miniature. In both, one sees suppression of the personality, lack of respect for individual goals and interests, repression, regimentation of life, centralism, the primacy of elders and tradition, inequality (women and the young did not participate in the exercise of power), and coercive collectivism founded on collective property (land in the case of the commune, and all property in the case of the family). The family and the commune fed off one another to a certain extent and, naturally, supported one another.

The authoritarianism of the family and commune found external support in Orthodoxy and autocracy, while internally it rested on the ignorance and, most important, the ethical outlook of the peasantry. M. Ia. Fenomenov expressed the essence of peasant ethics in these words: "The basic ethical worldview in the countryside lies in a unique and crude Darwinism: tacit recognition that the strong should take first place while the weak yield to them. The understanding of strength, except for physical strength, relies on factors such as wealth, intellect, and resourcefulness."[15]

Let us summarize and interpret in modern terms the main principles upon which familial-communal aspects of Russian village life rested—as did, in a concrete sense, all of Russian society, for which the peasantry served as the primary social base.

1. Communal property, which served as the material base of labor in Russia for centuries and provided the foundation of peasant life.

2. The right to work, which was guaranteed by the right of peasant males to possess land and by equal use of all communal property.

3. The right to rest. There were 140 days of each year on which the commune did not work, including 52 Sundays, 30 church and state holidays, and 58 popular (church and secular) holidays.[16]

---

[14] For a more detailed discussion of the commune, see B. N. Mironov, "The Russian Peasant Commune after the Reforms of the 1860s," in *The World of the Russian Peasant: Post-Emancipation Culture and Society*, ed. Ben Eklof and Stephen P. Frank (Boston, 1990).

[15] *Sovremennaia derevnia* (Moscow and Leningrad, 1925), 2:92.

[16] N. L. Peterson, comp., *Prosveshchenie: Svod trudov mestnykh komitetov po 49 guberniiam Evropeiskoi Rossii* (St. Petersburg, 1904), 12–14.

4. Maintenance of the solvency of each peasant family; the right to aid from the commune in the event of a crisis (fire, murrain among the livestock, and other situations). The right of invalids, the young, and others to social support and care.

5. Democratic centralism. The importance of the interests of the entire commune over those of the individual peasant. The subordination of the minority to the majority.

6. Collective accountability. The commune was held accountable for its members before the government, while the family answered for the individual before the commune. Collective responsibility in the payment of taxes.

7. The right of married males to participate in community and social matters (at village and township assemblies, in peasant courts, by holding elective office).

8. Egalitarianism as the ideal, as expressed both in the observance of equality in the distribution of rights and fulfillment of obligations and in efforts to impede significant differentiation among peasants.

9. Regulation of the entire life of the peasantry. The right of the commune to interfere in interfamilial and personal dealings of peasants if these contradicted norms and traditions or violated the interests of the commune as a whole. The suppression of individualism in the practical realization of the principles of communal life within the strict framework of traditions and norms.

10. Traditionalism—that is, an inclination to use the old as an example or model.

It should be noted that under the influence of authoritarianism, the commune viewed the rights granted to individual peasants as obligations. For example, the rights to work, rest, and participate in community matters were, in reality, obligations to do so.

The regulating principles of familial and communal life were institutionalized not only in the peasants' social, economic, and familial relations within the commune, but also in their ideals, ethical outlooks, and value systems. In combination, these principles transformed the Russian village into a traditional authoritarian society that, without interference from the market, city, state, or other external forces, was a direct reproduction of its material and spiritual values, much like the dissemination of the authoritarian personality discussed above. Insofar as the authoritarianism of peasant society was an important factor in supporting its traditionalism, the peasantry's authoritarianism and conservatism were two sides of the same coin.

To understand how peasant authoritarianism was transmitted from one generation to the next, we must examine the agents of socialization within the village. In the concrete conditions of peasant life in the late nineteenth and early twentieth centuries, the primary agency for socializing the younger generation was the family. Village schools did spread to many areas during this period, but they played only a secondary role in the socialization process. Education was elementary, lasting only a short time, and was not available everywhere. In addition, as Ben Eklof has shown, parents purposely allowed the school to operate only on a minimal basis, limiting its role to providing basic literacy so that they would not lose complete control over their children.[17] The village itself—that is, the commune, the church, and the local clergy—also played an important, although smaller, role in the socialization of young peasants.[18] Commune and church did not clash with parents in this process, but educated children in the same spirit as did the authoritarian peasant family. The city participated in socialization only to a very limited degree. Young peasants who left their village for the city, even for a short time, did so only after they had reached maturity and often only after marriage—that is, after socialization had largely been completed.

The effects of socialization within the family were somewhat curious. Children grew up early and became something akin to their parents' doubles. O. P. Semenova-Tian-Shanskaia noted that young peasant children developed very quickly:

> Any ten-year-old boy judges the world around him as would an adult. This is explained by the simple day-to-day life of the peasantry and, most important, by the inclusion of the child in almost all work and in all affairs of peasant life, where everything lies open before his eyes. . . . The child looks at everything and everyone with the eyes of his elders. There is no special children's point of view. If one were to ask a child, "Why is the land captain here?" he would answer, "To repress the peasants." . . . The child's representation of the world, in essence, differs very little from that of adults. . . . The school does not change the child's view of the life that surrounds him. There is school and there is life, and for the peasants there is always a line between the two.[19]

Semenova-Tian-Shanskaia's observations are seconded by another student of late-nineteenth-century peasant life, N. N. Zlatovratskii, who argued that "young peasants from ten to thirteen years of age are as developed as the adults; one may converse with them as thoroughly as one might with their fathers. . . . This is the result of being raised by life itself,

---

[17] *Russian Peasant Schools: Officialdom, Village Culture, and Popular Pedagogy, 1861–1914* (Berkeley, 1986), 474–82.

[18] M. M. Gromyko, "Sem'ia i obshchina v traditsionnoi dukhovnoi kul'ture russkikh krest'ian XVIII–XIX vv.," in Gromyko and Listova, *Russkie*, 7–23.

[19] *Zhizn' 'Ivana': Ocherki iz byta krest'ian odnoi iz chernozemnykh gubernii* (St. Petersburg, 1914), 21–31.

not by the school, not by the commune, and not by the regulations of a pedagogue."[20]

Socialization of the commune's younger generation thus took place primarily within the family, and secondarily "on the street." Socialization occurred mainly through direct experience—through life experiences passed from parents to children, from elders to the young. The oral tradition of peasant culture was an additional factor in that culture's traditionalism and dogmatism.

Social psychology argues that socialization results from a person's interaction with the totality of social phenomena. But among the various agents of socialization, first place belongs to the family—even in contemporary western European countries,[21] where the role of schools and the mass media is immeasurably greater than in the semiliterate Russia of the late nineteenth and early twentieth centuries. Indeed, I would argue that the effects of the media and the educational system upon the Russian peasantry were negligible by comparison with their effects in contemporary developed countries. For reasons connected with poverty, culture, and social life, the family was the main transmitter of social heritage and the fundamental agent of peasant socialization in the prerevolutionary Russian village.

To further expand upon the opinions of social psychologists, I would argue that socially inherited information was fixed—one might say ingrained—in the interpersonal relations of the peasant family, in the stereotyping of adult family members' behavior, and in their teaching of the child. From early childhood, when the young peasant began to act independently and clearly control his or her own behavior, the child rapidly, albeit unconsciously, acquired the language and faith, manners and norms of behavior, ways of thinking, worldview, value system, and opinions about the cardinal problems of daily life that belonged to and characterized the child's family. While socialization did not, of course, end in childhood, that which the peasant acquired as a child remained throughout his or her life. Fundamental change in the models of behavior—the so-called conversion—occurred in exceptionally few instances. The peasant family played an important role in modeling and structuring not only interpersonal, intimate, informal relations, but social, economic, and political relations as well.[22] This was the case for the overwhelming majority of people. Only a few individuals overcame what was created in child-

[20] "Ocherki krest'ianskoi obshchiny," in *Sobranie sochinenii* (St. Petersburg, 1913), 8:62.

[21] G. M. Andreeva, N. N. Bogomolova, and L. A. Petrovskaia, *Sovremennaia sotsial'naia psikhologiia na Zapade* (Moscow, 1978), 155–219; E. B. Shestopal, *Lichnost' i politika* (Moscow, 1988), 28–38.

[22] E. F. Vougel, "Sem'ia i rodstvo," in *Amerikanskaia sotsiologiia: Perspektivy, problemy, metody* (Moscow, 1972), 165–66.

hood; mutations of the "genes" of social heredity were as rare as mutations in human chromosomes.

Thus, the family gives birth not only to the person, but also to the citizen. This occurs because the family is a social microcosm in and of itself; its structure represents the closest thing to the "original" model of the larger society. It includes, in miniature, the gamut of society's human relations. It is the entire system of fraternal and familial, economic and legal, moral and psychological relations. Intrafamilial relations are intertwined with the social, national, political, and economic relations of society. From another perspective, the Russian peasant family concentrated its totality within itself, as a result of which children were included in the system of social relations from birth.[23]

What sort of citizens did the peasant family produce with the help of the commune? First of all, there were those who shared the established principles, accepting fully developed relations as a given and not demanding change. Second, there was the type that is typically produced by an authoritarian family.[24] If we summarize the observations of contemporaries and psychologists, we can say that the peasantry's model personality (by which I mean the typical system of character traits that develops in a given culture as the result of a specific system of socialization and social control)[25] possessed the features we will now discuss.

Those raised by the family and commune had to sacrifice individual interests for the sake of common interests. They experienced want because of the policies of the authorities and of their leaders; they tolerated coercion and regulation. There was a very strong leveling tendency both in the division of the social and economic pie and in community obligations. Peasants did not like significant differentiation in any form. They were oriented toward tradition, the old ways, and authority, in which they sought models, ideals, and answers to their questions. They treated new forms of behavior negatively and disliked changes, from which they expected only a worsening of their situation. As a result, the village did not hold enterprising, independent persons in high esteem. Peasants were collectivists, preferring to be together. At the assembly, they argued and then unanimously made decisions, even though not everyone was satisfied. Plurality of thought was foreign to them; they always strove for unity of thought or, at the least, unity of action. The Russian peasant was obsessed by a fear of defying the numerous prohibitions, rules, and de-

---

[23] *Sovetskaia sotsiologiia* (Moscow, 1982), 1:212; V. Ia. Titarenko, *Sem'ia i formirovanie lichnosti* (Moscow, 1987) 19–20.

[24] V. P. Levkovich, "Vzaimootnosheniia v sem'e kak faktor formirovaniia lichnosti rebenka," in *Psikhologiia lichnosti i obraz zhizni* (Moscow, 1987), 70; N. N. Obozov, *Mezhlichnostnye otnosheniia* (Leningrad, 1979), 62, 88; Titarenko, *Sem'ia*, 41–42, 61–63.

[25] M. I. Bobneva, *Sotsial'nye normy i reguliatsiia povedeniia* (Moscow, 1978), 89.

mands of the village world. People constantly looked to neighbors, to the commune, and to the church, fearing to stray from the proper path. And if anyone decided to leave this path, that peasant did so with the entire commune. The peasants manifested solidarity in their common interests, particularly in the face of an external threat such as a landowner or the police. In internal matters, however, their behavior was characterized by anarchism and an unwillingness to cooperate, making joint enterprises within the village very difficult. Peasants also displayed cruelty, hostility, and aggressiveness toward outsiders belonging to another social estate— particularly the privileged—and toward those who defied established norms or went against the interests of the peasantry. Examples of such behavior can be seen in the harsh treatment of landowners, horse thieves, unfaithful wives, and disobedient children. Peasants were contemptuous of the intelligentsia and intellectual work in general. Their thoughts and behavior were characterized by dogmatism and banality. The rebellious, anarchical spirit, the emotionality, and the spontaneity were easily provoked in social situations. Prejudices and fatalism permeated all of village life, which was closely bound up with magical rituals.[26]

In comparing the authoritarian personality described by Adorno, Marcuse, and social psychologists with the prerevolutionary Russian peasant's model personality, we discover their essential kinship. The similarity between them is striking given that the material for a generalized social psychology was drawn up in Germany, Italy, the United States, and other developed European countries between the 1930s and 1950s. It seems to me that one important circumstance that has no relationship to authoritarianism formed several traits among the peasantry that are, in

[26] See, for example, M. Gor'kii, *O russkom krest'ianstve* (Berlin, 1922); V. I. Dal', "Russkii muzhik," in *Polnoe sobranie sochinenii* (Moscow, 1883), 6:148–63; N. N. Zlatovratskii, "Ustoi," in *Sobranie sochinenii* (St. Petersburg, 1912), 3:4; P. Nebolsin, "Okolo muzhikov," *Otechestvennye zapiski* 138 (1861): 141; K. F. Odarchenko, "Russkaia krest'ianskaia obshchina v sviazi s narodnym kharakterom," parts 1, 2, *Russkaia mysl'*, no. 2 (1881): 266–331; no. 3 (1881): 195–244; Semenova-Tian-Shanskaia, *Zhizn' 'Ivana'*; G. I. Uspenskii, "Iz derevenskogo dnevnika," "Krest'ianin i krest'ianskii trud," and "Vlast' zemli," in *Sobranie sochinenii* (Moscow, 1956), vols. 4, 5; A. N. Engel'gardt, *Iz derevni: 12 pisem, 1872–1887* (Moscow, 1937); T. Ganzhulevich, *Krest'iane v russkoi literature XIX veka* (St. Petersburg, 1913); A. E. Kirillin, "V. I. Lenin i psikhicheskie osobennosti krest'ianstva," in *Nekotorye voprosy filosofskikh nauk* (Leningrad, 1968), 218–40; N. S. Kabytov, "O nekotorykh kharakternykh chertakh dukhovnogo oblika russkogo krest'ianstva nachala XX veka," in *Sotsial'no-ekonomicheskoe razvitie Povolzh'ia v XIX– nachale XX veka* (Kuibyshev, 1986), 60–69; I. M. Kolesnitskaia, "Analiz psikhologii krest'ian v literature kontsa 1850–1860-x godov," *Uchenie zapiski Leningradskogo gosudarstvennogo universiteta*, no. 355, pt. 76; N. Rybnikov, *Krest'ianskii rebenok* (Moscow, 1930), 27–45; and M. A. Rakhmatullin, "K voprosu ob urovne obshchestvennogo soznaniia krest'ianstva v Rossii," in *Voprosy agrarnoi istorii Tsentra i Severo-Zapada RSFSR* (Smolensk, 1972).

fact, characteristic of the authoritarian personality: a disposition to authority, dogmatism, conservatism, fatalism, and prejudice. That circumstance is the peasants' ignorance. In 1917, only 37 percent of the rural population over the age of nine—including the nonpeasant estates—had basic literacy skills, having spent only two years in school.[27] If we consider only the peasantry, the literacy level was lower still, with over two-thirds being illiterate.

The cognitive model of socialization set forth by Piaget and other psychologists suggests that the development of the cognitive, emotional, and moral structures of personality occurs during the process of schooling. In particular, the adult, "mature intellect"—which is capable of deductive reasoning and of constructing hypotheses, in contrast to the incapacity of the "childlike" intellect for formal operations—is formed in the concrete and situational learning process that occurs up to the age of fifteen.[28] As the research of A. R. Luriia indicates, a person who does not go through the instructional process in school will continue to possess a childlike intellect throughout life.[29] This has a strong influence on personality and behavior, especially in a realm where authoritarian relations function.[30] Perhaps it was from this shortcoming that the peasantry's "infantilism" stemmed—a characteristic occasionally referred to by scholars of the Russian countryside.

Of course, some peasants differed from the standard described above. But there were relatively few, and peasants who behaved differently were not respected in the village. They either left voluntarily or were compelled to do so. The commune, at least from the mid-eighteenth century, had the right to send "depraved members" into the army, to Siberia, or to another remote region.

It can thus be suggested that the peasant family, along with the commune, fostered citizens who became the most fertile social base for political absolutism—for authoritarianism in society at large, with all of its economic and social consequences. It is no wonder that Russian emperors, including Nicholas II, always counted on support for the autocracy from the peasantry and the commune. The last ruler, of course, miscalculated in this regard. It is not impossible to assume that the peasants, during the revolutionary years of 1905–7 and 1917, came out not against the autocracy in principle, but against a concrete, self-compromising mon-

[27] B. N. Mironov, "Literacy in Russia, 1797–1917," *Soviet Studies in History*, Winter 1986–87, 107.

[28] Zh. Piazhe, *Izbrannye psikhologicheskie trudy* (Moscow, 1969); B. M. Velichkovskii, *Sovremennaia kognitivnaia psikhologiia* (Moscow, 1982).

[29] *Ob istoricheskom razvitii poznavatel'nykh protsessov* (Moscow, 1974).

[30] B. N. Mironov, *Istorik i sotsiologii* (Leningrad, 1984), 140–62.

arch. Perhaps this is why the new man who reigned in Russia so soon after the overthrow of Nicholas II was a strong, menacing, and cruel figure, in complete accordance with the peasants' idea of the patriarch, the sovereign, the master.

There were contemporaries who detected the connection between the relations within the patriarchal peasant family and the commune on the one hand, and the political structure of the Russian state on the other. In 1851, for example, A. L. Leopol'dov noted, "There is one elder in the household and all must obey him. This is one of the distinctive characteristics of the Russian people. To look upon this little patriarchal administration is to see in embryo the unquestioning obedience of the Russian people to those in power, as if they were sent by God."[31] A similar point of view was expressed by Alexander von Hauxthausen, who wrote that "the real strength of the people is rooted in their familial and patriarchal life, in the Slavic land commune, in the free self-administration. . . . The father in the family, the elected communal elder, and the all-powerful tsar as head of state are linked to one another by an unbreakable bond of historical development and succession."[32]

The strong link between the patriarchal organization of the peasant family and the state is not a national characteristic of Russia, but rather a historical phenomenon typical of agrarian societies. This was pointed out repeatedly as early as the nineteenth century by such researchers as Alexis de Tocqueville.[33] Modern historians have also focused attention on this connection. Jean-Louise Flandrin, for example, describes the premodern European family in terms of a "monarchical model," justifiably suggesting that not only the absolutism of governmental authority, but also Christianity and other monotheistic religions found nourishing soil in the patriarchy of everyday life. "The authority of the father in family life and the authority of God were not only linked with one another, they legitimized all other forms of authority. Kings, lords, patrons, priests—all appeared as fathers and as deputies of God." As early as the seventeenth century, "to call authority patriarchal meant that it was legitimized by law and required absolute obedience."[34]

In Russia, the system of authoritarian relations within the peasant family and commune existed on a broader scale throughout society during the sixteenth and seventeenth centuries (for example, the famous *Domostroi*—a literary production of the mid-sixteenth century—contained a

---

[31] "Bol'shak i bol'shukha," *Saratovskie gubernskie vedomosti*, no. 9 (1851): 41–43.

[32] Cited in N. M. Druzhinin, "Krest'ianskaia obshchina v otsenek A. Gastgauzena i ego russkikh sovremennikov," in *Ezhegodnik germanskoi istorii* (Moscow, 1969), 33–34.

[33] A. Tokvill', *Demokratiia v Amerike* (Moscow, 1896).

[34] *Familles: Parenté, maison, sexualité dans l'ancienne société* (Paris, 1984), 119.

code of behavior, and the Russian family was presented as a classical authoritarian organization). Beginning in the eighteenth century, however, the Russian peasantry began to diverge from the Russian state and the nobility, bourgeoisie, and liberal intelligentsia. While the peasant family and commune preserved tradition or at least sought to limit change, elite society was gradually transformed in accordance with European cultural standards.

As far as can be determined from the historical data available, between the eighteenth and early twentieth centuries neither the peasant family nor the commune—the citadels of peasant popular culture—underwent fundamental changes, save for a slight decline in the average number of family members (the reason for this decline is not yet clear). The principles of peasant life that populists aptly called their foundation, while loosened somewhat during the 1905 revolution, remained so durable that in 1906 the government instituted a policy to eradicate the commune (the Stolypin reforms). Yet over the course of ten years, this policy failed to destroy the rural commune, though it was constricted (by 1917, about one-third of all peasant householders had left their communes).[35] For the great majority of the Russian peasants, the authoritarian family and the repartitional commune remained the standards, the reference points, and the social groups around which they oriented their entire lives. Peasants considered the morals and principles they shared to be inherently correct.

From the beginning of the eighteenth century, Russian society as a whole was experiencing a certain evolution of its ancient traditions, and that process was accelerated significantly by the reforms of the 1860s. But this evolution would have been quicker and more successful had it not run counter to traditional peasant culture. Indeed, one important reason the Russian state enjoyed only limited success with its reforms since the eighteenth century was the durability of the peasant family and commune. These reforms were not initiated from below, within the primary social groups—the family and commune—and they contradicted the traditional mode of the peasants' lives. Through its reforms, the government sought to create attitudes and relations that were unknown to Russian peasant culture. Hence these reforms received little support from a peasantry that by 1914 constituted 85 percent of the country's population.

A lawful government, the priority of law over the self-willed person, respect for the individual (including women and children), the right of the minority to autonomy, election of officials at all levels and their accountability before their constituents, private property, bourgeois relations, social and political equality of citizens, democratic freedoms, and representative institutions—all of this had little analogy within peasant popular

---

[35] *Krizis samoderzhaviia v Rossii, 1895–1917* (Leningrad, 1984), 358–60.

culture and, as a result, did not take root. Reform was distorted during the process of its realization. Only in the cities and among the upper strata of society did reforms meet with partial success within the primary social groups, engendering a transformation to a Western form of inter-personal relations.

It should be stressed that state-initiated reforms and the development of capitalism, whether it developed freely or not, created a new type of person in Russia—citizens not faithful but free; not passive but active; not traditional but creative; not dogmatic but rational; not loyal servants of God and tsar but critical, thinking individuals; not passive performers but enterprising actors. The peasant family and commune, as we have seen, created people of an entirely different type. Thus, a rift opened in Russian society between traditional peasant culture and its adherents on the one hand, and the Europeanized culture of the city, represented by the edu-cated and higher strata of society, on the other. This rift inevitably led to conflict between the two cultures.

Thus, the tragedy of the Russian reformation is twofold: first, reforms were created from above, before a broad layer of society felt them to be necessary; and second, radical, structural reforms ran counter to the foundations of peasant life—foundations that had been confirmed for centuries within the peasant family and commune. And custom, of course, is stronger than law. As Pushkin put it, "Custom is the despot of the people."

History has shown that as a rule, reformers lose their edge if their re-forms, whether willfully or not, damage traditional relations in the pri-mary social group—relations that still satisfy the broad mass of the popu-lation. More successful reforms from above affect relations within society as a whole; they are conducted in accordance with the relations of the primary social groups and thereby avoid popular opposition or resis-tance.

With these ideas in mind, let us now turn to examine several events in the history of the Soviet Union. It seems to me that one cannot understand the three Russian revolutions of the early twentieth century without tak-ing into account the conflict between traditional Russian peasant cul-ture—the culture of the vast majority—and the Europeanized culture of the ruling minority. Of course, the contradiction between these two cul-tures was not the sole reason for revolution, but it was an important factor. As the ideological and practical mouthpiece for popular culture, the Bolsheviks moved to the forefront of the popular movement and thereby found themselves in power. The political, economic, and social system established after the civil war was, in principle, organized for the peasantry and the working class, which largely had not yet parted with its peasant worldview. It seems to me that, in its basic features, the new regime reproduced the Russian rural repartitional commune on a national scale, and this commune, as noted above, rested on the following principles: democratic centralism, collectivism, the regulation of differentiation, a collective form of ownership and division of property, equality of rights and obligations, the right to work and to possess property, the right to social assistance, and the right to rest.

It may be argued, then, that in the 1920s an accord was at last reached between the character of human relations within the peasant family—that is, in the families of the vast majority of the country's population—and in the commune, on the one hand, and the character of the social, economic, and political relations within society and state on the other. Here one might see the victory of peasant popular culture, a unique form of revenge for the two hundred years of degradation that it had experienced since the time of Peter the Great.

Further events, I would suggest, represent the partial manifestation of certain principles of popular culture extended either to their logical conclusion or to the absurd. For example, collectivization in and of itself did not contradict the foundations of traditional peasant culture, which ideally strove for full equality in the distribution of material wealth. It is no accident that the collective farm (kolkhoz) adopted many characteristics of the peasant commune.[36]

The creation of a bureaucratic command system of rule and the personal dictatorship of Stalin, I would argue, were also in accord with the peasant understanding of power, which held that a ruler must be authoritarian. The Bolshevik party, reflecting the views of the broad masses (and with support from a significant majority of the party members), moved consciously to this style of rule toward the end of the 1920s. It seemed the most effective means to achieve the party's goals. Stalin simply utilized the situation and the objective possibility to establish a regime based on personal power—also with the support of a majority of party leaders and rank-and-file members. The authoritarian interpersonal relations of the Russian peasant family and commune served both as fertile ground and as sociopsychological prerequisites for the creation of an authoritarian regime within the country. This regime did not frighten the masses, nor did they protest it; rather, it suited them, because from childhood they had grown accustomed to authoritarian relations and simply knew nothing else. "And you [Bolsheviks]," Vladimir Korolenko wrote to Anatolii Lunacharsky, "were the natural representatives of the Russian people,

[36] On this point, see L. Volin, "The Russian Peasant Household under the Mir and the Collective Farm System," *Foreign Agriculture* 4, no. 3 (March 1940): 133–46; and idem, "The Peasant Household under the Mir and Kolkhoz in Modern Russian History," in *The Cultural Approach to History*, ed. S. P. Ware (New York, 1940).

with their leanings toward tyranny, with their naive expectations of 'everything right away,' and without even the rudiments of rational organization and creativity. It is no wonder that this explosion [the revolution] only destroyed, creating nothing."[37]

The use of the collective as a qualitative means for depersonalization and social leveling, the cult of collective rather than individual success, the socialization of private life (labor collectives took responsibility for the moral character of their members before official organs, resolved family problems, looked after health needs, and made community property out of members' abilities), the politicization of society (every person was formally or informally a hired worker or servant of the state, was assigned to a place of residence and often to a place of employment, and could not freely change either), alienation from property and power under a superficial democracy, and the decorative participation of the masses in various matters—all of these processes, in one way or another, were characteristic of communal relations. But under the new conditions they were speeded up, and their exaggerated development led to the formation of a totalitarian society.

The mass repressions, I believe, represented a case of taking to the absurd the striving for unity of thought and the disrespect for the individual and for minority opinion that were cultivated in the peasant family and commune. The exploitation of the village by government and city is possibly a distortion of popular notions of justice. But it cannot be forgotten that the authoritarian regime itself exploited as much as possible.

Thus, one can agree with those who believe the development of the Soviet Union from 1917 to 1940 was, so to speak, natural. Were there alternatives? There were, but they were not based on firm traditions, they had no broad support either in the rank and file of the Bolshevik party or among the mass of the population, and therefore the probability of their realization was not great. In concluding, I should note that my views on the continuity of the prerevolutionary and Soviet regimes are still intuitive and, of course, hypothetical. I have posed the problem in hopes of turning attention to the striking internal similarities of two authoritarian regimes, despite their external differences.

Translated by Rebecca Morrison

---

[37] "Pis'ma k Lunacharskomu," in *Svoevremennye mysli, ili proroki v svoem otechestve* (Leningrad, 1989), 45.

4

CONFRONTING THE DOMESTIC OTHER:
RURAL POPULAR CULTURE AND ITS
ENEMIES IN FIN-DE-SIÈCLE RUSSIA

Stephen P. Frank

IN AN 1889 REPORT on his field studies of Sarapul'skii district, Viatka province, the Russian ethnographer P. M. Bogaevsky noted that peasants who spent time working in cities served as pioneers of urban culture upon returning to their villages. Unfortunately, he added, repeating with dismay an already widespread observation, the rural population had interpreted this culture in the most undesirable manner, thereby allowing it to destroy ancient precepts and customs. Young peasants in particular now regarded with disdain the centuries-old traditions of their grandparents—traditions that had given the Russian peasantry its special form of communal life and shaped its worldview. In light of these developments, as Bogaevsky perceived them, "the most cheerless picture emerges" of the Russian countryside. The family principle "weakens more and more with each passing year," leading to a noticeable decline of morals, diminishing respect toward elders, and the replacement of a native worldview by one alien to the peasantry.[1]

Bogaevsky was but one among a growing number of educated Russians who, during the 1870s and 1880s, came to believe that the foundations (*ustoi*) of peasant life were crumbling. In consequence, a dangerous cultural and moral vacuum had emerged, which, because "new [foundations] have not yet been created . . . or molded into definite forms," threatened even greater corruption and deterioration of traditional vil-

Research for this article was supported by the National Endowment for the Humanities, the Social Science Research Council, the Kennan Institute for Advanced Russian Studies, the International Research and Exchanges Board, and the Academic Senate of the University of California, Riverside. Thanks to John Bushnell, Judith Coffin, Gregory Freeze, Abbott Gleason, Hans Rogger, and Mark Steinberg for their helpful comments.

[1] "Zametki o iuridicheskom byte krest'ian Sarapul'skogo uezda Viatskoi gubernii," in *Sbornik svedenii dlia izucheniia byta krest'ianskogo naseleniia Rossii*, pt. 1, ed. M. N. Kharuzin (Moscow, 1889), 1.

lage society.[2] The elite's fears of the lower classes—generated by the social problems and "degeneracy" that had accompanied urbanization and the growth of an urban proletariat—gradually extended to the countryside, where poverty, immorality, and crime appeared to be spreading unchecked among the nation's vast peasant population. As Russia entered its fin de siècle in the 1890s and the processes of social, economic, and cultural change accelerated, observers offered even gloomier assessments of a countryside sunk in "spiritual darkness."[3] Despite significant advances in areas such as literacy and education, officials, educators, and clergy all felt that Russia's network of primary schools was failing in its mission to "civilize" the rural population and break through centuries of cultural backwardness.[4] Worse, an impertinent younger generation lacking "rational" recreations and infected by individualism was turning at an alarming rate to crime, gambling, heavy drinking, debauchery, and wild carousing at holiday celebrations, markets, and fairs. Following the revolution of 1905, dismay became outright despair as a wave of "hooliganism" swept the country, sparing neither cities nor isolated rural hamlets. Peasant youths, some claimed, were being transformed into "a huge class of rural terrorists" akin to Parisian "apaches," committing random crimes in villages and provincial towns with no fear of punishment. The press also disseminated this troubling picture through regular columns that featured disturbing scenes from the darker side of village life, all of which testified to the serious state of peasant degeneration.[5]

[2] Marikovskii, "Narodnaia shkola i derevenskaia molodezh'," *Narodnyi uchitel'* 6, no. 6 (1911): 5. This view of a vacuum following the breakdown of "traditional" societies was especially widespread among European social reformers, and it has been accepted by several historians of popular culture. See, e.g., R. W. Malcolmson, *Popular Recreations in English Society, 1700–1850* (London, 1973). For a contrasting view, see J. M. Golby and A. W. Purdue, *The Civilization of the Crowd* (New York, 1984), 26–27.

[3] "Selo Mordovskoe Korino (T'ma dukhovnaia)," *Nizhegorodskii listok*, no. 106 (1899): 3; "Sviatki v derevni," *Nizhegorodskii listok*, no. 1 (1900): 4. On the "proletarian disease" and "social degeneracy" in cities, see Reginald E. Zelnik, *Labor and Society in Tsarist Russia* (Stanford, 1971); and Thomas A. McGivney, "The Lower Classes in the City of Moscow, 1870–1905" (Ph.D. diss., New York University, 1978), chap. 5. Educated Russians from populists to physicians published influential accounts of peasant life that stressed degeneration. See N. Flerovskii [V. V. Bervi], *Polozhenie rabochego klassa v Rossii* (St. Petersburg, 1869); A. I. Shingarev, *Vymiraiushchaia derevnia* (St. Petersburg, 1907); and V. S. Veressayev, *The Memoirs of a Physician* (New York, 1916).

[4] I. P., "Ideia narodnogo teatra i ee osushchestvlenie v Riazanskoi gubernii," *Vestnik Riazanskogo gubernskogo zemstva*, no. 10 (1913): 59; "Khuliganstvo i shkola," *Deiatel'* 19, no. 5 (1914): 118–23; "O narodnom teatre," *Sel'skii vestnik*, no. 266 (1913): 2; Ben Eklof, *Russian Peasant Schools: Officialdom, Village Culture, and Popular Pedagogy, 1861–1914* (Berkeley, 1986), 419–37.

[5] "Pis'ma iz Laishevskogo uezda," *Volzhskii vestnik*, no. 235 (1901): 4–5; "P'ianyi terror v derevne," *Trezvaia zhizn'*, no. 11 (1910): 430; "K voprosu o prichinakh khuliganstva v derevne i bor'be s nim," *Sel'skii vestnik*, no. 91 (1913): 2; Rossiiskii gosudarstvennyi istoricheskii arkhiv (hereafter RGIA; formerly TsGIA), f. 1405, op. 532, d. 439.

This article examines the ways in which Russia's educated public, clergy, and government perceived and responded to what they saw as a growing social and moral crisis that, by the first decades of the twentieth century, appeared capable of plunging the countryside into complete disorder, lawlessness, and decay.[6] I have focused on one prominent symbol of this crisis—leisure and its associated festivities. For here popular practices forcefully entered the world of educated society, where they not only intertwined and clashed with "higher" culture, but also influenced elite thinking and helped to shape an evolving public discourse over the condition of the lower classes and the most effective path to social reform. Itself the product of recent socioeconomic change, popular leisure became, during the 1890s, a complex and dynamic cultural arena in which educated Russians formulated notions of lower-class degeneration as a fundamental source of national crisis and subsequently sought to impose their own models of enlightenment, respectability, and moral improvement on the benighted masses.[7] In effect, they hoped to colonize the countryside using culture as their primary agent. Since it was thought to be irreparably corrupted and increasingly devoid of traditional modes of civility and deference, rural popular culture came under renewed assault in this period precisely because it conflicted so sharply with the new, Victorian sensibilities of an emerging yet insecure bourgeois culture. Peasant festivity, in particular, seemed to express most clearly the terrible darkness besetting country dwellers and the nation. Through the prism of elite perception, it thus served as a symbolic representation of the primitiveness and savagery of peasant life and a stark depiction of rural disorder and degeneracy, reminding Russia's middle and professional classes how tenuous the foundations of their "civilization" would remain until it took firm root among the peasantry.[8]

---

[6] The turn of the century witnessed national "crises" throughout Europe that pitted middle-class values against a stark vision of lower-class degeneration, best exemplified by the appearance of hooliganism. See, e.g., Seth Koven, "From Rough Lads to Hooligans: Boy Life, National Culture, and Social Reform," in *Nationalisms and Sexualities*, ed. Andrew Parker et al. (New York, 1992), 365–91; Robert A. Nye, *Crime, Madness, and Politics in Modern France* (Princeton, 1984), chaps. 6, 10; and Geoffrey Pearson, *Hooligan: A History of Respectable Fears* (New York, 1983), 51–116. On Russia, see Neil Weissman, "Rural Crime in Tsarist Russia: The Question of Hooliganism, 1905–1914," *Slavic Review* 37 (1978): 228–40; Joan Neuberger, *Hooliganism: Crime, Culture, and Power in St. Petersburg, 1900–1914* (Berkeley, 1993); and Stephen Frank, *Criminality, Cultural Conflict, and Justice in Rural Russia, 1856–1914* (forthcoming), chap. 6.

[7] However unconscious its application, an often simplified form of degeneration theory could be found in the ideologies of virtually all social-reform campaigns in late imperial Russia, the numerous publications of which are replete with images traceable to B. A. Morel's *Traité des dégénérescences* (Paris, 1857) and subsequent elaborations on his work.

[8] Cultural insecurity was a constant refrain in the Russian press—particularly in sketches of provincial town life, which openly acknowledged how thin and fragile was the veneer of

Fears about the collapse of lower-class morals were by no means unique to Russia. They proved a common theme among middle-class commentators and governments throughout Europe during the nineteenth century and were articulated with particular intensity as the century drew to its close.[9] Nor had such concern been unknown to earlier generations in Russia. The Orthodox church had long sought to raise the moral level of its rural flock, launching new efforts in the first half of the nineteenth century that emphasized schooling and religious instruction but which, according to one recent assessment, met with limited success at best.[10] Following the 1861 emancipation of the peasants, the government, the nobility, and the professional classes also worried about the countryside's cultural and material impoverishment as well as the lack of direct supervision over the newly freed peasantry. The Ministry of Internal Affairs found troubling evidence that a sharp upsurge of rural crime was occurring in the early 1860s, while A. V. Selivanov, an influential provincial councillor from Riazan', echoed many officials when he reported in 1873 that widespread drunkenness and depravity were the primary culprits behind rural poverty and the breakup of peasant families.[11] Only in the early 1890s, however, did a series of developments coalesce to fix educated society's attention firmly on the "peasant problem." A growing conviction that emancipation had failed to improve the lot of former serfs, the devastating 1891–92 famine and 1892–93 cholera epidemic; mounting evidence of the peasantry's moral and physical degeneration; increasing peasant migration to cities, which resulted in a greater

---

their "civilization." See, e.g., "Iz Livenskogo i Maloarkhangel'skogo u.," *Orlovskii vestnik*, no. 10 (1894): 1; "Iz zhizni v Kole," *Severnyi krai*, no. 191 (1899): 2; "Chistota eto ne nasha slabost'!" *Povolzhskii vestnik*, no. 123 (1906): 2; "Gorod Egor'evsk," *Riazanskii vestnik*, no. 34 (1909): 2; and "Sanitarnoe sostoianie g. Riazhska," *Riazanskii vestnik*, no. 140 (1909): 2.

[9] For example, see Edward J. Chamberlin and Sander L. Gilman, eds., *Degeneration: The Dark Side of Progress* (New York, 1985); Ruth Harris, *Murders and Madness: Medicine, Law, and Society in the Fin de Siècle* (Oxford, 1989); and Daniel Pick, *Faces of Degeneration: A European Disorder, 1848–1918* (Cambridge, 1989).

[10] Gregory L. Freeze, "The Rechristianization of Russia: The Church and Popular Religion, 1750–1850," *Studia Slavica Finlandensia* 7 (1990): 101–36. For self-evaluations of the church's mission, see "Odna iz prichin nedoveriia i nedruzheliubnogo otnosheniia prikhozhan k svoemu pastyriu," parts 1, 2, *Rukovodstvo dlia sel'skikh pastyrei* 27, no. 3 (1886): 53–61; 27, no. 49 (1886): 404–13; "Sushchestvenno-vazhnyi nedostatok v religiozno-nravstvennoi zhizni russkogo naroda," *Rukovodstvo dlia sel'skikh pastyrei* 30, no. 16 (1889): 469–74; and N. O. Osipov, *O prichinakh upadka vliianiia dukhovenstva na narod* (St. Petersburg, 1900).

[11] Frank, *Criminality*, chap. 1; "O merakh protiv narodnoi bednosti," Zaiavlenie glasnogo Selivanova, Gosudarstvennyi arkhiv Riazanskoi oblasti (hereafter GARO), f. 869, op. 1, d. 777, ll. 24–26ob. The government newspaper *Sel'skii vestnik* published numerous articles on this same point.

visibility of rural culture; and a corresponding rise in elite fears over this newly mobile but "uncivilized" class all led to calls for direct and forceful intervention and sparked wide-ranging public discussions over how best to help the rural population.

Having long believed that the peasantry's "backwardness" and "low level of culture" were the root causes of its present condition, many members of educated society felt popular enlightenment could provide the most effective remedy. But more recent images of social and cultural disintegration drawn from portraits of rural and urban lower-class life also suggested a need for innovative methods capable of initiating regeneration in the villages. If urban vices were accelerating a process of rural degeneration, it was argued, they should in all haste be supplanted by "rational" activities that would lead to a far-reaching transformation of peasant behavior. As anthropologist John Lubbock had concluded in his 1870 *Origin of Civilisation*, the "blessings of civilisation" must be extended to "countrymen of our own living, in our very midst, a life worse than that of a savage."[12] Rural popular culture therefore proved an ideal target to reformers who, much like their Victorian counterparts, defined the peasant problem largely in cultural terms grounded in a unique mingling of traditional Russian paternalism and elite insecurity, guilt, and fear, together with European theories of rational self-improvement, social progress, and sociocultural evolution.[13] In their efforts to construct new cultural foundations for the village world, however, reformers would—whether consciously or not—create a sanitized vision of an ideal peasantry, reject the communalism and other features of peasant life whose demise they had earlier bemoaned, and ultimately embrace the very forces that had been implicated in the breakdown of traditional society.

Although the nature of peasant festivity was clearly changing in the second half of the nineteenth century, critics charged that such changes merely worsened the already disorderly character of these all-too-numerous communal assemblages. Mediated primarily by educated Russians, descriptions of rural fêtes published from the 1890s on thus focused more directly than ever before on the violence, drunkenness, promiscuity, and depravity that many believed had come to dominate village leisure as a direct result of corrupting urban influences and the fall of traditional moral authority within peasant communities. Early on, those concerned about the state of Russian agriculture had set the stage for later criticisms

---

[12] Cited in George W. Stocking, Jr., *Victorian Anthropology* (New York, 1987), 218.

[13] These concepts are discussed at length in Stocking, *Victorian Anthropology*, 186–237. Their influence can be found in nearly all Russian treatises on education and social reform and in fields as diverse as anthropology and medicine.

by linking the excessive number of rural holidays with low productivity, laziness, and a decline of peasant industriousness.[14] By the 1890s, when the issue of popular recreation and leisure came before broad segments of educated society in conjunction with tentative experiments with the eight-hour workday, reformers drew from previous (and ongoing) clerical and official attacks on peasant celebrations to condemn not only the loss of work time, but also the squandering of money on liquor and food, the ruinous effects of drunkenness, and the immorality that accompanied it. Peasants, in short, celebrated too much and lost valuable hours, days, and even weeks that might be far better spent at material and moral improvement. Yet the often suggested imposition of labor discipline was not the entire answer to this problem; sober peasants, after all, knew very well the meaning of hard work. Even if peasant time could be colonized and work discipline imposed within the more controlled confines of a factory or estate, the sheer size of Russia's rural population precluded any general assertion of the middle-class dichotomy between work and leisure, at least in the short term.[15] For educated outsiders, the real problem was that peasants had no meaningful alternatives to the coarseness, disorder, and vice of their degraded culture. "If the peasants would really devote their holidays to rest and to exchanging ideas," wrote one critic, "there would be no talk about changing them." Since outsiders felt such a scenario remained unlikely, however, it appeared that only sustained colonization of village culture would replace the demoralizing elements of rural fêtes with more rational pursuits.[16]

---

[14] "Iz Rozhdestvenskoi volosti, Vetluzhskogo u., Kostromskoi gub.," *Sel'skii vestnik*, no. 3 (1893): 26–27; "O derevenskikh prazdnikakh (Pis'mo sel'skoi uchitel'nitsy)," *Saratovskie gubernskie vedomosti*, no. 99 (1895), pt. 2:3; "O derevenskikh prazdnikakh," *Novoe vremia*, no. 9752 (1903): 4. In 1902, Sergei Witte's Commission on the Needs of Agriculture estimated no less than 120 nonworking days in the countryside (including Sundays). "Narodnye prazdniki i predrassudki," *Obrazovanie* 12, no. 4 (1903): 108. For local figures, see GARO, f. 7, op. 1, d. 97, ll. 1–94ob. The church disputed this direct linkage between the number of holidays and productivity. "O vliianii prazdnikov i progul'nykh dnei na obshchee ekonomicheskoe polozhenie Rossii," *Vladimirskie eparkhial'nye vedomosti*, no. 7 (1865), pt. 2:399–407.

[15] Many believed that factory work had an especially corrupting influence on young peasants. "Vliianie fabrik na zemledelie," *Sel'skii vestnik*, no. 5 (1885): 51; Berendeev, "Derevenskie pis'ma: Pogonia za rublem," *Severnyi vestnik*, no. 7 (1888), pt. 2:47–56; "Narodnoe p'ianstvo i sovremennaia bor'ba dukhovenstva za trezvost'," *Trezvaia zhizn'*, no. 5 (1911): 445–47. On the clash of differing notions of time, see Frederick Cooper, "Colonizing Time: Work Rhythms and Labor Conflict in Colonial Mombasa," in *Colonialism and Culture*, ed. N. B. Dirks (Ann Arbor, Mich., 1992), 207–45.

[16] *Novoe vremia*, no. 9752 (1903): 4. *Colonization* is used here to denote the processes by which outside agencies seek to impose specific norms, values, or ideologies on what is believed to be a more primitive or backward population. Whether overtly political or not, the ideology of colonialism came to pervade nineteenth-century European and Russian social-

Peasant festivity was, above all, antithetical to the goal of civilizing village manners. Teachers, for example, saw traditional holiday celebrations as undermining rural education—the centerpiece of elite hopes for peasant improvement and the fundamental tool for creating a national culture that would unify all classes. In Griazovetskii district, Vologda province, a 1911 zemstvo-church survey estimated that because of the many local two- or three-day celebrations, pupils missed no less than 80 days in a 180-day school year.[17] Young peasants who watched their parents participate in the debauch of these communal drinking binges learned lessons that set them on the wrong path later in life. Teachers complained because adults kept their children away from school during the long festivals, allowing them to witness the corrupting revelry and depravity of the streets and listen to senseless talk and cursing, and often left them at home alone "where they drink vodka as a joke." Once the holiday ended in their own village, parents brought children to celebrations in neighboring parishes—a glaring example of "inexcusable simplemindedness." Students returning to school appeared exhausted and listless from lack of sleep because "guests have been shouting in their homes the entire night." In consequence, a rural teacher explained, "on the first day back at school [the pupils] understand nothing, as if they have forgotten all they knew, and only gradually do their heads become clear again." They also took from the fête precisely those things that schools sought to eliminate in young peasant minds: "The other day a young girl, returning to school after the holidays, wrote on the blackboard extremely foul words, the meaning of which she, of course, did not even understand."[18] Such damage was extremely difficult to repair.

According to contemporary accounts, drunkenness was by far the most ruinous aspect of village festivities. Much like children or primitives, reformers argued, peasants did not understand restraint and rational self-control but "spend every bit of money they have saved, and even sell their property" in order to purchase vodka for an upcoming festival. Poorer villagers let their fields deteriorate while they performed several days of

reform movements. See Eugen Weber, *Peasants into Frenchmen: The Modernization of Rural France, 1870–1914* (Stanford, 1976), 485–96; Michelle Perrot, ed., *A History of Private Life*, vol. 4, *From the Fires of Revolution to the Great War* (Cambridge, Mass., 1990), esp. 615–67; Harris, *Murders and Madness*, 76–79; and Nye, *Crime, Madness, and Politics*, esp. chap. 5.

[17] I. V., "Anketa o prazdnovanii razlichnykh prazdnikov v Griazovetskom uezde, Vologodskoi gubernii," *Izvestiia Arkhangel'skogo Obshchestva izucheniia Russkogo Severa 5*, no. 10 (1913): 446.

[18] "O derevenskikh prazdnikakh, 3; "O vliianii ulitsy na molodoe pokolenie," *Sel'skii vestnik*, no. 211 (1913): 2–3.

outwork, earning just enough money to buy holiday vodka. One writer claimed in 1911 that during the course of a three-day January holiday celebrated collectively by three villages of Tobol'sk province, peasants spent twenty-five hundred rubles at the state liquor shop. "For many, nothing remains after the holiday, not even bread."[19] Despite plentiful evidence that peasant communities were, on their own initiative, closing local taverns, banning holiday drunkenness, and prosecuting bootleggers more forcefully—and had been doing so long before moral reformers turned their attention to the countryside—outside observers and non-peasants living in rural areas nevertheless felt that liquor was destroying rural society, contributing to its physical, economic, and moral decline.[20]

Weddings were seen as especially onerous to the peasant budget because a single household had to supply food and drink to large numbers of guests, neighbors, and sometimes the entire village. Local government surveys of peasant liquor consumption conducted between 1911 and 1915 showed that patronal festivals accounted for the largest portion of annual household spending on drink, but that a wedding was the single most costly celebration. Studies calculated that marriage festivities cost poor families as much as 50 rubles, and that well-to-do peasants spent no less than 150 rubles.[21] In 1910, a correspondent from Rostovskii district, Iaroslavl' province, wrote that custom had established firm norms determining how much vodka should be provided at weddings—norms below

[19] "Selo Omutinskoe, Tob. g.," *Moskovskie vedomosti*, no. 22 (1913): 3; "O krest'ianskom p'ianstve," *Deiatel'* 10, no. 12 (1905): 259; V. Shchepotkin, "Prazdnik v derevne," *Russkii nachal'nyi uchitel'* 32, no. 6–8 (1911): 131. An outstanding survey of drinking practices is Patricia Herlihy, "Joy of the Rus': Rites and Rituals of Russian Drinking," *Russian Review* 50 (1991): 131–47. On patronal festivals and two- and three-day holidays, see "O provozhdenii khramovykh prazdnikov," *Rukovodstvo dlia sel'skikh pastyrei* 35, no. 51 (1894): 423–26; "Po voprosu o prazdnikakh," *Tserkovno-obshche-stvennyi vestnik* 10, no. 128 (1883): 4; "Anketa o prazdnovanii," 445–47; T. Pozdniakov, *Narodnye obychai v Aleksandrovskom uezde, Vladimirskoi gubernii* (Vladimir, 1902), 30–36; and D. N. Voronov, *Alkogolizm v gorode i derevne v sviazi s bytom naseleniia* (Penza, 1913), 37–41.

[20] Similar views of the physical and moral degeneration wrought by alcohol were already widespread in Europe. See Nye, *Crime, Madness, and Politics*, 155–58; Harris, *Murders and Madness*, chap. 7; and Eric T. Carlson, "Medicine and Degeneration: Theory and Praxis," in Chamberlin and Gilman, *Degeneration*, 130–33. For examples of peasant measures against drinking, see *Volzhskii vestnik*, no. 14 (1892): 2; *Tambovskie gubernskie vedomosti*, no. 10 (1894): 4; *Nedelia*, no. 49 (1894): 1574; *Orlovskii vestnik*, no. 9 (1894): 2; *Nizhegorodskii listok*, no. 152 (1899): 2; and *Riazanskii vestnik*, no. 68 (1909): 4.

[21] "Iz mest. Berezani, Pereiaslavskogo u., Poltavskoi gub.," *Sel'skii vestnik*, no. 41 (1892): 457. For additional estimates, see Statisticheskoe otdelenie Moskovskoi uezdnoi zemskoi upravy, *Derevnia i zapreshchenie prodazhi pitei v Moskovskom uezde* (Moscow, 1915), 31–32.

which a peasant family could not go without being shamed.[22] Contradicting their earlier assertions that the city was most responsible for rural vice, reformers now blamed custom itself for peasant excess, noting that even villagers who preferred sobriety could not escape the pressures and expectations of tradition. "The weaker the influence of cities in a given locality," the editors of a 1915 zemstvo survey argued, "the stronger the power of custom and the stricter the demands of public opinion that custom be observed."[23] Established local norms and the fear of public shame provided sufficient incentive even for reluctant peasants to spend as much as possible on a good banquet. As another survey stated in 1916, "The greater the drunkenness [at a wedding] . . . the more honored will be the marriage and the couple's happiness." Such celebrations "are remembered for years."[24]

In their strikingly similar representations of peasant behavior during the long holidays, critics of popular culture turned to analogies of the primitive, the natural, untamed world, and social disorder. They claimed that villagers took on "the likeness of beasts" in their drunken revelries, and pointed with great concern to the resulting epidemic of rampant promiscuity (another Victorian characterization of savage society and otherness) and violence spreading throughout the countryside.[25] The peasant "forgets he is a Christian" during patronal festivals, a temperance advocate asserted in 1908: "He does not go to church, but wanders around the market square from early morning in a drunken stupor, singing rowdy songs, using foul words. . . . And what happens on these holidays? They drink themselves into a complete frenzy, bite off one another's fingers, often thrash each other to death. . . . The same is true on religious

---

[22] According to this account, no less than sixty liters could be consumed at a "poor" wedding and ninety-six at a "good" (i.e., wealthy) wedding. "Svadebnyi sezon," *Golos* (Iaroslavl'), no. 19 (1910): 3. Though widespread in rural areas, such norms differed from one township to another. *Derevnia i zapreshchenie prodazhi pitei*, 26–29.

[23] *Derevnia i zapreshchenie prodazhi pitei*, 27.

[24] [D.] N. Voronov, *Zhizn' derevni v dni trezvosti* (Petrograd, 1916), 20. See also N. F. Sumtsov, *O tom, kakie sel'skie pover'ia i obychai v osobennosti vredny* (Khar'kov, 1897), 23–24; and "Svadebnoe razoren'e," *Sel'skii vestnik*, no. 12 (1888): 129.

[25] Mirianin, "Iz tekushchei zhizni,", *Trezvaia zhizn'*, no. 5–6 (1910): 533. See also *Severnyi krai*, no. 222 (1899): 3; and *Riazanskii vestnik*, no. 220 (1913): 3. On promiscuity among young peasants, see Riazanskii istoriko-arkhitekturnyi muzei-zapovednik, Rukopisnyi otdel, no. 313 (village of Shost'e), l. 2; "Razvrashchenie nravov derevni i mery k vrachevaniiu ikh," *Prikhodskaia zhizn'* 10 (1908): 566; "O krest'ianskikh posidelkakh," *Vestnik trezvosti* 7, no. 83 (1901): 6, 8; *Protiv khuliganstva, ozorstva i buistva molodezhi* (Kiev, 1915), 40, 42–43; and Stephen P. Frank, "'Simple Folk, Savage Customs?' Youth, Sociability, and the Dynamics of Culture in Rural Russia, 1856–1914," *Journal of Social History* 25, no. 4 (1992): 711–36.

holidays . . . [when] vodka flows like rivers and there is widespread immorality and disorder—it is difficult to describe."[26] On major holidays
like Christmas, Easter, and especially carnival (*maslenitsa*), the village
was transformed "into a veritable Sodom." Moralists charged that peasants "conduct themselves like pagans at weddings and holidays, acting as
servants of Satan."[27] The moment church services ended (and even earlier), "everyone turns to wild revelry. In the street there is great noise,
laughter, the sounds of accordions, songs and dancing. Loud conversation, singing, incoherent speech, and the clatter of dishes spill from open
windows. Young people stroll in large crowds, stopping at any given spot
to dance. Many are already so drunk that they cannot lift a hand or foot,
and lie down wherever they can—in a shed or simply on the street. By
evening everyone is drunk, barely able to stand."[28] Such depictions of
rural festivals abounded in newspapers and reformist literature, providing grim reminders of the task confronting educated outsiders determined
to stop these behaviors.

Equally disturbing evidence of moral decline came in the last years of
the nineteenth century with a growing perception that women, teenagers,
and even children had begun drinking and participating in holiday disorders together with adult men. "We remember the countryside when
drunkenness was rarely encountered," lamented an 1894 editorial in the
Saratov Provincial Gazette. Previously, "it was mainly adult men who
drank, but now . . . we find something quite different: not only the men,
but even women, even juveniles and young children drink, and this never
took place before." A correspondent for the *Riazan' Herald* noted in
1909 that while such corrupting behavior was especially evident during
parish festivals and carnival, children—including pupils—could be found
drinking, cursing, and smoking at virtually any village celebration.[29]
Peasant women also played an important role in the lucrative bootlegging
trade, as a parish priest from Dankovskii district, Riazan' province,
pointed out in 1911. This was especially terrible, he wrote, because "up
to now the woman was a symbol of sobriety, and she herself suffers from
the drunkenness of a husband or son." But now she was abetting the very
drunkenness "from which she will undergo still greater suffering."[30] Ear-

---

[26] "O p'ianstve (Pis'mo iz derevni)," *Deiatel'* 13, no. 6 (1908): 100.

[27] "O vliianii kazennoi vinnoi monopolii na otrezvlenie derevne," *Deiatel'* 9, no. 1
(1904): 36; "O svad'bakh i prazdnikakh," *Saratovskie gubernskie vedomosti*, no. 53
(1894): 3. See also *God trezvosti v Kazanskoi gubernii* (Kazan', 1916), 64–68.

[28] Shchepotkin, "Prazdnik v derevne," 131–32.

[29] *Saratovskie gubernskie vedomosti*, no. 68 (1894): 1; "Selo Tuma, Kasimovskogo
uezda," *Riazanskii vestnik*, no. 47 (1909): 3.

lier viewed as a beacon of hope in the struggle against liquor, peasant women, too, had become part of the problem.

Still more troubling, rural parents commonly sent twelve- or thirteen-year-old boys and girls to buy vodka and allowed their young children to drink. A 1915 zemstvo survey of Khar'kov province found that 6.4 percent of all female peasant children drank at least occasionally, as did 11.2 percent of male children. Among adolescents, these proportions were 21.2 percent and 38.9 percent respectively, while 51.8 percent of all adult women drank. Other surveys conducted in rural schools claimed that only 6 percent of all children questioned had never tasted vodka, and fully 25 percent had been drunk at least once.[31] Such behavior contributed greatly to the breakdown of the patriarchal family and to rural degeneration. But by the 1890s, educated Russians were placing much of the blame squarely on parents for not raising their children strictly or instilling good morals in the family, impeding efforts at primary education, setting bad examples through their own drunken, immoral conduct, and allowing youths to run wild at holiday gatherings without proper adult supervision.[32] As long as peasants themselves remained ignorant about "proper" methods of child rearing, and above all until their own behavior could be transformed, the cultural and moral salvation of their children would have to rest in the hands of educated outsiders.

To illustrate the degeneration of a "dissolute peasant youth," reformers published graphic details of the brutal, mass fistfights and turf battles between gangs from rival villages, the frequent stabbings and maimings, and the rash of other crimes that accompanied the revelries of teens and

---

[30] "Narodnoe p'ianstvo," 457. In this same survey, another letter from Riazan' province (Kasimovskii district) claimed that bootlegging was a direct cause of increased drunkenness among young people (450). Women continued to figure prominently in the illegal liquor trade after the Bolshevik revolution. See A. Uchebatov, "Tainoe vinokurenie v gorode i v derevne," in *Problemy prestupnosti: Sbornik*, pt. 2 (Moscow and Leningrad, 1927), 111–29.

[31] Voronov, *Zhizn' derevni v dni trezvosti*, 10; Mirianin, "Iz tekushchei zhizni," 548–49. See also I. Rozhdestvenskii, *K voprosu o p'ianstve v zemledel'cheskoi derevne (Po povodu ankety v Ufimskoi gubernii v 1913 g.)* (Moscow, 1914), 11; and V. A. Chernevskii, *K voprosu o p'ianstve vo Vladimirskoi gubernii i sposobakh bor'by s nim* (Vladimir na Kliaz'me, 1911), 11–14.

[32] "Vliianie fabrik na zemledelie," 52; "Iz Rozhdestvenskoi volosti," 27; P. P., "Staroe i novoe," *Tambovskie gubernskie vedomosti*, no. 11 (1894): 3–4; "O p'ianstve," 99; "Po povodu s"ezda o p'ianstve," *Deiatel'* 17, no. 1 (1912): 8; "O nepochtitel'nosti detei k roditeliam," *Sel'skii vestnik*, no. 5 (1888): 1; S. Ia. Derunov, "Selo Koz'modem'ianskoe," *Iaroslavskie gubernskie vedomosti*, no. 71 (1889), pt. 2; *Nizhegorodskii listok*, no. 63 (1899): 1; no. 65 (1899): 1. But see, by contrast, "Selo Gievka, Valkovskogo uezda," *Orlovskii vestnik*, no. 7 (1894): 3.

young adults during village fêtes. These "savage pastimes," reformers asserted, were spreading rapidly, "reaching into out-of-the-way corners
where previously . . . the peasant never dreamed of such things."[33] After
describing one bloody Christmas-season fight in rural Nizhnii Novgorod
province, a press account declared: "Seeing such a picture, one becomes
ill and terrified of these people. You want to shout at them to stop, to tell
them this is enough, but of course your words would have no influence on
the battle."[34] Drunken carousers threw themselves at one another "like
beasts," using not only fists but knives as well. Further stressing "the
extent that the savagery of morals has reached in our remote localities,"
commentators utilized images of primitive warfare in their attacks on
these often deadly fights. Thus, during the 1910 celebration of a single
holiday (Frolovshchina) in Luzhskii district, Petersburg province, "as
many people were killed within a circumference of thirty kilometers as on
a single day in a real war." Likewise, according to a 1912 Pskov zemstvo
resolution, "on the two holidays of Pokrov and Kuz'ma Dem'ian, the
murdered and wounded in Ostrovskii district were no fewer than during
a war." Even the weapons used by peasant youths and hooligans "are
quite similar to those of savages. In all their crudity, just as in the Stone
Age, these instruments for crushing human skulls carry traces of painstaking decoration."[35] As one correspondent from Iaroslavl' province
warned, "we are living in a time of barbarity, when human life has no
value."[36]

---

[33] "Razvrashchenie nravov," 565. Holiday fistfights had existed for centuries and survived long into the Soviet era. For descriptions of and attacks on this practice from Riazan'
province, see *Riazanskii vestnik*, no. 3 (1905): 3; no. 73 (1909): 4; no. 74 (1910): 3; no. 55
(1911): 3; no. 58 (1913): 3; "Kulachnye boi," *Riazanskaia zhizn'*, no. 42 (1914);
"Kulachnye boi," *Rabochii klich*, no. 29 (1923); "Dikie zabavy," *Rabochii klich*, no. 11
(1924); "Dikaia zabava," *Kollektiv*, no. 13 (1925); and "Dikost' eshche derzhitsia," *Rabochii klich*, no. 48 (1926). For other provinces, see *Orlovskii vestnik*, no. 10 (1894): 2;
Povolzhskii vestnik, no. 40 (1906): 4; and T. Segalov, "P'ianye draki v gorode i derevne,"
Problemy prestupnosti, 2 (1927): 88–99.

[34] *Nizhegorodskii listok*, no. 1 (1900): 4.

[35] "P'ianyi terror v derevne," 428; "Narodnaia anarkhiia," *Deiatel'* 18, no. 7 (1913):
218; "Derevenskie nravy," *Sudebnoe obozrenie* 1, no. 48 (1903): 928. See also Nikolai
Shiriaev, "O khuliganstve v derevne i o bor'be s nim," *Prikhodskaia zhizn'* 15 (May–June
1913): 247; N. Sakharov, "Iz t'my derevenskoi: Derevenskie prazdniki," *Deiatel'* 14, no. 11
(1899): 463–74; "Ubiistvo v drake," *Kazanskii telegraf*, no. 2718 (1901): 2; "Derevenskii
khuligan," *Severnyi krai*, no. 244 (1905): 2–3; "Nanesenie smertel'noi rany," *Povolzhskii
vestnik*, no. 52 (1906): 4; and "Za khuliganstvo," *Riazanskii vestnik*, no. 220 (1913): 2.

[36] "Dikost' nravov," *Golos*, no. 10 (1910): 3. Similar thoughts are expressed by Pskov
landowner I. M. Anichkova in her *Zametki iz derevni* (St. Petersburg, 1900); and in *Protiv
khuliganstva*, 49.

Theft was also on the rise, many believed, because peasant youths had turned to crime in order to pay for growing vices like drinking, smoking, and gambling at cards. Observers failed to note that a form of ritual theft by young villagers had long been a part of preparations for their evening gatherings. Girls pilfered food, fuel, and other necessities from parents or relatives, while boys "cut wood on the sly [and] swipe grain and money from their fathers." Such practices were "a common matter for rural youths," wrote a student of peasant life in the 1880s, and "almost no one complains against them."[37] By 1905, however, it was precisely this type of behavior, among others, that outsiders began to term hooliganism, claiming that rural lads would take grain from their fathers after the autumn harvest and sell it to bootleggers for vodka. If they could not manage to steal from the barn, then they went to another's field and took sheaves, potatoes, or other crops.[38] In his 1913 report to the Ministry of Justice's committee on measures to fight hooliganism, the governor of Pskov province listed theft of various food supplies, domestic fowl, and vegetables among the typical crimes of rural hooligans.[39] As in many other instances, "custom" had been degraded in the eyes of an educated society increasingly fearful of lower-class disorder.

Peasants who adopted urban tastes received a good deal of criticism as well, for if expenses on holiday vodka and food did not bring sufficient economic ruin to a village household, the growing slavery to fashion in rural areas would surely help to push it over the line between subsistence and poverty. Superfluous expenditures on samovars, tea, decorations for the home, and other consumer goods flooding the countryside by the century's last decades brought sharp condemnation from those whose image of village life clashed with the peasants' own notions of respectability. Here, too, critics singled out the young as primary culprits, for they in particular demanded the latest fashions so that they could attend evening gatherings in style.[40] One peculiar account in the *Voice of Moscow* even charged that hooliganism and the fall of morality among peasant women

[37] E. Ponomarev, "Artel'shchina i druzhestva, kak osobyi uklad narodnoi zhizni," *Severnyi vestnik*, no. 12 (1888), pt. 2:61–62. An intriguing analysis of ritual theft is Gerald M. Sider, "Family Fun in Starve Harbour: Custom, History, and Confrontation in Village New-foundland," in *Interest and Emotion: Essays on the Study of Family and Kinship*, ed. Hans Medick and David W. Sabean (Cambridge, 1984), 340–70.

[38] "Kak nashi muzhiki boriutsia s p'ianstvom," *Deiatel'* 15, no. 9 (1910): 167; Mirianin, "Khuliganstvo," *Trezvaia zhizn'*, no. 8 (1912): 597.

[39] RGIA, f. 1405, op. 532, d. 424, l. 12a.

[40] On changing fashions and peasant views of consumerism, see Frank, " 'Simple Folk, Savage Customs?' " 718; and "Iz sela Chulkovo, Skopinskogo u., Riazanskoi gub.," *Sel'skii vestnik*, no. 19 (1885): 208. Together with liquor, one author blamed tea drinking and expensive holiday foods for peasant poverty. "O prichinakh krest'ianskikh ubytkov," *Saratovskie gubernskie vedomosti*, no. 89 (1895): 4.

could be attributed to the cost and "splendor" of their newly fashionable tastes.[41] Reformers also fretted that young peasants were dressing above their social station. As one historian recently noted, "educators already worried about the effects of education on attitudes toward work and occupational choice were outraged at its apparent influence on taste in clothing and personal appearance." Others complained about "a heightened interest in tasteless and useless dandyism" among the rural school-age population.[42] Adult peasants, too, had begun imitating gentlemen, reformers mockingly charged. "Striving to be like the petty bourgeoisie [meshchanstvo]," they allowed themselves "all sorts of extravagances with which true peasants do not even bother."[43] Turn-of-the-century newspaper stories recounted the unfortunate consequences of these excesses. In 1901, for instance, a Kazan' daily told its readers of a young Warsaw worker who saw a dress in a shop window and wanted it so much that she toiled even harder at the factory (for which she received a raise) and went without food in order to save money. Two days after buying the dress, however, she died—the result, a doctor explained, of "the girl's organism being unable to sustain this systematic starvation."[44] These cautionary moral tales were aimed particularly at lower-class women, lest they bring themselves to ruin, but their warning was meant for men and young people as well.

Elite anxiety about peasant demoralization reached its peak with post-1905 fear that a new crime wave and widespread disorder were sapping the nation's strength and threatening the state's very ability to maintain order. As the most frightening apparition of Russia's "dangerous classes" (which included both peasants and urban workers), hooliganism made a timely appearance that served to bolster elite convictions about degeneracy. Though most critics of popular culture usually located the sources of hooliganism in towns and cities, they also remained convinced that its rural origins lay in the unrestrained debauch of evening gatherings, where "teenage village youths receive the first and most fundamental lessons of

[41] Cited in M. Rosliakov, "O khuliganstve na derevenskoi ulitse," Zhizn' dlia vsekh 4, no. 5 (1913): 660.

[42] Jeffrey Brooks, When Russia Learned to Read: Literacy and Popular Literature, 1861–1917 (Princeton, 1985), 56; Eklof, Russian Peasant Schools, 423. For descriptions of city dress at rural festivities, see, e.g., "Iz khutora Dubrovki, Novgorodskogo u.," Sel'skii vestnik, no. 44 (1888): 494–96; "Selo Nikol'skoe, Poshekhonskogo uezda," Severnyi krai, no. 191 (1899): 1; "S. Emetskoe," Severnyi krai, no. 222 (1899): 2; and "V derevne," Riazanskii vestnik, no. 220 (1913): 3.

[43] "Pod igom inostrannykh mod," Deiatel' 8, no. 4 (1903): 175–76; "Narodnoe p'ianstvo," 445. Similar attitudes found expression in Britain, among other countries, when workers were criticized for aspiring to "comforts and refinements." Golby and Purdue, Civilization of the Crowd, 33–34.

[44] "Neshchastnaia zhertva mody," Volzhskii vestnik, no. 250 (1901): 3.

hooliganism."[45] During and immediately following the 1905 revolution, newspapers began applying the label "hooligan" to protagonists of knife fights, assaults, murders, or general rowdiness at evening parties and other celebrations, in contrast to the term "mischief makers" (*ozorniki*) of earlier times.[46] In effect, nearly all the separate elements of rural festivity attacked in the past conveniently came to be united in this veritable peasant counter-evolution.

Although descriptions of rural hooliganism portrayed peasant life in even grimmer terms than had previous accounts of village popular culture, they meshed well with older perceptions. While peasant revelry and disorder had clearly been viewed as harmful—even dangerous—in earlier times, the onslaught of hooliganism seemed to make conditions in the post-1905 village simply intolerable. A 1906 report in the Kazan' newspaper the *Volga Herald* described "homegrown hooligans" shattering the usually monotonous life of one village in Makar'evskii district through their "savage" evening revelries, wounding passersby with knives and revolvers, breaking windows, and carrying on at the local tavern.[47] A similar complaint was heard from Iaroslavl' province in 1910: "Hooliganism has grown greatly among the local lads. They go around the village with sticks, banging on windows and doing other things they consider to be daring. Especially now, during the wedding season . . . drunken lads are encountered at every step. In the evening the local *intelligenty* dare not venture out into the village, for the drunken young men throw rocks at them. Can . . . nothing be done to put a stop to this disorder?"[48] At holiday time, "the fighting sometimes continues all night. People fall bleeding to the ground. Windows are broken. Gangs roam everywhere with rocks and sticks. On the following day blood covers the street." As a result of such frightening scenes, one writer declared, "it has become impossible to breathe in the countryside."[49] The rural population

---

[45] Shiriaev, "O khuliganstve v derevne," 226–27. See also GARO, f. 72, op. 18, d. 5, sv. 10a, ll. 1–2ob.; and B. S. Man'kovskii, "Derevenskaia ponozhovshchina," in *Khuliganstvo i ponozhovshchina*, ed. E. N. Krasnushkin, G. M. Segal, and Ts. M. Fainberg (Moscow, 1927), 113–29.

[46] For just a few examples, see "Derevenskii khuligan," 2–3; "Khuligany," *Povolzhskii vestnik*, no. 62 (1906): 3; "Pis'ma iz provintsii," *Russkie vedomosti*, no. 195 (1912): 5; "Za khuliganstvo," *Riazanskii vestnik*, no. 163 (1913): 2; and ibid., no. 165 (1913): 2. The earliest references to hooliganism in the provincial press, however, used the term to describe the activities of the reactionary Black Hundreds and pogromists. Only later did this label take on a broader usage.

[47] "S. Kovernini," *Povolzhskii vestnik*, no. 216 (1906): 3.

[48] "Selo Karash, Iaros. gub. Khuligany," *Golos*, no. 17 (1910): 4.

[49] Shchepotkin, "Prazdnik v derevne," 132; D. Zenchenko, "Prichiny ozorstva i bor'ba s nim," *Deiatel'*, 18, no. 10 (1913): 311. Similar acts are reported in RGIA, f. 1405, op. 532, d. 424, l. 45ob.

trembled in fear of hooligans, another report declared in 1913, and "not only degenerates and psychopaths are involved in this popular revelry and terror." Increasing numbers of peasant youths were being drawn into the ranks of a new, dangerous class of hooligans, who "boast openly about their crimes, brag about their debauchery, and brazenly demonstrate their complete impunity."[50]

Calmer voices did argue that there simply was no solid evidence attesting to a specifically hooligan crime wave. As the congress of Moscow justices of the peace stressed in its 1913 response to a Ministry of Justice proposal to stiffen penalties for hooligan acts, "one can hardly speak of a growth of hooliganism." Indeed, after a careful examination of local judicial statistics, the report declared that "it would be even more inaccurate to talk of hooliganism as a new phenomenon" because prior to that time it existed everywhere under different local names.[51] Yet many contemporaries still claimed that a rapid upsurge in juvenile crime—whether "hooligan" or not—had occurred after 1900 (especially in rural areas), although in the absence of figures on commissions, their assertions were most often based on flawed analyses of court convictions. Widely disseminated and mingled with local tales of hooligan outrages, assertions of this sort caused middle-class Russians as well as gentry landowners to agree even more readily with pronouncements that "rural hooliganism has become so savage, so crude, that there is no word to describe the terrible manifestation of disorder."[52]

This depravity encompassed young peasants above all. Those seeking to reform peasant life and popular culture had been moving toward such a position for some time. Although a collapse of village morality had led to hooliganism's widespread growth, said one temperance advocate, "it

[50] "Narodnaia anarkhiia," p. 218, citing a zemstvo resolution from Pskov province. See also "Rol' dukhovenstva v bor'be s khuliganstvom," *Deiatel'* 18, no. 7 (1913): 210.

[51] "Otzyv Moskovskogo stolichnogo mirovogo s"ezda o ministerskom zakonoproekte o merakh bor'by s khuliganstvom," *Iuridicheskii vestnik*, no. 3 (1913): 235.

[52] Zenchenko, "Prichiny ozorstva," 310. Figures for juvenile crime actually began growing at above-average rates as early as the mid-1880s, though contemporaries paid scant attention until the turn of the century. Also, in contrast to contemporary and some recent views, the rate of increase was quite high among females. Whether Russia experienced a real rise in juvenile crime remains open to serious question, however, for police repression, especially after 1905, focused on the young, and higher conviction rates may in large part reflect an increase in arrests prompted by public and state concerns. Indeed, during the entire period 1874–1913, the ten- to twenty-year-old age cohort grew from 15.1 percent to 17.8 percent of all persons tried—a statistically insignificant increase when population growth is taken into account. Furthermore, per capita crime rates based on age groups cannot be accurately calculated. See Frank, *Criminality*, chap. 3; and idem, "Women, Crime, and Justice in Imperial Russia, 1834–1913" (forthcoming), drawing on data from *Svod statisticheskikh svedenii po delam ugolovnym*, 42 vols. (St. Petersburg, 1873–1915).

should not be forgotten that the fall of morals does not refer to older peasants *who were born and raised in a regime of strict discipline*. Hooliganism in rural areas is almost entirely a phenomenon of the younger generation—the future of Russia."[53] As for causation, this, too, could be readily found in the very factors that had set off the process of decline: drunkenness, immorality, ignorance, lack of culture, migrant labor, and the infectious individualism of factory and urban life. A new element, however, drawn from the contemporary discourse of social reform, was being added to post-1905 analyses of Russia's crisis. Thus, while councillor N. N. Kolomarov echoed many of his contemporaries by declaring in a 1912 speech to the Bezhetskii district zemstvo assembly (Tver' province) that hooliganism was the "offspring of drunkenness," he also deployed the language of degeneration theory to construct an image of generational deformation.

> The widespread degeneration from alcoholism, the inherited traits of alcoholics, the immorality, unruliness, and intoxication—all of these factors condition the phenomenon of hooliganism. And thus we confront the fact that this riffraff society of hooligan scum has become master of the situation; these are the tramps, the sick, and those who have no conscience or fear of the law or God. . . . Peaceful inhabitants of the countryside have become slaves to vice, trembling in fear for every imprudent word. This is terror in the full sense of the term.[54]

Hooliganism, then, represented the final phase of lower-class degeneration. In this regard, it helped to finalize the conclusions of educated reformers: having imbibed the vices of their parents and the worst of urban culture, a new, frighteningly independent, and degenerate generation of peasants, raised under conditions of cultural backwardness without the discipline of serfdom, now represented the gravest threat to enlightenment, progress, and order in the countryside. The "future of Russia" and of civilization itself appeared to hang in the balance.

Rural revolution, crime, and hooliganism not only heightened elite fears about the lower classes, but convinced many that the "simple folk" of earlier times could no longer be found in the countryside. After the events of 1905–7, frequent reference was made to a time when these terrible problems had not existed. "Not long ago," claimed one proponent of this view, it was correct to assume "that our countryside was the reposi-

[53] "Ozdorovlenie derevni," *Deiatel'* 18, no. 5 (1913): 157 (my italics). For similar views from a member of the St. Petersburg zemstvo stressing both moral and religious decline, see "Khuliganstvo i neverie nashikh dnei," *Missionerskii sbornik* 24, no. 3 (1914): 170–73.

[54] RGIA, f. 1405, op. 532, d. 424, l. 53. For similar views, see the 1912 church survey of bishops in RGIA, f. 796 (Kantseliariia Sv. Sinoda), op. 195, d. 3223, ll. 1–194; and "Bor'ba s khuliganstvom i zemstvo," *Vestnik Riazanskogo gubernskogo zemstva*, no. 1 (1913): 115.

tory of moral purity, that the healthiest forces of popular life were cultivated in the villages, and that crude vices were a rare and uncommon
thing" among peasants. But this was no longer so.[55] Similarly, a military
officer remarked to the Simbirsk governor in 1914 that "the peasants [of
the 1850s] were more moral, honest, and religious." Indeed, added a temperance advocate, "half a century ago rural holidays were simply rural
holidays: [peasants] sang songs, danced the round dance, played catch,
and so on," without collective drunkenness, crowds of rowdy, promiscu-
ous teenagers, or bloody knife fights and brawls.[56] One author moved
this deferential, traditional life forward by two decades:

> I remember the seventies. There were few taverns then, and it was shameful
> for people to drink. We, too, had "free" time such as at holidays. But this
> free time was spent very simply. People went to church in the morning, . . .
> [then] they would have lunch and rest, after which they went out to the street
> to sit and chat with neighbors. Boys and girls organized games and sports, or
> went sledding in the winter. Even the elders took part. . . . There was so
> much humor and merriment—good, splendid, healthy merriment. . . . Now
> all this has receded into memory.[57]

Another commentator, recalling the winter holidays before railways had
pushed into the countryside around Moscow, claimed that young people
had conducted themselves innocently, gathering on a hill for sledding,
building snow fortresses, then assembling in a house when evening fell
and playing various games until the cock crowed, at which point they all
went home. But with the coming of the railroad, rural lads who worked
in Moscow regularly returned home at holiday time in their fine urban
outfits and, no longer enjoying the old village pastimes, spent entire days
in the local tavern getting drunk and setting bad examples for the yet-
unspoiled peasant youths. Peasants of this sort, along with those dwelling
in close proximity to cities, were no longer considered "real peasants";
rather, "the majority of them are drunkards."[58]

In much the same way as their counterparts from industrial and middle-class societies to the west, educated Russians reworked peasant culture in their own minds and in their presentations of village life, past and
present. Having created a culture of progress, enlightenment, science, ra-
tionality, legality, respectability, good manners, and cleanliness, to note

[55] "Derevenskie soiuzy prosveshcheniia," *Sel'skii vestnik*, no. 251 (1911): 2.
[56] "Khuliganstvo i shkola," 119; "P'ianyi terror v derevne," 429.
[57] "Ob uveseleniiakh dlia naroda," *Deiatel'*, 20, no. 6 (1915): 130. See also the compari-
sons in N. V. Davydov, *Iz proshlogo*, 2d ed. (Moscow, 1914), 161–62.
[58] "Derevenskie kartinki," *Vestnik trezvosti* 16, no. 184 (1910): 14; "Narodnoe p'ianstvo," 445. See also Ia. O. Kuznetsov, "O merakh protiv khuliganstva v derevne," *Vestnik
trezvosti* 18, no. 215 (1912): 9.

a few of its building blocks, they contrasted their culture to that of the lower classes and found the latter not only terribly primitive and deformed but, more ominous, stubbornly resistant to cultural colonization as a direct result of its continuing degeneracy. Swept up in Europe's fin-de-siècle insecurity over the impact of progress and equally insecure about their own social and cultural position, members of this far-from-homogeneous elite sought out a model for change by constructing a romanticized representation of the simple, uncontaminated traditions that, they believed, characterized peasant society before its infection by the insidious microbes of modern degeneration. The turn-of-the-century boom in folklore and ethnography was but one element in this new vision of the past. Another was the concerted effort to decisively transform rural popular culture and reshape the peasantry in a different image.

By the 1890s, then, educated Russians from various classes, professions, and political groups had determined that the peasantry could only be reformed through a broad range of measures designed to discourage villagers from the ruinous debauchery of their dying culture. Turning to philanthropy, voluntary associations, local government, and schools, they set out to take popular enlightenment into the village world on a scale far greater than attempted in any previous reform effort. They began a process that would, by the outbreak of the Great War, bring peasants and members of educated society into closer contact than ever before, though it would not necessarily lead to the much-envisioned cultural unity nor to a wholesale adoption of Victorian values by the rural population. This new "movement to the people" was, like all reform movements, anything but neutral or benign. For in attacking popular culture, reformers had already adopted the language and images of colonialism; now they armed themselves with the methods and ideology of Victorian social reform. Still beholden to an earlier moral obligation to guide peasants toward progress but with their perceptions of the peasantry (and the urban lower classes) rapidly changing, Russian reformers would attempt to colonize the rural population by means of an enlightened culture that was not yet dominant even in cities, seeking to rescue the peasantry from its very "lack of culture." In this respect, they closely resembled post-Risorgimento Italian social reformers who saw their national and cultural unity threatened by the "inherited backwardness" and degeneracy of the rural south, or French writers who described rural settlements as colonies "waiting to be 'claimed for civilization.'"[59] Success, Russia's *Kul-*

---

[59] For examples, see Alfredo Niceforo, *L'Italia barbara contemporanea* (Milan, 1898); Cesare Lombroso, *Delitti vecchi e delitti nuovi* (Turin, 1902); John A. Davis, *Conflict and Control: Law and Order in Nineteenth-Century Italy* (Atlantic Highlands, N.J., 1988); and

turträger believed, would stem the tide of degeneration, reverse centuries of neglect, and enable the country to overcome the crisis that beset it by constructing a national culture capable of blurring class boundaries; failure, by contrast, meant continued cultural fragmentation and a dangerous plunge into deeper decline. Their intentions in this "struggle for civilization" therefore went well beyond government efforts at a more limited, political colonization.[60]

The control and regulation of popular culture were important elements of these reform movements, elements deemed essential to rooting out the most harmful features of lower-class leisure activities. Suppression of rural youth gatherings, for example, became common practice after the 1905 revolution because they were viewed as potential breeding grounds for hooliganism as well as political opposition. During this same period, officials and reformers began calling for a reduction in the number of public holidays celebrated in Russia, but staunch church opposition succeeded in limiting legislation aimed at effecting such proposals.[61] Attempts to alter festive behavior could be found long before 1905, however. As early as the 1870s and 1880s, local governments introduced regulations forbidding commercial activities on Sundays and holidays as a means of encouraging rest and church attendance while allowing employees (and others) to spend time with their families. By 1901, nearly fifty cities and towns had either outlawed entirely or greatly limited holiday markets and trade, with a clear impact on peasants who usually filled provincial centers during the holidays.[62] Other regulatory measures initiated by clergy, police, or village and township authorities required more punitive tactics. Parish priests, for example, commonly pressured local officials to forbid drinking on Sundays and holidays, to ban festive assemblies before church services, or to abolish non-Christian celebrations like carnival. Some clerics would not perform marriages if drunken celebrations had preceded the ceremony, or refused to pay processional visits

---

Weber, *Peasants into Frenchmen*, 488. Lombroso, whose ideas on criminal anthropology were widely disseminated in Russia during the 1880s, was one of the most renowned proponents of such views. See also Daniel Pick, "The Faces of Anarchy: Lombroso and the Politics of Criminal Science in Post-Unification Italy," *History Workshop*, no. 21 (1986): 60–86; and Davis, *Conflict and Control*, esp. 326–28.

[60] On political colonization, see Francis W. Wcislo, *Reforming Rural Russia* (Princeton, 1990), 74; and idem, "The Land Captain Reform of 1889 and the Reassertion of Unrestricted Autocratic Authority," *Russian History* 15, no. 2–4 (1988): 285–326.

[61] For examples, see "O sokrashchenii prazdnikov," *Krest'ianskoe delo* 1, no. 14 (1911): 296; and "O sokrashchenii prazdnikov," *Prikhodskaia zhizn'* 11 (1909): 299–303.

[62] "Vospreshchenie torgovli v prazdniki," *Sel'skii vestnik*, no. 7 (1881): 49; "Spravka o prazdnichnom otdykh," *Kazanskii telegraf*, no. 2685 (1901): 2; *Saratovskie gubernskie vedomosti*, no. 2 (1894): 2–4; *Nedelia*, no. 23 (1897): 709–11; *Nizhegorodskii listok*, no. 85 (1899): 3; *Severnyi krai*, no. 200 (1899): 2.

to homes that allowed evening gatherings. Youth gatherings might be dispersed by the priest and police working together, sometimes forcing "sinners" to perform public penance at church.[63] Without direct police supervision and the complicity of the local administration, however, measures of this type were short-lived at best, finding little support among villagers hostile to outside interference in local affairs. Peasants themselves frequently passed resolutions banning holiday drunkenness and the sale of liquor, closed taverns, or prevented evening gatherings when they got out of hand, and they oversaw these rulings far more successfully through community enforcement. But the moralistic and sometimes humiliating regulations introduced by clerics, police, and other outsiders met with resistance, especially from younger peasants—who found many ways to voice their protest, such as refusing to attend church.[64]

Liberal reformers also rejected such measures, arguing that they had little educational benefit and ignored the realities of contemporary life. Education therefore remained the cornerstone of elite efforts to transform peasant culture. But by 1900, experiments at popular enlightenment had expanded the notion of learning far beyond the school walls to the broader realm of village life, making leisure itself a sphere of educational activity. Voluntary associations, educational societies, and individual activists now sought to draw the population into programs designed to expand literacy and introduce a new world of useful, uplifting literature through Sunday schools, public lectures and readings, and evening classes. Educators, clerics, zemstvo activists, and other professionals, together with a flood of volunteers and philanthropists, encouraged self-help among the peasantry by supporting the establishment of cooperatives, village or township libraries, and local theaters. Many organizations simply appropriated the popular tradition of group readings but regulated the material and message they delivered.[65] While the great interest that peasants displayed toward these activities was widely lauded, bit-

[63] *Sel'skii vestnik*, no. 27 (1888): 313; no. 32 (1888): 368–69; A. Liberov, "Okonchatel'noe izgnanie maslianitsy," *Kostromskie eparkhial'nye vedomosti*, no. 2 (1892): 27–32; "O krest'ianskikh posidelkakh," 8; *Severnyi krai*, no. 92 (1905): 4; "Kur'eznaia opeka narodnoi nravstvennosti," *Severnyi krai*, no. 104 (1904): 3. See also M. Senatskii, *Dukhovenstvo i intelligentsiia v dele religiozno-nravstvennogo i umstvennogo razvitiia naroda* (Nizhnii Novgorod, 1903).

[64] "Kur'eznaia opeka," 3. On suppression by peasant communities, see, e.g., *Sel'skii vestnik*, no. 6 (1885): 66; no. 34 (1888): 384–85; *Volzhskii vestnik*, no. 14 (1892): 2; no. 23 (1892): 3; *Tambovskie gubernskie vedomosti*, no. 10 (1894): 4; *Nedelia*, no. 49 (1894): 1574; *Vremennik Zhivopisnoi Rossii* 1, no. 20 (1901): 189; *Severnyi krai*, no. 84 (1904): 3; and "Epizody iz zhizni odnoi derevni," *Obrazovanie* 14, no. 5 (1905): 39–45.

[65] *Orlovskii vestnik*, no. 36 (1898): 3; "K voprosu o postanovke narodnykh chtenii," *Deiatel'* 4, no. 5 (1899): 222–28; *Severnyi krai*, no. 79 (1904): 3; "Na narodnom chtenii," *Prikhodskaia zhizn'* 7 (1905): 128–36; *Listok trezvosti*, June–August 1909, 50. Peasants

ter experience had proved that education alone did not always produce immediate results, particularly when it came to changing behaviors deemed harmful to villagers.

In addition to education, peasants needed alternatives to the holiday activities that were so greatly abetting the process of decline in rural society. Hence, a primary task of Russia's new reformers was to find "rational" recreations capable of raising the peasants' spiritual and cultural level while offering wholesome diversions from their reliance on bootleggers and taverns, ending the savagery of village brawls, and discouraging young people from debauchery, hooliganism, and crime. One of the most successful of these efforts was the organization of a broad network of popular theaters designed to bring culture to the lower classes in cities, towns, and larger villages. Sponsored by the state-financed Guardianship for Popular Temperance, local governments, schools, rural cooperatives, and private or philanthropic sources, popular theater grew rapidly in the years prior to World War I and, as Gary Thurston has shown in his insightful study of the movement, attracted large peasant audiences eager to experience this new form of entertainment.[66] Beginning in the 1890s, urban societies for the organization of popular entertainment also invested heavily in popular theater, along with People's Houses (narodnye doma)—which enjoyed similar popularity among peasants, particularly in provincial towns. After initial hesitation, even the church acknowledged the usefulness of this medium for instilling moral values in its rural flock. At least before 1905, Thurston argues, educated Russians saw popular theater as an ideal means through which the lower classes might appropriate elite culture.[67] As the Riazan' Zemstvo Bulletin stressed in

---

and rural officials played a primary role in initiating public readings and establishing libraries. *Tambovskie gubernskie vedomosti*, no. 83 (1894): 3; *Orlovskii vestnik*, no. 49 (1898): 3; *Severnyi krai*, no. 200 (1899): 2; "Krest'iane-bibliotekari," *Nizhegorodskii listok*, no. 25 (1900): 2–3; "Narodnaia shkola, ee polozhenie sredi krest'ian i vliianie na ikh nravy," *Obrazovanie* 3, no. 7–8 (1894): 40–49; M. M. Gromyko, *Mir russkoi derevni* (Moscow, 1991), 273–311.

[66] "O narodnom teatre," 2; Gary Thurston, "The Impact of Russian Popular Theater, 1886–1915," *Journal of Modern History* 55 (June 1983): 237–67. See also "Krest'ianskii spektakl'," *Nizhegorodskii listok*, no. 43 (1899): 3; "Otkrytie teatra O-va trezvosti," *Riazanskii listok*, no. 83 (1902): 2; "Sel'skii narodnyi teatr," parts 1, 2, *Golos*, no. 2 (1910): 3; no. 19 (1910): 3; and Anton Petrov, "O teatral'nykh spektakliakh v derevne," *Narodnyi zhurnal* 2, no. 5 (1913): 151–54.

[67] Thurston, "Russian Popular Theater," 240, 242, 251; "O narodnom teatre," 2; "Narodnye razvlecheniia," *Sel'skii vestnik*, no. 277 (1913): 2; *Otchet Riazanskogo Obshchestva ustroistva narodnykh razvlechenii za 1898* (Riazan', 1899), and subsequent years. See also "Narodnye razvlecheniia i ikh znachenie," in *Pamiatnaia knizhka dlia chlenov Obshchestv trezvosti na 1894 god* (St. Petersburg, 1894), 139–42; I. Ivaniukov, "Ocherki provintsial'noi zhizni," *Russkaia mysl'* 18, no. 11 (1897): 130–31; "K voprosu o teatral'nykh predstavleniiakh dlia naroda," *Rukovodstvo dlia sel'skikh pastyrei* 39, no. 16 (1898): 381–84; and "Narodnyi teatr," *Nedelia*, no. 38 (1897): 1213–14.

1913, popular theater was "one of the best means for raising the cultural level of the population, for softening the morals of the countryside, and for halting the growth of hooliganism among peasant youth."[68]

Social and moral reformers experimented with a broad range of "rational" entertainments, combining various media and holding these events—whether popular readings, theater, or lectures—during traditional holidays. Popular readings, for example, were regularly accompanied by magic-lantern shows to provide enjoyment and hold audience interest while imparting educational information. Some reformers organized musical concerts or established local peasant choirs in the villages, often linking the latter with charity work by recruiting the poor.[69] New ideas and technologies from abroad were adapted to the purpose of popular enlightenment and entertainment. By 1913—earlier in some localities—entrepreneurs had brought moving pictures to towns in Riazan' province. Phonographs appeared in rural "clubs" or at dances sponsored by various societies for popular improvement.[70] Drawing on the success of holiday excursions among the urban working class (often financed by benevolent factory owners), rural educators also spoke of employing school excursions to remove children from festive violence and drunkenness in the villages. Utilizing degeneration theory, which emphasized the importance of milieu on the organism, medical practitioners, educators, and temperance advocates had long argued that drunkards, much like diseased persons, should be removed from society to prevent further corruption and degradation of the larger social organism. But if this could not be achieved, then society's most innocent—the children—should be protected from infection by "social disease." Hence the growing discussion about the value of excursions, though most rural schools and reform societies lacked sufficient funds to provide such recreation for their adopted wards. Cheaper and equally beneficial was organized sport, which many teachers felt offered children rational pastimes while instilling discipline and self-reliance.[71] Finally, a number of societies, such as

[68] "Ideia narodnogo teatra," 59.

[69] See for example, *Volzhskii vestnik*, no. 20 (1899): 3; I. Mintslov, "Narodnye khory v Iaroslavskoi gubernii," *Vestnik Iaroslavskogo zemstva*, no. 14 (1904), pt. 4:29–35; "Sel'skii khor liubitelei peniia," *Prikhodskaia zhizn'*, 6 (October 1904): 381–83; *Severnyi krai*, no. 237 (1905): 3; and I. Anan'ev, "O normal'noi postanovke peniia v nachal'noi shkole," parts 1, 2, *Russkii nachal'nyi uchitel'* 32, no. 3 (1911): 54–62; no. 6–8 (1911): 126–28.

[70] *Riazanskii vestnik*, no. 166 (1913): 3.

[71] M. Novikov, "O vrede p'ianstva," *Krest'ianskoe delo* 1, no. 10 (1911): 215; L. G. Karchagin, *Spirtnye napitki i prazdniki na Rusi: Potreblenie spiritnykh napitkov na prazdnikoi i nekotorye posledstviia ego* (St. Petersburg, 1912); N. Kolosov, "Odna iz shkol'nykh mer bor'by s p'ianstvom," *V bor'be za trezvost'* 2, no. 10 (1912): 41; Kuznetsov, "O merakh protiv khuliganstva," 8; G. R., "Russkii sport i uchashchaiasia molodezh',"

the Union against Tobacco Smoking and the various groups of the better-known temperance movement, confronted popular vice directly. Among their numerous activities, temperance societies organized popular theater and readings, opened free libraries and tearooms, and established a series of educational "temperance museums" on train cars at railway stations around the country—a tactic later used by Bolshevik enlighteners as well.

The reformist zeal of educated Russia also targeted custom itself, with efforts to restore dying practices whose passing many viewed as contributing to the decline of traditional peasant culture, or to purify popular festive activities by ridding them of their most corrupting elements. Critics of recent, peasant-initiated cultural innovations—such as urban dances and the "vulgar" songs (*chastushki*) that were sweeping the countryside by the 1890s—proposed using peasant choirs to revive the old folk songs "that are now nearly forgotten," and called for Rural Unions of Enlightenment to sponsor entertainments like the round dance (*khorovod*), which was dying out in many areas.[72] In their rejuvenated and culturally cleansed form, of course, these recreations were expected to be devoid of the drunkenness and disorders that accompanied the fall of village morals. Similar attempts were made to "shatter drunken customs" and rituals that degraded holiday fêtes and celebrations. Clergy and temperance activists, for example, fought for "sober weddings" in peasant communities, at which tea or kvass would replace the customary vodka and decorum would reign in place of wild revelry. Prior to prohibition, however, these experiments met with little success; and after liquor was outlawed in 1914, surveys found peasants generally gloomy and depressed not only about the war, but also because celebrations had become terribly boring without vodka. Weddings were reported to be poorly attended and "as merry as funerals." In Poltava province, godparents could not be found for christenings now that the traditional treating with vodka was illegal. Even funerals proved more difficult to arrange, since payment could no longer be made in vodka for coffins or the digging of graves.[73]

Increasingly popular by the turn of the century was the intriguing notion of creating new holidays and festive "traditions" to replace the violent practices of the old popular culture, for many believed that "the

Vestnik vospitaniia 20, no. 9 (1909): 162–78; Harris, *Murders and Madness*, 74–76. On excursions and other activities organized for the working class, see Mark D. Steinberg, *Moral Communities: The Culture of Class Relations in the Russian Printing Industry, 1867–1907* (Berkeley, 1992), esp. 58–61.

[72] "Derevenskie soiuzy prosveshcheniia," *Sel'skii vestnik*, no. 251 (1911): 2; Kuznetsov, "O merakh protiv khuliganstva," 9; *Vladimirskie gubernskie vedomosti*, no. 3–6 (1912).

[73] "Svad'ba bez vina," *Prikhodskaia zhizn'* 5 (1903): 459–60; "Trezvaia svad'ba," *Riazanskii vestnik*, no. 197 (1909): 2; "Bez vodki," *Izvestiia Kostromskogo gubernskogo zemstva*, no. 8 (1915): 63; Voronov, *Zhizn' derevni v dni trezvosti*, 20–23.

people would willingly engage in cultured entertainments if they only existed."[74] The invented Victorian tradition of the Christmas tree, already adopted in Russian towns and cities well before the century's close, had appeared in rural schools by the 1890s and became widespread in the countryside after 1900. Educators and reformers, again centering their efforts on children, established school holidays designed to wean pupils away from activities "not at all suited to their age."[75] Typically organized around nationalist and religious themes, the new holidays saw rural schoolhouses transformed by decorations, flags, pictures, and portraits of the imperial family, while students busily trimmed the Christmas tree, set up scenery for plays they would perform, and practiced songs and patriotic hymns or prose for public readings. These activities were carefully planned not merely to provide alternatives to the old culture, but also to develop the pupils' aesthetic senses and, in the process, draw them into other intellectual pursuits. Teachers claimed that on such occasions, "you cannot drive the children away from school. They refuse to go home for dinner, but instead wait patiently at the schoolhouse or near it" for the festivities to begin.[76] When a teacher at a zemstvo school organized the first Christmas Tree celebration in the village of Shurma, Viatka province, "so many people attended that the schoolhouse could not accommodate them, and many stood in the street watching through the windows."[77]

Temperance societies also played an active role in arranging school holidays (and inventing others, like "holidays of sobriety"), as did the reactionary Union of the Russian People, with which the temperance movement became associated after 1906. At Christmas Tree celebrations held in parish schools, for example, antialcohol activists added poems about the dangers of drinking, hymns honoring sobriety, and lectures against tobacco smoking to the general program.[78] But if lower-class be-

---

[74] S. Vanin, "Derevenskie razvlecheniia," *Krest'ianskoe delo* 1, no. 10 (1911): 213.

[75] "Detskie prazdniki," *Vestnik trezvosti* 5, no. 55 (1899): 5. See also *Volzhskii vestnik*, no. 5 (1892): 2; *Orlovskii vestnik*, no. 4 (1894): 2; and *Golos*, no. 2 (1910): 3. The tradition of the Christmas tree was introduced in Britain (from Germany) during the 1840s and soon spread elsewhere, along with the notion of family-centered festivity. In England, by the 1920s, "children were forbidden to leave the house on Christmas Day because it was 'for family'." Susan Easton et al., *Disorder and Discipline: Popular Culture from 1550 to the Present* (Brookfield, Vt., 1988), 73. On the invented fête, see Mona Ozouf, *Festivals and the French Revolution* (Cambridge, Mass., 1988); and Charles Rearick, "Festivals in Modern France: The Experience of the Third Republic," *Journal of Contemporary History* 12, no. 3 (1977): 435–60.

[76] "Shkol'nye prazdniki v derevne," *Vestnik Riazanskogo gubernskogo zemstva*, no. 11–12 (1912): 80. See also "Detskie prazdniki," 6; "Detskii prazdnik," *Orlovskii vestnik*, no. 8 (1898): 2; "Elka v chastnoi voskresnoi shkole," *Riazanskii listok*, no. 32 (1902): 1; and "Dva shkol'nykh prazdnika," *Narodnoe obrazovanie* 13, no. 9 (1908): 275–77.

[77] "D. Shurma, Viatsk. gub., Mamyzh. u. (Elka)," *Volzhskii vestnik*, No. 20 (1899): 3.

[78] N. Poretskii, "Opyt bor'by s alkogolizmom v tserkovnykh shkolakh Moskovskogo uezda," *V bor'be za trezvost'* 3, no. 5–6 (1913): 28.

havior was to be changed decisively, temperance supporters argued, it would be necessary to establish a network of permanent "unions of sobriety" in rural schools, "as in America," or religious-patriotic organizations that could sponsor and regulate the new festivals, "as in Germany." Others looked to countries like Britain, Finland, and France, where "May Unions" had enjoyed great success among schoolchildren, and suggested that Russia follow their example. During the 1911–12 academic year, thirteen Moscow-district schools organized such unions, which continued to grow in number thereafter.[79] The purpose of these unions and societies, a temperance activist explained, was to give holidays like the Christmas Tree a stronger moral foundation while creating "a healthier (both physically and morally) new generation in our fatherland."[80]

Another new festival was the tree-planting holiday (*prazdnik drevonasazhdeniia*), which mirrored reformist and educational uses of trees from Sweden to France—though not on the scale of the United States' 1872 creation of Arbor Day. Unlike other Russian invented traditions, the honoring of trees was first practiced in rural areas during the 1890s and only gradually made its way to cities. In Moscow, for instance, the first such celebration was held on October 5, 1913.[81] Tree-planting holidays were especially useful to Russia's diverse strands of social and moral reformism, for they united nearly all the concerns of educated society over peasant culture; they not only provided "rational" recreation and thus helped to fill the village's cultural vacuum, but were also expected to instill in peasants respect for nature, the forests, and private property. The 1902 Witte Commission on the Needs of Agriculture expressed great enthusiasm for the new holiday in the hopes that it would futher popular enlightenment as well as keep future farmers from engaging in illegal woodcutting, as so many of their parents now did. As one proponent argued, "tree-planting holidays and school gardens will teach pupils to respect others' property and treat it with care."[82] Rural teachers and officials began petitioning for permission to establish this holiday in their

[79] "Detskie prazdniki," 7; Kuznetsov, "O merakh protiv khuliganstva," 8; "Dukhovenstvo v bor'be s khuliganstvom," *Prikhodskaia zhizn'* 15 (October 1913): 415–16; Poretskii, "Opyt bor'by," 28. For movements in Germany and Britain, see George L. Mosse, *The Nationalization of the Masses* (Ithaca, N.Y., 1975); and Lilian Shiman, "The Band of Hope Movement: Respectable Recreation for Working-Class Children," *Victorian Studies* 17, no. 1 (1973): 49–74.

[80] Poretskii, "Opyt bor'by," 25. See also *Vestnik trezvosti* 20, no. 229 (1914): 18–20.

[81] "Prazdnik drevonasazhdeniia," *Riazanskii vestnik*, no. 250 (1913): 4. The new holiday came earlier to provincial towns, however. See *Riazanskii listok*, no. 10 (1902): 1–2. On earlier festivals centered on trees and tree planting, see Ozouf, *Festivals and the French Revolution*, 233–61.

[82] D. S. Shilkin, *Lesnoe khoziaistvo*, vol. 19 of *Svod trudov mestnykh komitetov po 49 guberniiam Evropeiskoi Rossii* (St. Petersburg, 1904), 21; Kuznetsov, "O merakh protiv khuliganstva," 8.

locales; and, after seeing its apparent success in test cases approved by the Ministry of Internal Affairs (for example, in Chernigov province), provincial governors instructed land captains, zemstvos, and schools to organize tree-planting holidays. Following a 1901 order by the governor of Riazan' province, for example, at least nineteen schools and peasant communes in Riazan' district alone were celebrating the holiday by 1903. During Russia's 1911 festivities commemorating the centennial of victory over Napoleon, land captains in Samara province united nature and nation by inducing rural townships to establish patriotic tree-planting holidays in honor of this occasion.[83]

Tree planting, proponents of the new tradition pointed out, had its aesthetic and practical sides as well, because trees served as ideal decorations for bringing beauty and order to village streets ordinarily strewn with refuse or "covered by stagnant, fetid puddles," in the words of a former justice of the peace.[84] They also offered protection from the elements, gave shelter to birds, and kept the air fresh and healthy. Yet however innocent these goals appeared from the urban perspective, their impact on peasant society was potentially far-reaching. As did middle-class reformers elsewhere in Europe who attempted "to create a common national identity in a period of sharpened class conflicts," advocates of the "greening of Russia" envisioned a domesticated, recreational rural landscape into which morally reformed peasants could be comfortably situated.[85] This was to be accomplished, in part, by means of their invented traditions, which they hoped would reify the myth of an older, more peaceful village community and give birth to a new class of country dweller—one that was educated, sober, hardworking, and more deferential. Through the ritualized yet practical act of planting trees, this holiday celebrated the majesty and power of nature's rejuvenation (aided, however, by human agency), symbolizing educated society's hopes for a similar regeneration of the peasantry and, by extension, of the nation.

Many reformers felt that the monotony and boredom of rural life that encouraged drinking and hooliganism also had "a dulling effect on one's sense of the beauty of nature."[86] The villagers' closeness to the soil, moral

---

[83] "Perepiska ob ustroistve prazdnika drevonasazhdeniia," GARO, f. 76, op. 14, d. 17, sv. 7, ll. 1–29; Sel'skii vestnik, no. 238 (1911): 3. Compare Jonas Frykman and Orvar Löfgren, Culture Builders: A Historical Anthropology of Middle-Class Life (New Brunswick, N.J., 1987), 58.

[84] Davydov, Iz proshlogo, p. 162.

[85] Frykman and Löfgren, Culture Builders, 60–61, writing of late-nineteenth-century Sweden. Compare the discussion in "Zelenaia Rossiia," Sel'skii vestnik, nos. 239, 240, 245, 256 (1911).

[86] Kuznetsov, "O merakh protiv khuliganstva," 8. This was also the reason that young peasants drank vodka and engaged in hooligan acts, according to Kuznetsov.

impoverishment, and "bestial" behavior exhibited during festivals led critics of popular culture to associate peasants not merely with the primitive, but directly with the natural and animal world. In other words, their very nearness to nature alienated peasants from its true appreciation. Some reformers therefore urged that schools organize excursions to large villages or district towns so that rural children would gain a fresh perspective of their surroundings when they returned.[87] This altered outlook was critical to the achievement of the goals of educated society, for nature itself could not be successfully colonized or tamed as long as the population remained in a savage, "natural" state; as with milieu and degeneration, the two were tightly intertwined. Hence the conscious linkage of moral reform, the inculcation of new views of nature, and a transformation of the landscape. The new rural landscape described by Russian reformers would look strikingly similar to the idyllic descriptions found in contemporary belles lettres (especially in translations from European literature), while its more individualistic inhabitants came increasingly to resemble an ideal type of middle-class farmer. As one commentary in a government-sponsored publication told its imagined peasant readers:

> Plant a garden around [village] homes and everything will change: all of the surroundings will come to life. . . . In early spring, . . . people can sit in the shade of trees. The greenery will attract others by its beauty. It is nicer still to drink tea in a garden created with one's own hands, to dream in the quiet evening on a bench beneath a tree grown by one's labor, to eat fruit from the trees and to know that you did all of this [so that] others will . . . remember you with good words. [In a garden] one can escape life's worries and rest one's soul. It is especially healthy for children, because here a good mother can find many useful and intelligent entertainments for them. . . . Fathers and mothers! Build a garden for your children . . . and God will bless your work. . . . [O]ne neighbor after another will follow your example.[88]

With their gardens, pride in individual achievements, family-centered recreation, and tea drinking in the shade, peasants would lose their communal character and be made over into the likeness of the educated classes, whose members might then take their own recreational excursions into a domesticated yet still exotic countryside without fear of the savage Others.

Church and secular organizations similarly sought to instill a different view of the animal world as a means of softening and moralizing peasant behavior. "Being surrounded from childhood by cruelty toward ani-

---

[87] Ibid. Already practiced in the Baltic provinces by 1911, this type of excursion was known as *vykhod v zelen'*.

[88] "Zelenaia Rossiia," no. 256:2.

mals," argued one proponent of this movement, "creates callousness in the young heart [that] is later transferred to people."[89] A more rational and sensitive outlook toward animals would therefore lead to a lessening of rural violence and better treatment of others. Chief among the efforts to propagate this new vision was that sponsored by the Russian Society for the Protection of Animals, founded in 1865 and patterned after Britain's Royal Society for the Prevention of Cruelty to Animals (established in 1824).[90] With eighteen branches in urban centers throughout the empire by 1875, the Society focused its early activities primarily on cities, where it led campaigns to improve the treatment of horses by cabbies and carters, for example. But members also sought legislation regulating or forbidding popular entertainments that involved animals in both town and country (such as cockfighting or the use of bears in various entertainments), voiced concern over cruel hunting and trapping methods, called for better treatment of livestock and domestic animals, and assisted in fighting epidemics and establishing veterinary hospitals.[91]

To change lower-class views of the animal kingdom, however, meant a vast literature campaign aimed at propagating middle-class sensitivities and sentimentalities while spreading a still young but growing "cult of nature"—which itself reflected "changing middle-class perceptions of animals and nature." One important element of civilization at the turn of the century, after all, was believed to be the "kind treatment of domestic animals and other living creatures."[92] Since hooligans were renowned for, among their other heinous deeds, tormenting, maiming, and killing animals, the Society's civilizing mission gained willing and widespread support within educated society. Its many pamphlets and treatises on proper treatment of animals also won official approval for use at public readings. Seeking to humanize the natural world, authors presented simplified depictions of maternal instincts and family life within the animal kingdom and stressed the usefulness of domestic animals, likening them to friends if treated kindly. Several of the most successful publications contained illustrations reproduced from popular European prints showing well-dressed, bourgeois children in tender domestic scenes with cats, dogs, and other pets. That such books had a broad urban audience can-

[89] Kuznetsov, "O merakh protiv khuliganstva," 8.

[90] The Russian Society's history and goals are elaborated in *Pervoe desiatiletie Rossiiskogo obshchestva pokrovitel'stva zhivotnym: Istoricheskii ocherk ego deiatel'nosti v 1865–1875 gg.* (St. Petersburg, 1875). On the British Royal Society, see F. M. L. Thompson, *The Rise of Respectable Society* (Cambridge, Mass., 1988), 278.

[91] *Pervoe desiatiletie*, 9–91; *Vzgliad na obiazannosti Gg. chlenov i uchastkovykh popechitelei Rossiiskogo obshchestva pokrovitel'stva zhivotnym* (St. Petersburg, 1880); "K zashchite zhivotnykh," *Riazanskii listok*, no. 1 (1902): 2.

[92] Frykman and Löfgren, *Culture Builders*, 75, 84.

not be doubted; A. Bogdanov's *How One Must Treat Animals* reached a
fifth edition by 1912.[93] More striking is evidence that the Society also had
a clear impact in rural areas, where schools and popular readings introduced villagers to the new, morally superior views on treatment of animals with the aim of creating a more humane (and less bestial) peasantry.
Nor were the Society's legislative efforts without effect in the countryside;
even in the early 1870s, some peasant township courts imposed strict
punishments for cruelty to animals, basing their decisions on rules established by the Society.[94]

Activists engaged in these diverse attempts to transform popular culture
repeatedly revealed that their ultimate goal was the creation of a new
peasant class capable of filling what they saw as the moral and cultural
vacuum of Russia's dangerous countryside. Hence their focus on the
younger generation—especially primary-school children—"who can
form a new, cultured layer of the rural population." Properly reared and
educated, "they will be unswerving enemies of vice in the village," helping to re-create the moral foundations of peasant life.[95] But another,
equally important source for rural regeneration appeared at the turn of
the century when the state bureaucracy, local governments, and (in part)
educated society turned away from the traditional peasant commune as a
basis for organizing rural society.[96] Moral reformers, too, now reversed
their positions; by the early 1900s, though not entirely abandoning earlier assertions about the corrupting influence of cities, they were blaming
rural degeneration on the commune itself. A decade of decrying the tyranny of communal customs, mass holiday revelry, and the inability of
peasant elders to educate their children or halt the growth of hooliganism
convinced many that individualism itself, if properly channeled, could
serve as the new bulwark of social order. Certain that the deferential
peasantry of old was nearing extinction, they began to view a radical
restructuring of peasant life as the key to civilizing the countryside, for
within traditional communes, they believed, widespread vice, corruption,

[93] A. Bogdanov, *Kak nuzhno obrashchat'sia s zhivotnymi*, 5th ed. (Moscow, 1912). See
also Ia. Levandovskii, *Posledstviia zhestokogo obrashcheniia s zhivotnymi* (St. Petersburg,
1879); and A. B. Bratchikov, *O rasprostranenii v narode razumnogo i krotkogo obrashcheniia s zhivotnymi* (Zhitomir, 1901). Examples of state-approved publications for popular
readings can be found in *Vestnik Iaroslavskogo zemstva*, nos. 3–8 (1905).

[94] *Trudy komissii po preobrazovaniiu volostnykh sudov* (St. Petersburg, 1873–74),
3:208.

[95] "Derevenskie soiuzy prosveshcheniia," 2.

[96] Opinions on the commune can be found in *Trudy mestnykh komitetov o nuzhdakh
sel'skokhoziaistvennoi promyshlennosti*, 58 vols. (St. Petersburg, 1903). See also David A.
Macey, *Government and Peasant in Russia, 1861–1906* (De Kalb, Ill., 1987); and Wscilo,
Reforming Rural Russia.

and oppressive collective institutions made it impossible for an industrious, honest peasant to lift his family from poverty or raise its cultural level.[97]

It is no surprise, then, that those seeking improvement in rural life hailed the Stolypin reforms of 1906, which allowed peasants to consolidate their holdings and escape the corrupting influence of the commune by withdrawing to individual farmsteads. Reformers resolutely—and literally—accepted Stolypin's wager "on the strong and sober," praising it for "giving free range to the individuality of the peasant" and allowing a unique class to be born "with a new relationship to the land, new views toward life, and . . . a consciousness of the value of their labor."[98] Indeed, as peasant separators "threw off the chains of the commune" and became petty landed proprietors, reformers compared them directly to the rational, hardworking, independent farmers who, it was believed, provided stability in much of the European countryside, symbolizing progress and rural civility.[99]

Together with a stream of laudatory writings immediately following the reforms, journals appeared offering this new agrarian class extensive advice and information on agriculture, horticulture, animal husbandry, the legal procedures necessary to consolidate one's land and leave the commune, how best to organize and run a private farm, and the advantages of becoming a property owner.[100] These and other publications sought to allay uncertainty among peasants and to entice them out of their communes by describing the productivity and peaceful living conditions to be enjoyed on an individual homestead. Citing evidence from newly independent farms across the country, authors of such works claimed that separators produced larger harvests and raised superior livestock on less land than average communal peasants farmed, and were safer from the epidemics that periodically ravaged village livestock. The petty disputes that commonly disrupted village communities and shattered families disappeared on the new farms because separators worked together harmoniously, largely immune to the devastating wave of household divisions that had wreaked havoc in traditional settlements for decades. The new system also strengthened family life and the morality of

<hr/>

[97] See, e.g., "Khutora i ikh budushchee," *Volost' i derevnia*, no. 5 (1910): 3–11.

[98] "Nasha obshchina i nashe zemledelie," *Sel'skii vestnik*, no. 157 (1912): 3; "Khutora i khuliganstvo," *Sel'skii vestnik*, no. 16 (1913): 3.

[99] "Zhizn' na khutorakh russkikh i angliiskikh," *Vestnik trezvosti* 18, no. 214 (1912): 14–24; "Obshchina nyneshniaia i obshchina budushchaia," *Sel'skii vestnik*, no. 256 (1907): 3.

[100] The major journals, largely overlooked in research on the Stolypin reforms, were *Khutor* (1906–17), *Khutorianin* (1909–17, with an earlier effort in 1896–97), and *Khutorskoe khoziaistvo* (1906–17).

youth, for there was less corruption and vice by contrast with the disorderly streets of communal villages. As one staunch supporter of the reforms claimed in 1910, "the consolidated farmstead represents salvation from the commune."[101] When combined with the greater wealth that consolidated farms promised, these pictures of social and familial harmony meshed particularly well with the reformist ideal for combatting and reversing the insidious process of degeneration.

Separators, in effect, came to be viewed as a social basis for cultural renewal, enlightenment, and order in the countryside. As petty proprietors, they had a greater interest in improving their farms and increasing family wealth; but because property conferred both respectability and individual responsibility, they were also less inclined toward the ruinous holiday drinking, carousing, and debauchery that beset most communes. Reformers argued that as the "sober and strong" freed themselves from the power of the wealthy exploiters (*kulaki*) and drunken "bawlers" (*gorlana*) who ruled their villages, occasions for communal drunkenness would eventually disappear entirely, along with hooliganism and other consequences of drinking. As one reform enthusiast noted, "it is not so easy to drink away one's own farm as it is the communal meadows. . . . By giving land into the private ownership of honest and sober peasants, we will see an end to the mass of hooligans . . . who are destroying the countryside, abandoning their families, and spreading drunkenness" and vice. Others claimed that hooliganism had completely disappeared in areas where the reforms had been widely accepted.[102] Perhaps most important from the perspective of educated society, ownership of private farms seemed to be creating respect for the property of others—a historical and cultural deficiency of the peasantry long decried by observers of rural life—and contributing to a greater acceptance of social- and moral-reform movements.[103]

There is, in fact, sufficient evidence to suggest that Russia's social engineers were at least partially correct in their assessment. The Stolypin reforms set in motion a process that encouraged forces already at work in

[101] "Khutora i ikh budushchee," 3, 7; "Issledovanie khutorskogo khoziaistva," *Sel'skii vestnik*, no. 135 (1908): 3; "Novaia zemledel'cheskaia Rossiia na khutorakh i otrubakh," *Sel'skii vestnik*, no. 142 (1910): 5–6. See also I. G. Doronin, *Kak zhivut liudi na khutorakh* (Glubokoe, 1913); and *Zapiski khutorianina* (Mogilev, 1914). Such sentiments were far from universal, of course, and widespread opposition to the Stolypin reforms continued until the collapse of the old regime. E. G., "V zashchitu obshchiny," *Rukovodstvo dlia sel'skikh pastyrei* 52, no. 49 (1912): 323–32; A. V. Shapkarin, ed., *Krest'ianskoe dvizhenie v Rossii, iun' 1907 g.–iul' 1914 g.* (Moscow and Leningrad, 1966), 107–10, 132, 139–43, 165–70, and passim.

[102] S. Ivanov, "Narodnoe otrezvlenie i zemel'naia reforma," *Deiatel'* 19, no. 6 (1914): 148–49; "Khutora i khuliganstvo," 2; "O p'ianstve," 99.

[103] "Khutora i ikh budushchee," 9.

the countryside, particularly social differentiation and the emergence of a rural petty bourgeoisie. Certainly communal peasants knew this to be the case, as their frequent and violent attacks on separators attested. Those who left the communes found that former fellow villagers cut them off from participation in local cultural activities, and they therefore began to establish their own recreations or to accept more readily the invented traditions of outsiders.[104] Separators took clear pride in their new status and sought to use it as a symbol of respectability. Many joined rural temperance societies, for example, and, when signing their names to membership lists, identified themselves as independent farmers and specified the amount of land they owned. Others contributed signatures to petitions calling for prohibition and supported rural cooperatives.[105] The reforms may, at last, have provided a foundation for the efforts of educated outsiders by forming small islands of sobriety and enlightenment that could be used as a springboard to further cultural improvements.

Implicit in this belief that separators represented a new force for rural regeneration were powerful hopes that they would sow the seeds of civilization among the peasantry not only through hard work, but by their willing acceptance of moral reform, education, and rational forms of recreation. Indeed, contemporaries again turned to the language and rationale of colonialism when describing the benefits that Stolypin's reforms would bring to backward peasants throughout Russia, and they used rural opposition to separators as a means of reinforcing these characterizations. "The separators want to work and are trying to propagate a new culture," declared an article on peasant disorder, "but they literally find themselves in a hostile country, enduring partisan raids and sieges from the beasts who are running wild. . . . At the present time, a real *civil war* is taking place in the depths of the peasantry . . . which threatens destruction far worse than an external invasion."[106] After 1907, peasants who fought against the reforms or resisted enlightenment from above were classified in starkly alien terms of "otherness" that transformed them into colonial objects representing the antithesis of culture and progress. For the most vehement antagonists of rural life and culture, the undisciplined, depraved peasant youth became "rural outlaws," "wild savages" displaying "beastly morals," "degenerates," and, finally, "apaches" and "hooligans."[107] By the 1930s, they would become "enemies of the people."

---

[104] See, e.g., Frank, " 'Simple Folk, Savage Customs?' " 35; and Shapkarin, *Krest'ianskoe dvizhenie*, passim.

[105] See, for example, M. D. Chelyshov, *"Poshchadite Rossiiu!" Pravda o kabake, vyskazannaia samim narodom po povodu zakona o merakh bor'by s p'ianstvom* (Samara, 1911), 77–86.

[106] "Narodnaia anarkhiia," 218, 221. See also "P'ianyi terror v derevne," 430.

[107] "Narodnaia anarkhiia," 218–19, 220; I. A. Rodionov, *Nashe prestuplenie (Ne vred, a byl')* (St. Petersburg, 1909); RGIA, f. 1405, op. 532, d. 440, l. 36; d. 424, l. 53; f. 1276, op. 9, d. 116, l. 24ob.; f. 796, op. 195, d. 3223, passim.

As with the attacks on rural festivity and peasant degeneration from which they arose, such formulations shed important light on the nature of moral-reform movements sponsored by the educated classes, clergy, and government in fin-de-siècle Russia. Whether the goal was to seek a revolutionary peasant ally, a class of solid, property-owning farmers to buttress state and civilization, or a God-fearing and deferential peasantry that would restore an imagined rural tranquillity of old, the means for achieving such ends remained much the same from one group to the next. Domination of rural popular culture—through education, invented traditions, transformation of worldviews, or even suppression—was fundamental to the goals of church, government, liberal reformers, and socialists alike, much as it would be to their Bolshevik successors (who used "red weddings," *komsomol* evening gatherings, and other new celebrations). Fearful of the "dark" lower classes and far more insecure than most of their European counterparts, Russia's reformers aimed to sever peasants from the degenerative practices of a corrupted popular culture and instill their own vision of respectability in the village (or factory). By transplanting their culture, ideals, and values across class lines, they would create a radically different peasantry beholden to the forces that spread enlightenment and order. Hence the sharp hostility toward the continued vitality of many popular practices—particularly autonomous innovations such as peasant appropriation of tearooms or libraries established by outsiders, which were frequently transformed into local "clubs" for gambling, drinking, and other forms of socializing.[108] In these cases, villagers willingly used the tools of cultural transformation provided by moral reformers but ignored or openly rejected the values and morality that accompanied them. Similarly, autonomous visions of respectability (such as peasant-sponsored and peasant-controlled sobriety movements, reading rooms, and self-education), which could be found throughout the countryside, were often greeted with suspicion from reformers precisely because they did not conform to the enlightened goals of educated society. By contrast, villagers who participated in the new holidays, joined official temperance societies, planted gardens and trees, or set up independent farmsteads became small but promising beacons of hope for reformers terrified about the state of their fragile civilization. These peasants, at least, most resembled the colonizers.

---

[108] For examples, see *Severnyi krai*, no. 114 (1904): 3; *Povolzhskii vestnik*, no. 181 (1906): 3; and *Sankt-Peterburgskie vedomosti*, no. 224 (1911): 5.

5

DEATH OF THE FOLK SONG?

Robert A. Rothstein

I
T IS AN unquestionable fact," wrote an anonymous American observer in 1893, "that in Russia all the principal outward adjuncts of modern civilization—large towns, factories, railroads, hotels, etc.— exercise a blighting effect on the beautiful old folk-song. This disappears at the sound of the steam whistle, and is gradually superseded by commonplace melodies with stupid words, not seldom of doubtful propriety."[1] Similar expressions of concern at the alleged demise of traditional folk music were being voiced at the same time in Russia itself in the course of an extended public discussion that lasted from the 1870s until the early years of the twentieth century. Ostensibly, this discussion was about "the perversion of folk-song creativity" or "the decline of the folk song," to cite the titles of two contributions to the debate.[2]

More was at issue, however, than aesthetic judgments or feelings of musical nostalgia. The folk song was not dying, but rather changing with the times, gradually becoming part of a common (urban and rural) musical culture. The new song repertoire brought messages of social and cultural change that were not always welcome to contemporary commentators: more independence for youth, greater sexual equality, and, in general, an increased stress on the concerns of the individual. In what follows we shall examine the way folk songs changed in form and content, as well as the reactions to these changes.[3]

This article is based in part on research made possible by a fellowship from the Russian Research Center, Harvard University, and sabbatical-leave support from the University of Massachusetts at Amhurst.

[1] Cited by Eugenie Lineff [E. E. Lineva], *Russian Folk-Songs As Sung by the People and Peasant Wedding Ceremonies Customary in Northern and Central Russia* (Chicago: C. F. Summy, 1893), 60.

[2] V. O. Mikhnevich, "Izvrashchenie narodnogo pesnotvorchestva," in *Istoricheskie etiudy russkoi zhizni* (St. Petersburg: F. S. Sushchinskii, 1882), 2:377–420 (first published in *Istoricheskii vestnik*, December 1880); P. I. Tikhovskii, "Padenie narodnoi pesni" (summary of paper and discussion), in *Izvestiia IX arkheologicheskogo s"ezda v Vil'ne*, no. 13 (August 13, 1893), *Protokol zasedaniia IV-go otdeleniia*, 6–8.

[3] Various elements of the common song culture that had developed by the twentieth century are discussed in Robert A. Rothstein, "The Quiet Rehabilitation of the Brick Factory:

In earlier times, the cultural life and traditions of the lower classes had not been a concern of Russian upper-class society. For most of the eighteenth century, Russian aristocratic society viewed the lower classes and the Russia of previous centuries with disdain, freely applying the term *podlyi*, "lowly, plebeian." When the Western orientation and especially the Francomania of the Russian upper classes began to be the subject of satirical literature in the 1770s, however, some writers started searching for native resources as a counterweight to foreign imports.

One reflection of this search was the appearance of the first printed collections of songs, starting with M. D. Chulkov's *Collection of Various Songs* (texts only) in the 1770s (reprinted in an enlarged version by Novikov in the 1780s), V. Trutovskii's *Collection of Russian Simple Songs with Music* (published between 1776 and 1795), and the most influential collection, the *Collection of Russian Folk Songs with Their Melodies* (1790), compiled by the Russian architect and poet Nikolai L'vov and the Czech musician Jan Bogumir Prač (in Russian, I. G. Prach).[4]

There is an interesting difference between the 1790 edition of the L'vov-Prač collection and an enlarged edition that appeared in 1806. In the introduction to the second edition, the word *muzhik*, "peasant," is replaced by what the editor of a 1955 Soviet reprint calls "the more democratic word" *prostoliudin*.[5] Since at the time the former was a stylistically neutral synonym for *krest'ianin*, while the latter was a more general term referring to members of the lower classes, the change seems to reflect not so much a more democratic attitude as a recognition that the folk repertoire belonged to a broader stratum than just the (rural) peasantry.

The Chulkov, Trutovskii, and L'vov-Prač collections contained a variety of material, songs by known authors and composers as well as folk songs. Even the latter were recorded not in the countryside, but in St. Petersburg or Moscow. Although L'vov, for example, writes in his introduction of the difficulty of collecting songs "dispersed over the broad territory of Russia," his cousin later described how L'vov and Prač com-

---

Early Soviet Popular Music and Its Critics," *Slavic Review* 39, no. 3 (September 1980): 373–88; and idem, "Popular Song in the NEP Era," in *Russia in the Era of NEP: Explorations in Soviet Society and Culture*, ed. Sheila Fitzpatrick, Alexander Rabinowitch, and Richard Stites (Bloomington: Indiana University Press, 1991), 268–94. The centrality of individual emotions in Russian songs of World War II is addressed in Robert A. Rothstein, "Homeland, Home Town, and Battlefield: The Popular Song," in *The Heart of War: Soviet Culture and Entertainment, 1941–1945*, ed. Richard Stites (Bloomington: Indiana University Press, forthcoming).

[4] M. D. Chulkov, *Sobranie raznykh pesen*, 4 vols. (St. Petersburg, 1770–74); V. Trutovskii, *Sobranie russkikh prostykh pesen s notami*, 4 vols. (St. Petersburg, 1776–95); N. A. L'vov and I. Prach, *Sobranie narodnykh russkikh pesen s ikh golosami. Na muzyku polozhil Ivan Prach* (St. Petersburg, 1790; repr., ed. V. M. Beliaev, Moscow: Muzgiz, 1955).

[5] L'vov and Prach, *Sobranie*, 14, 41, 46.

piled their collection "with the aid of amateurs and relatives who were always singing in [L'vov's] house."[6] It was not until the 1830s that serious collecting of village folk song began, largely under the inspiration and leadership of the Slavophile publicist Petr Kireevskii.

Kireevskii and his collaborators (among whom were Pushkin and Iazykov) made a point of authenticity. Kireevskii wrote that his collection contained only "pure folk songs," explaining that he had excluded "so-called romances and imitations of folk style."[7]

The efforts of Kireevskii and his circle were motivated in part by a desire to counter negative views of Russia, such as those expressed in Petr Chaadaev's *Philosophical Letters* of 1829–31,[8] and to find evidence supporting their preconceptions about Russia's "ancient spiritual and religious culture."[9] These efforts also reflected a concern for the imminent disappearance of Russian folklore. In his public appeal to collect folk songs, published in the *Simbirsk Provincial Gazette* in 1838, Kireevskii wrote, "Experience has shown us that it is necessary to hurry with the collecting of these priceless remnants of olden times, which we can observe disappearing from the memory of the folk with the changes in its mores and customs."[10]

The old songs, Kireevskii observed elsewhere, were not merely fading away but were being driven out by new ones, which replaced the beauty and nobility of the old songs with the "affectations of the servant class."[11] Kireevskii's judgment may have been harsh, but it was the dominant view among nineteenth-century observers, even those writing long after his death (1856). A few argued for the generally progressive character of change, suggesting that Russia (and Russian folklore with it) was in a transitional period and that the task of the *intelligent* was to help guide change in a positive direction. One such author was the village school-

[6] Ibid., 48, 54.

[7] Kireevskii's comments are paraphrased by M. N. Speranskii in his introduction to the posthumous *Pesni, sobrannye P. V. Kireevskim*, n.s., pt. 1 (Moscow: Obshchestvo liubitelei rossiiskoi slovesnosti pri imp. Moskovskom universitete, 1911), lv, and are cited in A. M. Novikova and A. V. Kokorev, eds., *Russkoe narodnoe poeticheskoe tvorchestvo* (Moscow: Vysshaia shkola, 1969), 377, from P. V. Kireevskii, "Russkie narodnye pesni, sobrannye Petrom Kireevskim," *Chteniia v Obshchestve istorii i drevnostei rossiiskikh pri Moskovskom universitete*, 1848, no. 9, pt. 4:vi.

[8] Peter Yakovlevich Chaadayev, *Philosophical Letters and Apology of a Madman*, trans. Mary-Barbara Zeldin (Knoxville: University of Tennessee Press, 1970).

[9] Abbott Gleason, *Young Russia: The Genesis of Russian Radicalism in the 1860s* (New York: Viking Press, 1980), 237.

[10] A. D. Soimonov, "'Pesennaia proklamatsiia' P. V. Kireevskogo," *Sovetskaia etnografiia*, 1960, no. 4:148.

[11] Cited by M. N. Speranskii in his introduction to *Pesni, sobrannye P. V. Kireevskim* (lv) as "uzhimistyi kharakter sosloviia lakeiskogo."

teacher I. Ia. L'vov, whose thirty-nine-page brochure *New Times—New Songs* (1891) was frequently cited.[12] For L'vov, change demonstrated the "youthfulness of the [Russian] national spirit" and its *élan vital*, which he described in an elaborate extended metaphor as "an excess of life force that is boiling and overflowing, but flowing in the wrong direction because of the dirty scum that has formed on its surface from contact with the rusty cover."[13]

The changes that were taking place in the Russian folk song in the second half of the nineteenth century involved the loss of some genres, the reworking of others, and the spread of at least one new genre, the *chastushka*. Let us examine these changes in turn, commenting on their causes, mechanisms, and significance.

By the second half of the nineteenth century, the old narrative genres (the epic poem, or *bylina*, and the traditional ballad) had disappeared from central Russia. Collectors seeking to record epic poetry had to travel to the far north of European Russia or to the Ukraine to indulge what poet and critic Apollon Grigor'ev mockingly called their "archaeological passion."[14] These narrative forms, with their accounts of Vladimir's court or other ancient aristocratic milieux, must have seemed less and less appropriate to Russian peasants and to workers and servants of peasant origin. They also served no particular national function—unlike the Balkan epics, with their tales of anti-Turkish struggles, or the Ukrainian *dumy*, which sang of the exploits of specifically Ukrainian heroes, the cossacks.

Then, too, the epics and the ballads—like the traditional ritual songs (*obriadovye pesni*), which were becoming less common—were typically long and slow (*protiazhnye*), and their poetic form (tonic verse, lack of

---

[12] *Novoe vremia—novye pesni* (Ustiug: P. N. Lagirev, 1891). This was only one of the many contributions to the discussion mentioned at the beginning of this essay. I have seen over forty of them, dating from 1862 to 1915. Many are listed in V. M. Sidel'nikov, *Russkaia narodnaia pesnia: Bibliograficheskii ukazatel', 1735–1945 gg.* (Moscow: Izd. AN SSSR, 1962) and/or in M. Ia. Mel'ts, comp., *Russkii fol'klor: Bibliograficheskii ukazatel', 1901–1916* (Leningrad: Biblioteka AN SSSR, 1981).

[13] *Novoe vremia*, 23 ("kipiashchii i l'iushchiisia cherez krai izbytok zhiznennoi sily, no l'iushchiisia ne po tomu napravleniu, blagodaria griaznoi nakipi, obrazovavsheisia na ee poverkhnosti ot soprikosnoveniia s izorzhavsheisia kryshkoi").

[14] A. G. Grigor'ev, "Russkie narodnye pesni s ikh poeticheskoi i muzykal'noi storony," parts 1, 2, *Otechestvennye zapiski*, 1860, nos. 4, 5, reprinted in *Sochineniia*, ed. V. S. Krupich (Villanova, Pa.: Villanova University Press, 1970), 1:327. Some of the "archaeologists" were optimistic about the survival of epic poetry. Writing of the area to the north and east of Lake Onega, where Petr Rybnikov had collected *byliny*, Isabel Florence Hapgood suggested that "so long as schools and trade do not penetrate to this secluded region, there is no danger of epic poetry dying out." *The Epic Songs of Russia*, 2d ed. (New York: C. Scribner's Sons, 1916), xxviii.

rhyme) was out of keeping with the latest urban musical fashions (to which we shall shortly return). Contemporary observers noted the preference among young people for shorter and livelier songs.[15] The explanations were sometimes rather simplistic—involving, for example, the rhythm of factory work versus that of agricultural work. One author cited the "rapid and monotonous sound" of factory wheels as well as the lack of opportunity for choral singing brought about both by work in a noisy factory and by the individual farming that had replaced serf labor.[16] Even the role of songs in kissing games was seen as a factor in the shift away from long, slow songs: the shorter the song, the sooner the couple got to kiss.[17]

The ritual songs, some of which originated in pagan observation of the agricultural cycle, had less of a role to play in a society in which young people were seeking nonagricultural occupations and in which agriculture itself was becoming more individualized.[18] In the case of those rituals that continued to involve collective participation, such as weddings, the older songs were sometimes replaced by newer, more "fashionable" ones.

The changes that affected songs involved both form and content. The Soviet folklorist Sergei Lazutin has pointed to the processes of reduction and contamination by which older songs were shortened or their elements combined to produce a new song. Lazutin calls attention as well to the elimination of older folk-song conventions and symbols as part of the modernizing process.[19] Another aspect of this process was the shift to more regular metrical schemes (iambic and trochaic meters) and the in-

---

[15] Eugenie Lineff cites without attribution the following comment on the difference between the tempo and also the degree of stylistic ornamentation of the old and new song: "The ancient song flows like a river with its own bends and twists, and the new song runs like a railway." *The Peasant Songs of Great Russia As They Are in the Folk's Harmonization* (St. Petersburg: Imperial Academy of Sciences, 1905), xxvii.

[16] K. S. Kuz'minskii, "O sovremennoi narodnoi pesne," *Etnograficheskoe obozrenie 55*, no. 3 (1902): 95.

[17] Kissing games in the Vologda district are described in V. Aleksandrov, "Derevenskoe vesel'e v Vologodskom uezde," *Sovremennik*, 1864, no. 7:175.

[18] Note, by contrast, the use of the "Internationale" and other workers' anthems in the new rituals ("red weddings," civic burials) of the Soviet period. See Richard Stites, "Bolshevik Ritual Building in the 1920s," in Fitzpatrick, Rabinowitch, and Stites, *Russia in the Era of NEP*, 202–3.

[19] S. G. Lazutin, *Russkaia chastushka: Voprosy proiskhozhdeniia i formirovaniia zhanra* (Voronezh: Izd. Voronezhskogo universiteta, 1960), 46–47, 37. The "recycling" of folksong material is discussed in an analysis of the late-nineteenth-century soldier and student song "At the Smithy" (Vo kuznitse) in Robert A. Rothstein, "'Vo kuznice': Historical Notes on a Musical Repertoire," in *Alexander Lipson in Memoriam*, ed. Charles E. Gribble et al. (Columbus, Ohio: Slavica, forthcoming). The three phenomena of reduction, contamination, and elimination of symbols had been cited earlier in V. N. Peretts, "Iskazheniia v sovremennoi narodnoi pesne," *Bibliograf*, 1892, no. 12:414–15.

creasing use of rhyme, both under the influence of literary poetry. Rhyme, of course, was not foreign to folklore; it can be found in children's folklore and in proverbs, for example. Traditional folk songs, however, were not often rhymed, and such rhyme schemes as *abab* were not in the traditional repertoire. Sometimes the forced rhymes led to weak texts, as contemporary critics were fond of pointing out with examples like "Prodam karty, prodam tuz / Kupliu milomu kartuz" ("I'll sell my cards, I'll sell my ace / I'll buy my beloved a cap").[20]

At the same time, the language of the folk song was changing, reflecting both the sentimental tone of popular literary poetry and the new realia of urban and (to a certain extent) rural life. A very early example of what one author called "servant Don-Juanism" (*lakeiskoe don-zhuanstvo*) is a song found in an eighteenth-century manuscript songbook. It contains such lines as "Akh ty, chernaia brov', / Ty sklonis' ko mne v liubov'" ("Oh you, dark brow, / Incline toward me in love").[21] Later a more cynical attitude appeared, as in lines cited in an 1895 article: "Ne khodite, devki, parom / Ne liubite rebiat darom" ("Don't walk the fallow field, girls / Don't love the boys for free").[22] Yet another tone—love as melodrama—dominated in the so-called new ballad (with its subtype, the "cruel romance"), which replaced the largely extinct traditional ballad.[23]

The vocabulary of newer songs included terms for newly fashionable articles of clothing (*pidzhak*, "sports coat" and *kaloshi*, "galoshes" for men; *kofta*, "blouse" and *plat'e*, "dress" [as opposed to the traditional sarafan] for women) and for items from the urban or upper-class household (*lombernyi stolik*, "card table" and *fabrichnaia salfetochka*, "factory-made napkin"); even rum (exotic in comparison to native vodka) is mentioned. "Learned" vocabulary was not always used appropriately, as in the case of a girl described as *shkol'naia, manernaia*, presumably meaning "educated" and "well-mannered"; the adjectives were not used that way in standard Russian.[24]

The literary historian Vladimir Peretts used the New Testament metaphor of "new wine in old wineskins" to describe the destructive effect of new elements in old songs.[25] The last quarter of the nineteenth century

[20] L'vov, *Novoe vremia*, 9.

[21] V. G. Varentsov, *Sbornik pesen Samarskogo kraia* (St. Petersburg: N. A. Serno-Solov'evich, 1862), 241–42.

[22] D. Uspenskii, "Fabrichnaia poeziia," *Knizhki "Nedeli"*, 1895, no. 9:11. The word *parom* could also be understood as meaning "in pairs."

[23] S. G. Lazutin, *Russkie narodnye pesni* (Moscow: Prosveshchenie, 1965); Robert A. Rothstein, "The Cruel Romance" (forthcoming).

[24] Mikhnevich, "Izvrashchenie," 391–95; F. M. Istomin, "Otchet ob ekspeditsii dlia sobiraniia russkikh narodnykh pesen s napevami v 1893 godu F. M. Istomina i S. M. Liapunova," *Izvestiia imp. Russkogo geograficheskogo obshchestva* 30 (1894): 349.

[25] "Iskazheniia," 414.

also saw the spread of "new wine in new wineskins" in the form of a new genre—the *chastushka*, a short, usually four-line, rhymed song.[26] Russian folklorists have disagreed about the time of the earliest appearance of the chastushka (or its prototype), but there is no doubt that it spread rapidly and widely in the period under discussion here.

Contemporary observers often blamed chastushki for driving out the old folk songs; one compared their effect to the "conquest of the Australian continent by weeds of European origin."[27] (The intended analogy was to the supposedly urban chastushka's spreading over the Russian countryside and choking out the native "musical flora" of the village.) Such critics cited the worst possible examples of the genre, those that were least poetic in form and most decadent or crass in content. For example:

> Ia sidela na luzhku,
> Pisala tainosti druzhku,
> Ia pisala tainosti
> Pro liubovnye krainosti.

> I sat in the meadow,
> And wrote secrets to my boyfriend,
> I wrote secrets
> About romantic excesses.[28]

or

> Gde ty milyi skrylsia?
> Gde ty zapropal?
> Ili s kruga spilsia,
> Il' v tiur'mu popal!

> Where are you hiding, darling?
> Where have you disappeared to?
> Either you've become a total drunkard
> Or you've wound up in jail.[29]

Other observers, however, starting with the writer Gleb Uspensky in 1889, cited the chastushka as evidence of the "freshness" and "youthful-

---

[26] This genre has a vast literature, including two particularly useful monographs: Lazutin, *Russkaia chastushka*; and Brigitte Stephan, *Studien zur russischen Častuška und ihrer Entwicklung* (Munich: Otto Sagner, 1969). For additional references, see the several volumes of bibliography compiled by Mikaela Mel'ts, starting with M. Ia. Mel'ts, comp., *Russkii fol'klor: Bibliograficheskii ukazatel', 1917–1944* (Leningrad: Biblioteka AN SSSR, 1966).

[27] L'vov, *Novoe vremia*, 16.

[28] Ibid., 22.

[29] P. I. Bogatyrev, "Russkaia pesnia," *Novoe vremia*, January 27, 1895, 2.

ness" of folk creativity. In his article, which is credited with popularizing the term *chastushka*, Uspensky pointed to its function as a medium for nearly instantaneous reaction to the phenomena of everyday life. Most of the examples he cites deal with love (happy or unhappy), but the tone is often far from traditional. For example:

> Bat'ka rozh' molotil,
> Ia podvorovala—
> Ponemnozhku, po lukoshku,
> Vse milomu na garmoshku.

> Father threshed the rye,
> I pilfered
> A little bit at a time, a little basketful at a time,
> All for my love [so he could buy] an accordion.[30]

The folklorist Vasilii Simakov, writing in 1913, expanded upon Uspensky's observation about the function of the chastushka, arguing that its role was not that of a song, but rather that of an impromptu epigram, an *ostroe slovtso*. Indeed, in the northern Russian villages where he had collected chastushki, he had never heard them called songs. Musically, he added, they were not designed for choral singing, but for the individual, "for the expression of passing feelings, moods, and experiences."[31] Uspensky and Simakov were not alone in noticing a shift in folk song toward the expression of individual emotions—a phenomenon that we shall return to shortly after examining the sources and mechanisms of change.

The prophets of the death of the folk song were nearly unanimous in blaming the influence of the cities (especially St. Petersburg and Moscow) for its decline. Young people were leaving the villages to seek urban employment in factories or shops, or as servants. Some of them were seasonal workers who spent part of the year back home in the village. These "visitors from the capital" had an attractive aura about them. They were the most literate members of the village community, and with their education (or at least a veneer of *obrazovannost'*), they had enough prestige to set the tone for dress, language, behavior, and songs. But their horizons were limited; as one contemporary observer put it, "their world is small

---

[30] G. I. Uspenskii, "Novye narodnye stishki," in *Sobranie sochinenii* (Moscow: Goslitizdat, 1957), 8:554–55, 558 (first published in *Russkie vedomosti*, April 23, 1889).

[31] V. I. Simakov, comp., *Sbornik derevenskikh chastushek* (Iaroslavl': By the compiler, 1913), xiii. A contemporary analogue to chastushki might be found in rap songs, with which they share not only topicality, but also the strong sense of rhythm and rhyme.

and impoverished, limited to deadening mechanical work during the week and the tavern on holidays."[32]

Folklorists have been less certain that the big cities were the source of all change. There has been disagreement, for example, about whether the chastushka was in its origins an urban or a rural genre. The most convincing hypothesis seems to be the one proposed by Lazutin, who argued that the chastushka arose at points of contact between village and city, between traditional folklore and literary poetry: in "the small *guberniia* (province) and *uezd* (district) capitals, the outskirts of large cities, the bustling villages on major roads, and the areas of railroad construction." It was the traditional gatherings of young people, the *khorovody* and *posidelki*, that served as the incubator of the new genre.[33]

The "visitors from the capital" were not the only agents of change. Itinerant craftsmen and workers such as tailors, fullers, and woodcutters brought new songs with them, as did villagers returning from visits to neighboring villages or from military service.[34] Yet another source of new songs were the cheap songbooks turned out by the publishers of popular literature (*lubochnye izdateli*)—each of which put out not just one songbook, but several, in "complete and abridged editions, more expensive and cheaper ones."[35] The ethnographer Dmitrii Zelenin reported in 1901 that in some villages, when he asked peasants about their songs, they brought out songbooks from well-known Moscow publishers.[36]

Popular literature also had an effect on the rural song repertoire. A song about the bandit Churkin became very popular in the mid-1880s

---

[32] N. A. Nadezhdin, "Perevorot v narodnoi pesne," *Zhivopisnaia Rossiia*, 1902, no. 64:146. See also N. I. Kostomarov, "Istoricheskoe znachenie iuzhno-russkogo narodnogo pesennogo tvorchestva," *Beseda*, 1872, no. 4:8–l0; and M. I. Sokolov, comments in Tikhovskii, "Padenie narodnoi pesni," 7.

[33] Lazutin, *Russkaia chastushka*, 54–59. The *posidelki* are discussed in Stephen P. Frank, " 'Simple Folk, Savage Customs?' Youth, Sociability, and the Dynamics of Culture in Rural Russia, 1856–1914," *Journal of Social History* 25, no. 4 (Summer 1992): 711–36. See also the references to the Ukrainian "fall and winter socials," the *vechernytsi*, in Christine D. Worobec, "Temptress or Virgin? The Precarious Sexual Position of Women in Postemancipation Ukrainian Peasant Society," *Slavic Review* 49, no. 2 (Summer 1990): 233.

[34] V. Magnitskii, "Pesni krest'ian s. Belovolzhskogo, Cheboksarskogo uezda, Kazanskoi gub.," *Izvestiia i uchenye zapiski Kazanskogo universiteta* 13 (1877): 156, cited in Lazutin, *Russkaia chastushka*, 55. In his report to the Imperial Russian Geographic Society on an 1893 expedition to collect folk songs, Fedor Istomin cited with approval the comment of a village ecclesiastical official (*blagochinnyi*) who had lived for twenty-five years in a village in the Vologda district; the official blamed the institution of universal military service for the disappearance of the traditional folk song. Istomin, "Otchet," 348.

[35] A. S. Prugavin, *Zaprosy naroda i obiazannosti intelligentsii v oblasti umstvennogo razvitiia i prosveshcheniia* (Moscow: I. N. Skorokhodov, 1890), 165.

[36] D. K. Zelenin, *Novye veianiia v narodnoi poezii* (Moscow: Vestnik vospitaniia, 1901), 9.

DEATH OF THE FOLK SONG? 117

after the newspaper *Moskovskii listok* (The Moscow Sheet) serialized Nikolai Pastukhov's novel *Razboinik Churkin* (The Bandit Churkin). The song, beginning with the words "In the midst of the dense forest" ("Sredi lesov dremuchikh"), remained popular into this century; new texts were being set to its melody as late as World War II.[37]

As we have seen, the new songs of the late nineteenth and early twentieth centuries differed from older ones in form as well as content. Contemporary observers attributed the growing tendency to use rhyme and regular, literary meters (in chastushki, for example) in part to the influence of school. Readers for the elementary grades contained simple, melodious poems, which schoolchildren learned by heart and recited at home. "The sonorous rhymed lines appeal to the musical ear of the folk," even if the text was not always understood. "The music [of this poetry] leaves a permanent trace," and new songs were composed following literary models.[38]

Most contemporary critics had little more to say about the musical side of the new songs that they found so objectionable. Yet the new songs did differ musically from more traditional folk music. Just as their texts showed the influence of literary poetry, so, too, their music was influenced by Western musical styles and harmonies. A few authors criticized what the ethnomusicologist Nikolai Lopatin called "voluntary servility to Western fashion."[39] Lopatin's views were shared by the composer César Cui, who blamed much of the decline of the Russian folk song on the standardizing influence of the street organ (*sharmanka*) and especially the accordion (*garmon'* or *garmoniia*), which he called "a barbarous instrument that reduces any song to two chords."[40] Cui heaped similar scorn on his composer colleagues Aleksandr Diubiuk and Aleksandr Varlamov (his particular *bête noire*), whose classically influenced settings

[37] Churkin and Pastukhov's novel are discussed in Jeffrey Brooks, *When Russia Learned to Read: Literacy and Popular Literature, 1861–1917* (Princeton: Princeton University Press, 1985), 177–83 and passim. The effect of the novel is cited by N. M. Lopatin in his introduction to part 1 of N. M. Lopatin and V. P. Prokunin, *Russkie narodnye liricheskie pesni*, ed. V. M. Beliaev (Moscow: Muzgiz, 1956), 50 (first published Moscow, 1889). Churkin was a peasant-worker who protested conditions at a dye factory, was arrested, escaped from prison, and spent the next twenty years as a highwayman. The song about him was based on Fedor Miller's 1846 translation of a German poem by Ferdinand Freiligrath. See V. E. Gusev, ed., *Pesni russkikh poetov* (Leningrad: Sovetskii pisatel', 1988), 2:401–2, 495–96. On the new texts from World War II, see Rothstein, "Homeland."

[38] Nadezhdin, "Perevorot v narodnoi pesne," 146; L'vov, *Novoe vremia*, 8.

[39] Lopatin's phrase, *dobrovol'noe kholopstvo pered inozemnoi modoi* (Lopatin and Prokunin, *Russkie narodnye liricheskie pesni*, 68), had a later echo in Stalinist attacks on *nizkopoklonstvo pered zapadom*, "servility toward the West."

[40] César Cui [Ts. A. Kiui], " 'Krest'ianskie pesni', zapisannye N. Pal'chikovym," in *Izbrannye stat'i*, ed. I. L. Gusin (Leningrad: Muzgiz, 1952), 386 (first published in *Grazhdanin*, no. 42 [November 11, 1887]).

of texts written by poets in imitation of folk style and whose arrangements of authentic folk songs were being sung in place of original folk
songs.[41]

Most contemporary critics, however, were less concerned with musical
innovations than with the texts that were being sung and the negative
aspects of lower-class life that they revealed (or, in the view of some,
helped to cause). The author of an 1895 article, for example, lumped
together the replacement of old songs by new ones, the weakening of
parental authority and of religiousness, the development of fashion in
clothing, and the new freedom in relations between the sexes.[42] One
writer's parental authority, however, is another's "patriarchal despo-
tism";[43] fashion may be read as conformity or as the desire of the individual villager to stand out among peers by adopting the latest urban innovations. Sexual freedom may mean simply the demand for freedom in
choosing one's mate.[44]

In any case, it is clear that the new songs reflected what Zelenin, writing in 1903, called "an immense shift" (*grandioznyi perelom*) in the life
of the people—namely, the growth of individualism.[45] The expression of
emotion in song was not new; that, after all, is one of the functions of the
lyric song. But the old lyric song tended to portray generic situations and

---

[41] César Cui, "Sbornik malorossiiskikh pesen Rubtsa," in Gusin, *Izbrannye stat'i*, 168
(first published in *Sankt-Peterburgskie vedomosti*, 1870). Cui used the terms *khutorok*,
"farmstead" and *sarafan*, "sarafan" (traditional Russian sleeveless dress) as symbolic generic designations for this kind of "composed folk song," alluding to Diubiuk's setting of
the poem "The Farmstead" by Aleksei Kol'tsov and to Varlamov's setting of "Do Not Sew
a Red Sarafan for Me, Mother" (Ne shei ty mne, matushka, krasnyi sarafan) by Nikolai
Tsyganov. Outside of Russia, the latter became the classic Russian folk song, turning up, for
example, in chapter 25 of John Galsworthy's *End of the Chapter*.

[42] D. Uspenskii, "Fabrichnaia poeziia," 10–11.

[43] V. Popov, *Narodnye pesni, sobrannye v Cherdynskom uezde Permskoi gubernii*
(Moscow: A. I. Manukhin, 1880), iii.

[44] There were, to be sure, songs that presented more extreme matters, such as premarital
pregnancy or even incest. E. Shurygin, "Novye pesni," *Zhizn'*, 1897, no. 16–17, for example, includes texts such as "U garmoshki ital'ianki / Otorvalos' ushko; / U moei-to li mi-
lashki / Naduvaetsia briushko" ("The handle broke off the Italian accordion; my darling's
belly is swelling" [147]) and a song about brother-sister incest (149–50), a variant of which
was still current in Latvia in the 1930s. I. D. Fridrikh, *Fol'klor russkikh krest'ian Iaun-
latgal'skogo uezda* (Riga: Kultras fonds, 1936), 1:314. Then, too, the evidence cited by
contemporary commentators was not always pertinent. For example, a song about the
choice of a husband, cited by N. A. Smirnov in *Russkie narodnye pesni noveishego vremeni
(Etnograficheskii ocherk)* (St. Petersburg: I. Gol'dberg, 1895), 15–17, to demonstrate new
ideas of sexual equality, can in fact be traced back to medieval Latin student poetry from
Bohemia. Robert A. Rothstein, "The Mother-Daughter Dialogue in the Yiddish Folk Song:
Wandering Motifs in Time and Space," *New York Folklore* 15, no. 1–2 (Winter–Spring
1989): 51–65.

[45] "Cherty sovremennogo narodnogo byta po 'chastushkam,'" *Russkie vedomosti*, January 8, 1903, 3.

emotions, while the new songs—both the chastushka and the new ballad—were more individualized, more concrete, more topical. If in the old songs, for example, unhappily married young people (both men and women) simply bemoaned their fate, in the new songs unmarried young people insisted on freedom of choice. In one song cited by Zelenin, the daughter responds to her mother's objections about her getting married: "Ia skazala na otvet / Tebe dela, mati, net" ("I said in reply / It's no business of yours, mother"). Another girl threatens to tear off the wedding crown (*venets*) if her parents try to marry her to someone other than the one whom she has chosen.[46]

Analyzing the songs that he had collected in the Tver', Klin, and Moscow districts, the linguist Vasilii Chernyshev came to the conclusion that "the girl of our day is a free Héloïse who values her own feelings and does not recognize any dependence on other people." He illustrated this with a text in which the young man, abandoning his lover, tells her not to cry, lest people say that he had lived with her. She replies:

> Puskai liudi skazhut,
> a ia ne baiusa:
> Kavo [*sic*] ia liubila,
> s' tem ia rastaiusa.

> Let people say it,
> I'm not afraid:
> I'm parting with
> the one I loved.[47]

Chernyshev found the main characteristic of many of his songs to be the dramatic nature of their content, which most often portrayed "restive individual feelings that could not accept constraints imposed by others." Even the frequent depiction in newer songs of suicide as a response to being abandoned by one's lover (rare in older songs) represented greater respect for and attention to individual feelings. Such attitudes were characteristic of sentimentalism and romanticism in literature: indeed, Chernyshev compared the appeal of such motifs for the composers of new songs and their (lower-class) audience with a similar focus on the individual among the (upper-class) writers and readers of Nikolai Karamzin's time. The readers of Karamzin's 1792 novella *Bednaia Liza* (Poor Liza) had shown extraordinary sympathy for Liza, the story's abandoned heroine, who took her own life.[48]

---

[46] Ibid.

[47] V. I. Chernyshev, "Svedeniia o nekotorykh govorakh Tverskogo, Klinskogo i Moskovskogo uezdov," *Sbornik otdeleniia russkogo iazyka i slovesnosti imp. Akademii Nauk* 75, no. 2 (1903): 156.

[48] Ibid., 153–54.

The expression of individual feelings in new songs, the references to elements of urban material culture in their texts, the shift toward rhyme and literary meters as well as Western harmonies—all of these were signs of the ongoing cultural transformation of the village. But songs were also a force for change: more rapidly and effectively than underground literature, they spread subversive ideas like greater sexual equality, more independence for youth, or even criticism of the mistreatment of workers.[49] By themselves, these notions were hardly likely to bring down the empire; but they helped pave the way for a more revolutionary consciousness.

Writing in 1901, Zelenin saw the "first beginnings" of a new folk poetry that would develop its final shape only in the more or less distant future. He felt confident, however, in predicting the direction that development would take: "The time will come—and apparently it is already beginning—when our people will no longer have their own poetry, but rather will have the very same poetry as the educated [*intelligentnye*] strata of society. Chastushki (as well as romances) show us that the transition of folk poetry from purely folk literature to artificial, book literature is near."[50]

Zelenin was right in part, but he failed to anticipate the degree of convergence involved in the development of the twentieth-century common song repertoire. That repertoire is beyond the scope of this essay; here we should only note that it was the product of a complex interaction between the traditional folk song and songs sung in Moscow and St. Petersburg. That process had its beginnings in the eighteenth century, as poets and composers reworked or imitated folk songs and then found their compositions in turn reworked into new folk songs. The process was fed by other streams: Ukrainian melodies, underworld songs, Western fox-trots and tangos. It was mediated at various times by choruses of serfs, Gypsy ensembles, and songwriters born into the musical milieu of the Pale of Settlement. The serfs and the Gypsy choruses, as well as most of the Jewish composers, are gone. The old folk songs are preserved mostly by folkloric ensembles; the nineteenth-century critics discussed above were not able to "preserve a living past . . . by setting up human natural sanctuaries for isolated corners of archaic life."[51] Yet the assimilation of variegated musical material continues, as does the creation of new texts to old melodies and the oral transmission of new songs. The folk-song process, in other words, did not die along with the Russian Empire.

[49] Smirnov mentions briefly two topics of recent songs: the situation of the worker, "whose boss gives him only warm water, neither cabbage nor grain," and the situation of the Siberian prisoner. (*Russkie narodnye pesni*, 23–24). He refrains from commenting on them because of the paucity of examples in the available published collections.

[50] *Novye veianiia*, 6.

[51] Eric Hobsbawm, introduction to *The Invention of Tradition*, ed. Eric Hobsbawm and Terence Ranger (Cambridge: Cambridge University Press, 1983), 8.

6

SHOWS FOR THE PEOPLE:

PUBLIC AMUSEMENT PARKS IN

NINETEENTH-CENTURY ST. PETERSBURG

Al'bin M. Konechnyi

S T. PETERSBURG, capital of the Russian Empire, was known as a city of high culture, famous for its artificiality and its grandiose architecture. Refined court life and displays of imperial symbolism were accompanied by a rich world of opera, ballet, dramatic art, concert halls, musical societies, and literary salons. The imperial theaters reflected both the high standards of a common European elite culture and the expectations of a sophisticated cosmopolitan audience.

St. Petersburg, however, like most other European capitals in the nineteenth century, was not only an extension of the imperial court. It was above all a city of bureaucrats, small shopkeepers, merchants and entrepreneurs, the demimonde, and, toward the end of the century, a rapidly increasing number of workers. The vast majority of these people never went to the imperial opera or to a ballet performance, nor did they attend classical-music concerts. Their leisure time was spent on other, more "democratic" kinds of diversion, such as the circus and public amusement parks (*uveselitel'nye sady*). The latter in particular became popular attractions in nineteenth-century St. Petersburg. Although they were the centers of urban show business and an important part of the cultural life of the old capital, amusement parks have gone largely unnoticed by urban and cultural historians.

Until the middle of the nineteenth century, the main entertainment for a majority of St. Petersburg's citizens was the *narodnoe gulian'e*. This traditional folk fair included a variety of amusements, rides, booths, and games. During carnival (*maslenitsa*) and Easter week, gulian'ia regularly took place on Petrovskaia, Teatral'naia, and Admiralteiskaia squares. Ekateringof was the location for fairs on May Day and Whitsunday, while Whitmonday fairs were held in the Summer Garden, in order, it was said, "to seek out brides of merchant background." Name days, anniversaries of coronations, and other commemorative days of the imperial family were usually occasions for festivals featuring shows and fire-works on the Field of Mars, on Elagin and Kamennyi islands, in Aleksan-drovskii Park, and in Petergof.[1]

Ordinary people particularly liked to visit Ekateringof, Poliustrovo, or Krestovskii Island for their recreation, while high society relaxed at dachas along Petergofskii Road and on the islands around the city. At some of these locations, fairground attractions had already begun to ap-pear by the beginning of the nineteenth century. Elagin Island, for exam-ple, was known for its ice slides (*ledianye gory*). On Krestovskii Island, "Swiss hills" (*shveitsarskie gory*, an early form of roller coaster) and swings were set up during the summer season. Some of these rides were inspired by similar, though more elaborate, structures in the parks of the imperial summer residence in Tsarskoe Selo.[2]

Other amusements were available at the resorts as well. Wealthy citi-zens and "people dressed in a decent manner" frequented dances and musical evenings in summer gardens located in fashionable dacha dis-tricts.[3] They also went to taverns such as the Little Red Bar (Krasnyi ka-bachok) and the Tashkent on Petergofskii Road, the Russian Pub (Rus-skii traktir) on Krestovskii Island, or the Lübeck (Liubek) on Petrovskii Island. These places featured shows by Gypsy singers and itinerant thea-ter groups similar to the programs of such pleasure domes as the Villa Monplaisir (Villa monplezir) on Aptekarskii Island and the Hermitage (Ermitazh) in Poliustrovo.[4] In the 1830s, outings to balls, concerts, and musical soirées became fashionable. These events took place in Novaia Derevnia, in Poliustrovo, in Aleksandrovskii Park, and, from the end of the decade onward, "at the Vauxhalls [*vokzaly*]," meaning the new gar-

---

[1] See, for example, "Ob ustroistve narodnykh gulianii v 1867 godu," Tsentral'nyi gosu-darstvennyi istoricheskii arkhiv Sankt-Peterburga (hereafter TsGIA SPb; formerly LGIA), f. 514, op. 1, d. 510.

[2] Depictions of these amusements are available on contemporary lithographs by such artists as V. Patersen, A. P. Briullov, S. F. Galaktionov, and A. E. Martynov. On lower-class recreation at Ekateringof, see Evgenii Mikhailovich Kuznetsov, comp., *Russkie narodnye gulian'ia po rasskazam A. Ia. Alekseeva-Iakovleva* (Moscow and Leningrad, 1948), 37–40; M. Marina, "V Peterburge 60-kh godov proshlogo stoletiia," *Russkaia starina*, no. 3 (1914): 698–99; and TsGIA SPb, f. 792, op. 1, d. 10551, l. 6ob. On the imperial amuse-ments in Tsarskoe Selo and their role as models for popular rides, see A. M. Konechnyi, "Obshchestvennye razvlecheniia i gorodskie zrelishcha v Tsarskom Sele (XVIII–nachalo XX v.)," in *Etnografiia Peterburga–Leningrada: Materialy ezhegodnykh nauchnykh chtenii no. 2* (Leningrad, 1988), 14–17.

[3] According to *Severnaia pchela*, January 10, 1839, there were 1,054 "public and private gardens" in St. Petersburg in 1838.

[4] For detailed information on these establishments, see M. I. Pyliaev, *Zabytoe proshloe okrestnostei Peterburga* (St. Petersburg, 1889).

dens of Ekateringof and Pavlovsk and the railroad station of Tsarskoe Selo.[5]

Public amusement parks became a regular feature of summertime relaxation and entertainment for most of the citizens of St. Petersburg by the second half of the nineteenth century. They included elements of the gulian'ia, the taverns, and the summer gardens and are thus difficult to define as a specific genre of popular culture. They shared, however, a common geographic and aesthetic quality. Amusement parks usually stretched along a river on land leased from the owners of suburban dachas, and they often included a pond or small lake. The layout of the parks and the exotic, often Moorish or Chinese style of architecture of their wooden buildings—in particular the theaters, the *estrada* (variety) stages, the open podiums, and the pavilions—were meant to surprise and enchant visitors. Temporary structures of the traditional fairground such as the *balagan* (show booth) and the merry-go-round, together with other attractions aimed at the broadest audience, helped to evoke a festive atmosphere.[6]

"The urban amusement park has always interested me as a special mixture of show and entertainment that is able to communicate the latest achievements of culture and technology in a witty and fascinating way," wrote Aleksei Alekseev-Iakovlev, a director and producer of mass festivals.[7] Many amusement-park directors also owned balagan theaters and could draw on their long experience in fairground entertainment. Like Alekseev-Iakovlev, they displayed a certain didactic vein in the organization of their parks. They wanted to enlighten their audience by transforming elite into popular culture, by making high art accessible to a mass public.

The theater reform of 1882 played a crucial role in the development of amusement parks. It abolished the monopoly of the imperial theaters on

[5] The Russian word for railroad station, *vokzal*, is derived from the Vauxhall Gardens, a London amusement park that was closed in the late 1850s. *Vokzal* was first used in Russian in the sense of "Vauxhall" and only later acquired its current meaning. See Max Vasmer, *Russisches etymologisches Wörterbuch* (Heidelberg, 1953), vol. 1, s.v. "vokzal."

[6] The architectural characteristics and layout of public parks are discussed by E. I. Kirichenko, "K voprosu o poreformennykh vystavkakh Rossii kak vyrazhenii istoricheskogo svoeobraziia arkhitektury vtoroi poloviny XIX v.," in *Khudozhestvennye protsessy v russkoi kul'ture vtoroi poloviny XIX v.* (Moscow, 1984).

[7] *Russkie narodnye gulian'ia*, 140. Alekseev-Iakovlev (1850–1939) produced shows in a number of St. Petersburg parks, such as the Livadiia (1875–76), the Arkadiia (1877–80), the Krestovskii sad (1881–82), and the Zoologicheskii sad (1886–97), as well as in the balagan theater Razvlechenie i pol'za, or Entertainment and Benefit (1880–98). On Alekseev-Iakovlev, see *Opis' pamiatnikov russkogo teatra iz sobraniia L. I. Zheverzheeva* (Petrograd, 1915), 83; and *Rabochii i teatr*, no. 20 (1935): 17.

all forms of theatrical and concert activities. Operas and serious drama could now be staged in the parks. Estrada shows in particular experienced a boom, which was evident not only in an increase of concerts by professional musicians and orchestras (the concert stage, or *kontsertnaia estrada*), but especially in the formation of the entertainment stage (*divertismentnaia estrada*) and the café chantant stage (*kafeshantannaia estrada*). These were vaudeville shows in the broadest sense, and they drew on a wide range of Russian and western European models of urban entertainment.

The *divertismentnaia estrada* initially borrowed extensively from opera, ballet, and drama. But there was a strong tendency to come up with a distinct style, to create something like a separate genre. Humor and satire directed at current events, the *zloba dnia*, became important ingredients. Folk singers and dancers, accordion players, storytellers, reciters of couplets, clowns, acrobats, and magicians were regular participants. Popular urban performance culture in its broadest variety thus became part of the repertoire of the amusement parks, where it mixed with productions of the Russian classics, pantomimes, detective plays, farces, operettas, and reenactments of historic battles and military victories.

The *kafeshantannaia estrada* drew its inspiration more from western European cabaret, in particular from the Parisian café chantant.[8] It was closely connected with the demimonde and featured not only burlesque shows with special "female numbers," but also some borrowings from the *divertismentnaia estrada*, such as Russian choirs and dance groups, circus attractions, and Gypsy ensembles. According to the artist V. I. Kozlinskii, "the café chantant with its music and grotesque repertoire was deeply rooted in the consciousness of Russian society." The greatest impression, however, was made by Gypsy performers. In the words of A. A. Pleshcheev, "Gypsies were at the top of the program in all parks. Gypsy romances and dances were audiences' ultimate favorites."[9]

One of the prototypes of St. Petersburg amusement parks was the Artificial Mineral Waters Establishment (Zavedenie iskusstvennykh mineral'nykh vod). It opened in 1834 in Novaia Derevnia near the banks of the Bol'shaia Nevka, on property belonging to the dacha of Countess Stroganov. Although this enterprise was initially intended for a wealthy

---

[8] The first public performances of French chansons in Russia took place in the early 1860s in St. Petersburg amusement parks, according to A. F. B., "Teatr 'Opera-buff' i frantsuzskie pevtsy v Peterburge," *Peterburgskii listok*, February 21, 1878.

[9] V. I. Kozlinskii, "Vospominaniia," Otdel rukopisei, Rossiiskaia natsional'naia biblioteka, St. Petersburg (hereafter OR RNB), f. 1226, ed. khr. 101, l. 103; P. Stolpianskii, "Kaskadnyi zhanr v starom Peterburge," *Stolitsa i usadba*, no. 49 (1915); A. Pleshcheev, "Ostrova (V kontse proshlogo stoletiia)," ibid., nos. 19–20 (1914): 9; idem, "Tsygane (Iz zhizni starogo Peterburga)," ibid., nos. 38–39 (1915).

clientele, it was here that the foundations were laid for shows and entertainment in parks accessible to the broader public.[10]

The Mineral Waters was a beautifully laid out park that included a theater in Moorish style and a number of other buildings. "At Izler's"— Johann Izler was the manager of the park between 1840 and the 1860s— one could enjoy musical soirées, "physico-magical performances," recitals by Gypsies and Tyrolean singers, and shows with Hungarian dances. *Tableaux vivants* such as "Peter the Great at Lake Ladoga" could be seen alongside French chanteuses, circus acrobats, a marionette theater featuring Punchinello, and Weinert's balloon flight. Izler was also famous for his fireworks and Chinese illuminations at the close of the evening. After his departure, the park was taken over by Vasilii Egarev, but it closed after a fire in 1875 destroyed all the buildings.[11]

During the 1860s, a number of other amusement parks opened for the public. Beginning in 1863, for example, Iusupov Park became popular, "especially among artisans and the middle class." It was famous for having Russia's first public skating rink, which opened in 1865; and it featured such sensational attractions as the balloon flights of the "maestro" of the balagan, Wilhelm Berg, alongside regular narodnye gulian'ia.[12] In 1862, Tauride Park (Tavricheskii sad) was opened. Its ice slides were popular, especially among "the aristocratic youth, the diplomats, and the guards officers." The park also housed a People's Theater, founded there in 1898 by the local Guardianship for Popular Temperance.[13]

---

[10] *Opisanie Sanktpeterburgskogo Zavedeniia iskusstvennykh mineral'nykh vod* (St. Petersburg, 1834).

[11] Johann (Ivan) Izler (1810–77) was the owner of a famous café on Nevsky Prospect and of the "Vauxhall" park in Poliustrovo. In the 1860s, he had a balagan on Admiralteiskaia Square. *Literaturnaia gazeta*, January 20, 1840; Pyliaev, *Zabytoe proshloe*, 60; TsGIA SPb, f. 792, op. 1, d. 1028. The merchant Vasilii Nikitich Egarev (d. 1897) was a longtime St. Petersburg entrepreneur; he was active in organizing public amusements and was said to own "the best entertainment businesses of the city and its environs." Between 1875 and 1879, he ran a balagan on the field of Mars, the Theater of English Pantomimes. *Novoe vremia*, May 31, 1875. For more about the Mineral Waters, see *Sanktpeterburgskie vedomosti*, July 27, 1849; *Peterburgskii listok*, July 1, 1865; K. Gubert, *Gulian'e na iskusstvennykh mineral'nykh vodakh bliz Novoi derevni v Sanktpeterburge* (St. Petersburg, 1852); and Pyliaev, *Zabytoe proshloe*, 10–12. See also the lithographs with views of the park by V. Timm in *Russkii khudozhestvennyi listok* (1852).

[12] V. Mikhnevich, *Peterburg ves' na ladoni* (St. Petersburg, 1874), 120; *Severnaia pchela*, April 24, 1863. Wilhelm (Vasilii) Berg (1819–86) was born in Hamburg. From the 1840s to the 1860s he organized balloon flights in amusement parks, and from the 1850s to the 1880s he ran a pantomime theater at urban fairgrounds. *Novoe vremia*, 28 July 1888; TsGIA SPb, f. 514, op. 1, d. 644; f. 513, op. 64, d. 538. On the gulian'ia in Iusupov Park from 1866 to 1911, see TsGIA SPb, f. 792, op. 1, d. 1112, 1533; f. 514, op. 1, d. 593, 644; f. 513, op. 47, d. 39; op. 50, d. 111, 185; and op. 137, d. 955.

[13] N. V. Drizen, "Staryi Peterburg," *Ves' mir*, no. 10 (1918): 10; *Niva*, no. 35 (1898): 693.

Egarev, the enterprising manager of the Mineral Waters, founded another park in 1863 called the Russian Family Park (Russkii semeinyi sad). Its location, Demidov Garden at Ofitserskaia Street 39, already had a tradition in St. Petersburg garden culture. According to the local historian Mikhail Pyliaev, it was where the first public amusement park of the city had opened its doors in 1793: for those who could afford the cover charge of one or two rubles, the Vauxhall at Naryshkin Garden (Vokzal v Naryshkinom sadu) offered masquerades, balls, itinerant actors, pantomimes, and Bengal lights.[14]

The Russian Family Park (which in the early twentieth century became Luna Park and saw the first Russian futurist theater performance in 1913) was a haunt for devotees of the chanson. The appearance and promulgation of the French operetta and the café chantant in St. Petersburg was closely connected to the park and to Egarev himself. His successor as manager, the actress V. A. Nemetti, broke with that tradition in the 1880s and focused more on Russian operettas, which were even more popular and attracted huge crowds. She also built separate theaters for use in the summer and the winter seasons, thus enhancing the park and giving it a "light and animated" atmosphere.[15]

V. O. Mikhnevich reports that by 1870 there were seven amusement parks in St. Petersburg "serving as a place of entertainment for an indistinct audience from the lower strata." He names Egarev's Russian Family Park as the "most fashionable and most amusing establishment in the capital." The other parks were the Concert Garden (Kontsertnyi sad), also owned by Egarev, near Izmailovskii Bridge; Krestovskii Park on Krestovskii Island; the Mineral Waters; Bekleshovskii Park in Lesnoe; the merchant Sosov's Family Park (Semeinyi sad), located eight miles beyond the Shlissel'burg Gates; and Shukhardin's tavern and garden on Liteinaia Street, near the Church of the Transfiguration. Over the following decade, a number of other gardens were added to this list. The Taiwan Vauxhall (Vokzal Taivani) and the Bavaria (Bavariia) opened on Petrovskii Island, and a number of smaller establishments sprang up along the Fontanka River.[16]

---

[14] M. I. Pyliaev, *Staryi Peterburg* (St. Petersburg, 1887), 407.

[15] *Novoe vremia*, February 17, 1897; A. Pleshcheev, "Kak veselilis' v stolitse," *Stolitsa i usad'ba*, no. 44 (1915): 21. See also *Novoe vremia*, July 28, 1888; and S. Andreevskii, "Demidov sad," *Stolitsa i usad'ba*, no. 56 (1916). Material about Luna Park for the years 1900–1917 is in TsGIA SPb, f. 513, op. 13, d. 397; op. 132, d. 236; op. 137, d. 638, 801; op. 139, d. 180; and f. 569, op. 14, d. 199. See also I. Petrovskaia, *Teatr i zritel' rossiiskikh stolits, 1895–1917* (Leningrad, 1990), 74, 105–6.

[16] Mikhnevich, *Petersburg ves' na ladoni*, 233–35; idem, "Peterburgskie sady i ikh etnografiia," in *Peterburgskoe leto* (St. Petersburg, 1887); TsGIA SPb, f. 961, op. 4, d. 47. Beside the parks mentioned by Mikhnevich, Egarev still owned the Pleasure (Udovol'stvie) on Petergofskii Road, the Arban near Izmailovskii Bridge, the comedy theater Opera-Bouffe

The right bank of the Neva, with its islands and Novaia Derevnia, became the main resort area for the residents of St. Petersburg in the last quarter of the nineteenth century. Here the biggest and most popular public amusement parks were concentrated. One of the most important was Krestovskii Park. Its precursor was the Russian Pub, which since the 1830s had been a notorious hangout and workplace for itinerant actors. In the 1860s and 1870s, the park was run alternately by Egarev and Berg.[17]

The repertoire of Krestovskii Park included street theater in the broadest sense. Drama groups appeared on an open stage, followed by a variety show. During the Russo-Turkish War, battles were elaborately reenacted under the open sky. In the 1877 production "The War with Turkey" (Voina s Turtsiei), for example, about five hundred people participated, along with aeronauts in balloons, horses, carrier pigeons, and dogs; guns were fired and a fortress was attacked by artillery. The audience could watch amphibious maneuvers, explosions, sea battles, and, of course, a victorious finale in a purely patriotic spirit. Toward the end of the century, Krestovskii Park also offered concert evenings with light music.[18]

Comparable in popularity to Krestovskii Park was the Zoological Garden (Zoologicheskii sad), a park next to the zoo, which was opened in the 1870s by the merchant E. Rost. The clientele of this park consisted predominantly of petty-bourgeois and lower-class inhabitants of the neighboring Petersburg Side and Vasil'evskii Island. Next to the entrance was a summer concert hall for symphony orchestras, attesting to the pedagogical intentions of the park's founder. The theater of the Zoological Garden showed one-act vaudevilles, numbers by circus and estrada artists, and performances of satirical couplets and factory ditties. There were also grandiose spectacles and enchanting fairy tales that included the whole troupe and a corps de ballet. Fairground attractions were located in an open square outside the theater. Gymnasts performed their tricks while

on Aleksandrinskaia Square, and the café chantant Folies-Bergère (Foli Berzher). *Novoe vremia*, March 8, 1880; July 28, 1888. On Shukhardin's tavern and garden, see N. Leskov, "Kartiny proshlogo," *Novoe vremia*, January 12, 1883, and *Peterburgskii listok*, March 7, 1874. Gardens along the Fontanka were located at embankment numbers 9, 13, 81, 80–86, and 114. TsGIA SPb, f. 513, op. 159, d. 74, 133; op. 137, d. 1322; op. 139, d. 182. In 1901, the theater Bouffe opened in the park at Izmailovskii Bridge. *Teatr i iskusstvo*, no. 17 (1901): 333.

[17] "Okrestnosti Peterburga: V voskresen'e vecherom v Novoi derevne," *Vsemirnaia illiustratsiia*, no. 3 (1878): 50–51; TsGIA SPb, f. 514, op. 1, d. 2097, l. 137; f. 513, op. 64, d. 538.

[18] K. A. Maksimov, "Krestovskii ostrov," *Nasha starina*, no. 7 (1915): 674–75; P. N. Stolpianskii, *Staryi Peterburg* (Petrograd, 1916), 50–51; *Russkie narodnye gulian'ia*, 130–31; *Delovoi i veseliashchiisia S.-Peterburg* (St. Petersburg, 1894), 266.

flying in an aerostat; acrobats balanced on balls on a high spiral track. A balagan with waxworks made by V. Schulz in 1862 was on permanent display.[19]

Almost all of St. Petersburg's amusement parks were organized and sponsored by merchants and entrepreneurs. These people obviously knew what was popular; they knew that money could be made from people's leisure activities; and they may well have simply enjoyed the prestige and social status connected with a visible role in local entertainment culture. In 1875, three of them, G. A. Aleksandrov, A. F. Kartavov, and D. P. Poliakov, leased a stretch of land from Princess Volkonskaia in Novaia Derevnia on the embankment of the Bol'shaia Nevka and opened the Livadiia, which distinguished itself from the other parks by featuring exclusively Russian artists. Beside the customary *divertismentnaia estrada*, the Livadiia also offered arias from operettas and "fantastic illuminations." Under the sole direction of Kartavov in the early 1880s, the park turned to programs with predominantly Russian operettas, thus following the same popular trend as Nemetti's Russian Family Park. In later years, the Livadiia was renamed the Kin'grust' by its new manager, M. V. Lentovskii. Its repertoire also changed; it concentrated more on so-called adventure revues (*prikliuchencheskie obozreniia*), which combined operetta with fairy tales and classical ballet.[20]

In 1880, two of the founders of the Livadiia, Aleksandrov and Poliakov, decided to build the most spectacular and grandiose amusement park of the Petersburg Side. Other establishments in this district, like the Monplaisir (Monplezir), the Pompeii (Pompei), and the Aquarium (Akvarium), which also opened in the 1880s, would pale in comparison to the new enterprise, which was to be called the Arcadia (Arkadiia). Aleksandrov and Poliakov chose the empty space of the former Mineral Waters in Novaia Derevnia for their new park. The reputation of Izler's establishment, the venerable and shady park, and the nearby terminus of a horse-drawn tram were a recipe for easy success. Count Stroganov rented out a huge part of his land for the park, which was planned and constructed under the supervision of the architect A. V. Malov. It included a theater, a multipurpose building with a winter garden, an open

[19] N. V. Drizen, "Sorok let teatra," *Stolitsa i usad'ba*, nos. 40–41 (1915): 24; *Kuplety, ispolniaemye v S-Peterburgskom "Zoologicheskom sadu"* N. N. Bogdanovym (St. Petersburg, 1879); "Novaia feeriia v S-Peterburgskom 'Zoologicheskom sadu'," *Niva*, no. 29 (1887): 730; *Russkie narodnye gulian'ia*, 134–38; TsGIA SPb, f. 514, op. 1, d. 589; f. 569, op. 14, d. 2; f. 921, op. 45, d. 6.
[20] Pleshcheev, "Kak veselilis' v stolitse," 21; Drizen, "Sorok let teatra," 24. See also the material about the Livadiia in the archive of P. A. Kartavov, OR RNB, f. 341; and TsGIA SPb, f. 513, op. 159, d. 101.

podium and an estrada stage, a roller coaster, and other structures. In May 1881, the Arcadia opened with a gala performance.[21]

The repertoire of the Arcadia was geared to a very diverse audience. For the more urbane, Russian opera was performed by some of the best singers in the country. The theater featured single acts of operas and medleys of arias, drama, operetta, comedy, vaudeville, and ballet, as well as guest performances by artists from France, Italy, and Belgium. Military bands and ballroom orchestras played continuously in band shells in the park, while on the estrada stage the Russian choir of V. M. Umants, the Moscow Gypsies of N. I. Shishkin, or the Ozroni clowns appeared. It goes without saying that there were grandiose fireworks in the evenings, accompanied by all sorts of decorative lighting. Other outdoor attractions were balloon flights, the wild beasts of the animal tamer Gugo, and, from 1884, a "Colony of Indians" from North America. A special place was designated for the shows of the tightrope walker Fedor Molodtsev. In another section of the park, huge inflated likenesses of ballerinas, Arabs, or devils were launched. Military pantomimes such as "The Taking of Plevna" (Vziatie Plevny) or "Our Heroic Victors" (Nashi geroi-pobediteli) could be enjoyed around a pond. In one of them, the "Battle of Sinope" (Sinopskoe srazhenie, 1886), five Russian ships fought against eight enemy crafts. The adversary's fleet was, of course, thoroughly blown up and burnt. With a program as variegated as this, the Arcadia quickly became the most popular and most "democratic" amusement park in the city.[22]

The last ten years of the nineteenth century saw a development that seriously threatened the popularity and profitability of the public amusement parks. All sorts of associations, especially the Guardianship for Popular Temperance, more and more often organized their own fairs and opened People's Theaters in such places as Smolensk Field on Vasil'evskii Island, Tauride Park, Poliustrovo, Ekateringof, and Petergof. In addition, the character of the amusement parks changed to some extent. Restaurants and buffets became more important than diversified entertainment, and shows relied more on the lurid style of the café chantant. In

[21] The Monplaisir was located at Kamennoostrovskii pr. 57–59, the Pompeii on the embankment of the Bol'shaia Nevka 87. TsGIA SPb, f. 513, op. 160, d. 134, 23. The Aquarium was at Kamennoostrovskii pr. 10; for more on this park, see Drizen, "Sorok let teatra," 24; Pleshcheev, "Kak veselilis' v stolitse," 22; Kozlinskii, "Vospominaniia," OR RNB, f. 1226, l. 101–2; and TsGIA SPb, f. 513, op. 137, d. 992. The Arcadia was on the embankment of the Bol'shaia Nevka 93, and later on the Novoderevenskaia embankment 13. TsGIA SPb, f. 513, op. 159, d. 89.

[22] "Arkadiia": Desiatiletie so dnia ee osnovaniia (St. Petersburg, 1891); Drizen, "Sorok let teatra," 24; Pleshcheev, "Kak veselilis' v stolitse," 21–22; Russkie narodnye gulian'ia, 131–32; TsGIA SPb, f. 569, op. 11, d. 182.

Pleshcheev's opinion, the amusement parks of earlier years, especially the 1880s, were much more grandiose, fun, and relaxed than those around the turn of the century.[23]

Public amusement parks played a leading role in the leisure activities of the majority of the citizens of St. Petersburg especially in the last quarter of the nineteenth century. Through the peculiar mixture of their repertoire, they were instrumental in spreading elite art and folk culture (albeit in a rather watered-down and folkloristic aspect) among a large and diverse audience. People from various walks of urban life came to the parks and enjoyed the same entertainment together. In addition to this democratizing effect, the parks also gave rise to new genres, such as the urban romance, and promoted others, such as the *kafeshantannaia estrada*. Moreover, they advanced the refinement of garden architecture and of elaborate stagings of attractions.

Without its amusement parks, the capital of the Russian Empire would have been a much less interesting place for its inhabitants to live and work. Like the cinema in later years, the parks offered a form of entertainment that was specifically urban and open to everyone. Going to the amusement parks meant going to a world of fantasies and social discourse, to a place where the metaphor of the big city as a melting pot became reality in a rather civilized way.

Translated by Hubertus F. Jahn

---

[23] E. Karpov, *Desiatiletie narodnykh gulianii za Nevskoi zastavoi, 1885–1895* (St. Petersburg, 1895); "Iz istorii teatrov peterburgskogo popechitel'stva o narodnoi trezvosti," *Teatr i iskusstvo*, no. 52 (1907); *Russkie narodnye gulian'ia*, 140–46; TsGIA SPb, f. 492, op. 1, d. 6304; f. 792, op. 1, d. 4328, 6373, 8116; f. 513, op. 81, d. 497; op. 132, d. 249; op. 134, d. 109; Pleshcheev, "Kak veselilis' v stolitse," 22.

7

FOR TSAR AND FATHERLAND?

RUSSIAN POPULAR CULTURE AND

THE FIRST WORLD WAR

Hubertus F. Jahn

ORLD WAR I broke out in Europe at a time of major transformations in cultural life. As a result of industrialization and the ensuing social changes, an urban mass culture developed that centered on such new media as the cinema or the music hall but that also included older forms of entertainment, like the circus or the fairground. At the same time, the traditional high culture of opera, concert hall, and the fine arts continued to flourish. The war was reflected in the cultural life of Europe in many ways, and for some countries more or less detailed studies have already been published on this issue.[1]

Russia, which industrialized relatively late, developed a somewhat different cultural scene, made up of a Western-oriented elite culture and a rapidly growing mass culture based on new Western forms of entertainment and on Russian traditions that had been part of the urban fairground or that were imported by the masses of workers migrating from rural areas into the big cities. Thus, around 1914 a variety of entertainments coexisted—from the imperial opera houses, art academies, and concert halls to political cabaret and futurist counterculture; from the traditional fun fair (*narodnoe gulian'e*) and the circus to People's Theaters, cinemas, and the wide field of *estrada*, which comprised everything from Gypsy music and nightclubs to cafés chantants, dance shows, and "theaters of the miniature."

World War I had a considerable impact on all genres of Russian culture. Audiences changed because masses of soldiers and officers departed for the front. Actors and musicians were drafted and the contents of the shows often changed, adopting the war theme and all sorts of patriotic

---

[1] See, for example, Arthur Marwick, *The Deluge: British Society and the First World War* (New York: Norton, 1965); Ann Purser, *Looking Back at Popular Entertainment, 1901–1939* (Wakefield, Eng.: EP Publishing, 1978); and Robert Eben Sackett, *Popular Entertainment, Class, and Politics in Munich, 1900–1923* (Cambridge, Mass.: Harvard University Press, 1982). More theoretical and with a wider temporal scope is John M. MacKenzie, ed., *Imperialism and Popular Culture* (Manchester: Manchester University Press, 1986).

motifs. Publishing houses put out countless editions of visual patriotic material in the form of postcards, posters, and the traditional *lubki*, or broadsheets. Artists painted battle scenes and contributed a large number of war caricatures to journals and newspapers. Right from the beginning of the war, many forms of charity developed and left their imprint on the cultural life of the time. While all these activities were undertaken by society, official nationalist propaganda was rather weak and had little impact on wartime culture. Studying this patriotic culture, as one might call it—looking not at official propaganda and philosophical concepts such as Pan-Slavism, but at the entertainment that people enjoyed (and paid for)—may provide a clue as to how the Russian population related to the war and to how strongly nationalism, commonly seen as the driving force of World War I, was developed in Russian society.

No study of the culture of a society as variegated as was Russia's early in this century can claim to present an all-encompassing picture. Statistics about audiences, for example, are barely available and not always trustworthy; artists' personal impressions and memoirs are not necessarily representative and have to be read with caution. Mass culture, by definition, eludes a quantitative, in-depth investigation. Yet there are trends, fashions—or, put rather pompously, the sociocultural climate—that can be pinned down by samples taken from various genres. Assuming that there exists a close connection and a mutual conditioning between artists and audiences—reflecting what Ruth Benedict has called a situation of give-and-take between an individual and society—one should thus be able to detect recurring images, clichés, themes, and motifs that occupied the minds of people, that were the "keywords" of a specific communication group.[2]

Popular and elite cultures are usually seen as two separate entities, as parts of two different communication groups. They customarily refer to categories of artistic quality, intellectual competence, and social status. A division of culture into "high" and "low" may even reveal a specific historical and social situation; but with the rise of mass media and the increased mobility within European societies, it becomes more a useful tool for classifications by cultural historians than a reflection of sociocultural realities. Consequently, it has been called into question and redefined many times in order to fit changing social settings.[3]

---

[2] Frank Kämpfer, *"Der rote Keil": Das politische Plakat: Theorie und Geschichte* (Berlin: Mann Verlag, 1985), 111; Jeffrey Brooks, *When Russia Learned to Read: Literacy and Popular Literature, 1861–1917* (Princeton: Princeton University Press, 1985), xviii–xxi, 353–54, and passim (on the use of the "thematic" approach); Ruth Benedict, *Patterns of Culture* (Cambridge, Mass.: Riverside Press, 1961), 253.

[3] For examples, see Ray B. Browne, "Popular Culture: Notes toward a Definition," in *Popular Culture and the Expanding Consciousness*, ed. Ray B. Browne (New York: Wiley, 1973), 22; or Herbert J. Gans, *Popular Culture and High Culture: An Analysis and Evalua-*

In Russia, a similar dilution of categories took place toward the end of the nineteenth century. Classical forms of elite entertainment such as books and theater were actively adopted by or taken to the people; upper-class consumers of elite culture also enjoyed popular amusements such as folk bands and the circus. The cinema, finally, attracted everyone, regardless of social background. Mass and elite cultures thus converged and overlapped; they inspired rather than excluded each other. This phenomenon was particularly evident during World War I, as an investigation of patriotic motifs shows. There were exceptions: the motif of the famous hero Kuz'ma Kriuchkov, a cossack who was said to have killed eleven Germans at once with his lance, was simply too unsophisticated and implausible to find its way into high culture. On the other hand, heraldic animals, symbolizing competing principles of the European nations, were too abstract for a wider distribution. They led an exclusive life in the apocalyptic lithographs of Natalia Goncharova, in the pictures that the famous book illustrator Georgii Narbut contributed to the literary-satirical journal *Lukomor'e* (Bay of the Sea), and in an unpublished poem that Osip Mandelstam presented on New Year's Eve of 1916–17 in the Petrograd cabaret Prival komediantov (The Comedians' Halt).[4]

Many patriotic motifs, however, could be found on all levels of Russian culture during World War I. Clearly, Russian society consisted of a single communication group, at least at the beginning of the war and with respect to it. Kaiser Wilhelm, German atrocities, the fate of Belgium, "oriental" topics and the Turkish sultan, as well as national symbols like the flag or the national anthem, were able to build a thematic bridge between high and popular culture in the face of a common enemy. They were present at evenings of the literary elite, on cheap postcards, and in films, theater performances, and circus shows.[5]

No patriotic motif was distributed more widely than the vilified or mocked figure of the German kaiser. This was not a peculiarly Russian phenomenon. In all Allied nations, Wilhelm II was seen as the personification of the enemy, of German militarism and aggression. To identify

tion of Taste (New York: Basic Books, 1974), 10, 67–71; An interesting and amusing approach to the problem in the American context is Paul Fussell, *Class: A Guide through the American Status System* (New York: Summit Books, 1983).

[4] J. F. Kowtun [Evgenii Fedorovich Kovtun], *Die Wiedergeburt der künstlerischen Druckgraphik: Aus der Geschichte der russischen Kunst zu Beginn des zwanzigsten Jahrhunderts* (Dresden: VEB Verlag der Kunst, 1984), 59; Platon Beletskii, *Georgii Ivanovich Narbut* (Leningrad: Iskusstvo, 1985), 114–15; *Lukomor'e*, no. 28 (1914), cover; Al'bin Mikhailovich Konechnyi et al., "Artisticheskoe kabare 'Prival komediantov'," in *Pamiatniki kul'tury: Novye otkrytiia: Pis'mennost, iskusstvo, arkheologiia: Ezhegodnik 1988* (Moscow: Nauka, 1989), 133.

[5] A convergence of high and popular culture during the war has also been noted for England by MacKenzie in his introduction to *Imperialism and Popular Culture*, 4.

the enemy in such a personal way was, of course, easier than to project one's hatred onto something as complex as a whole nation. In addition, Wilhelm himself and his behavior made it easy to ridicule him and the "Prussian" spirit that he embodied. His appearance invited attacks on him, his whiskers and spiked helmet being the most prominent and most frequently exaggerated attributes. His comic figure was so fascinating that even serious Russian film journals published detailed analyses of the kaiser's facial wrinkles as seen in German newsreels.[6]

Not surprisingly, Wilhelm was the main target of caricatures in the press; about one-third were devoted exclusively to him. A similar percentage can be found among patriotic postcards, with many more cards showing the kaiser in connection with the Austrian and Turkish rulers. He also appeared prominently in satirical lubki and was often the "hero" in the *raek*, or peep show—a traditional fairground amusement that consisted of a lubok picture mounted in a box with magnifying glasses and commented on by a *raeshnik*, or barker.[7]

Visual arts catering to a broad social spectrum, consequently, adopted the kaiser as their main patriotic theme. Famous artists, including members of the World of Art group as well as later Soviet celebrities like Vladimir Lebedev and Aleksei Radakov, contributed kaiser cartoons to intelligentsia journals like *Novyi Satirikon* (New Satirikon). Ivan Bilibin, for example, portrayed Wilhelm on a playing card as the king of spades with a crown, neck decoration, and sword on the upper side and, on the reverse, with a fool's cap, a necklace of sausages, a decoration in the form of a stein, and a fork instead of the sword. Lebedev showed Wilhelm trapped in a cage that he supposedly had built for protection against air raids but that turned out to be his prison. Radakov gave an example of

---

[6] On Wilhelm as the personification of the enemy in the Allied countries, see Harold Dwight Lasswell, *Propaganda Technique in the World War* (London: Kegan Paul, 1938), 89–90. Changes in Wilhelm's face are discussed in "Kino-kaizer," *Sine-Fono*, no. 6–7 (1915): 60; and in a short note in *Vestnik kinematografii*, no. 105 (January 1915): 27.

[7] The calculation of the frequency of the kaiser motif in the press is based on a sample of 194 caricatures from the journals *Lukomor'e*, *Novyi Satirikon*, and *Voina*, as well as on albums with caricatures from the press such as F. I. Shol'te, comp., *Grimasy voiny, 1914–1915 g.: Plakaty, karikatury, lubki*, 2d ed. (Petrograd: Biokhrom, 1916); *Karikatury "Voina i Pem"—Caricatures "La Guerre et Pême,"* 2d ed. (Petrograd: B. A. Suvorin, 1915); and V. B. Lekhno, *Voina: V sharzhakh i karikaturakh periodicheskikh izdanii* (Moscow: Reklama, n.d.). The calculation for postcards is based on 360 patriotic cards in the Slavonic Library of the University of Helsinki (where large numbers of war lubki and two raek pictures of Wilhelm can also be found). For more about raek, see Al'bin Mikhailovich Konechnyi, "Raek v sisteme peterburgskoi narodnoi kul'tury," *Russkii fol'klor* 25 (1989): 123–38; and A. F. Nekrylova, *Russkie narodnye gorodskie prazdniki, uveseleniia i zrelishcha: Konets XVIII–nachalo XX veka*, 2d ed. (Leningrad: Iskusstvo, 1988), 95–125.

what would happen if the Germans took Paris: Notre Dame cathedral would get towers in the form of spiked helmets and the rose window would be changed into a portrait of the kaiser.[8]

Traditional media of popular patriotism like lubki or the raek, which had attacked Napoleon in the nineteenth century, now made fun of Wilhelm II. Experiencing a last renaissance during World War I, these multicolored prints, made not by the people but by professional and usually anonymous artists, were mass-produced in big publishing houses like Sytin i Ko in Moscow. To judge by their output and by the comments of contemporary observers, lubki were very popular among the rural and urban lower strata, to whom they brought not only the kaiser, but also fascinating war technology, heroic battle scenes, and allegorical pictures of Russian might.[9]

The lubok and the raek as parts of Russian patriotic folklore were consciously revived by some elite artists in 1914. Under the name Segodniashnii lubok (Contemporary Lubok), people like Kazimir Malevich, Aristarkh Lentulov, Il'ia Mashkov, and Vladimir Mayakovsky published colorful and rather crude pictures with biting captions by Mayakovsky. In one of them, Mashkov showed the kaiser sitting on a collapsing iron horse, a symbol of German industry, that has whiskers and wears a spiked helmet like Wilhelm's. Along comes a brave cossack with his lance and runs it through the kaiser's head. Not quite so brutal were pictures for the raek. The later-famous poster artist and caricaturist Dmitrii Moor, for example, drew a raek picture that showed the metamorphosis of an onion into Wilhelm II in the garden of the devil. The theme of Satan is also taken up in the picture *Raek: Vil'gel'm satana i nemetskaia voina* (Raek: The Devil Wilhelm and the German War) by A. Lebedev. The artist, a caricaturist who regularly worked for the Petrograd weekly *Voina* (War) and produced patriotic postcards for the publishing house

[8] "Bitaia karta," *Novyi Satirikon*, no. 41 (1914); Lebedev's cartoon is in *Novyi Satirikon*, no. 43 (1914): 6; and Radakov's is in *Novyi Satirikon*, no. 36 (1914). On Radakov's and Lebedev's later careers, see Stephen White, *The Bolshevik Poster* (New Haven, Conn.: Yale University Press, 1988), 104–5, 116; and Nicoletta Misler, "A Public Art: Caricatures and Posters of Vladimir Lebedev," *Journal of Decorative and Propaganda Arts* 5 (Summer 1987): 60–75.

[9] V. Denisov, *Voina i lubok* (Petrograd: Izd. Novago zhurnala dlia vsekh, 1916), 18–20, 26, and passim; A. F. Nekrylova, "Komicheskii batal'nyi lubok v sostave raeshnogo obozreniia," *Russkii fol'klor* 25 (1989): 53–56; G. Miasoedov, "Russkii lubok kontsa XIX–nachala XX veka," in *Illiustratsiia*, comp. G. V. El'shevskaia (Moscow: Sovetskii khudozhnik, 1988), 243–44; A. Kalmykova, "Russkie lubochnye kartiny v ikh prosvetitel'nom znachenii dlia naroda za poslednee 75-letie nashei zhizni," in *Polveka dlia knigi: Literaturno-khudozhestvennyi sbornik, posviashchennyi piatidesiatiletiiu izdatel'skoi deiatel'nosti I. D. Sytina* (Moscow: Sytin, 1916), 190–92.

Sovremennoe iskusstvo (Contemporary Art), portrayed Wilhelm as a satanic madman pinned up on the raek box and ridiculed by the barker.[10]

The kaiser motif could also be found on large numbers of Russian postcards. A relatively new (and so far little-studied) medium of mass communication, postcards with patriotic contents were produced in large series with millions of copies during World War I. Their artistic and aesthetic quality covered a wide range, from highly imaginative and ironic color prints to utterly primitive black-and-white sketches on cheap paper. Patriotic postcards—the "buttons" of World War I, as they have been called for their individualistic and declaratory qualities—offered the kaiser for all the tastes of an increasingly literate public. But, as a contemporary observer noted, they could also be found among illiterate people, who used them like lubki to adorn the walls of their rooms.[11]

Wilhelm blowing soap bubbles that symbolized the German air force appeared on a postcard by an artist signing himself Nevskii. Its toned-down colors and decorative style suggest that upper-class aesthetes would have used this card. Not quite as moderate was a card depicting Wilhelm as a ragged marauder with red eyes, a boozer's nose, and a rucksack full of stolen treasures. On the crudest postcards, he sat in a cage at the Moscow zoo or was given the finger from Paris and Warsaw—a sign certainly more widely used by people of the street than by people of the salons.[12] While lubki and press caricatures still catered to people from different cultural levels, postcards obviously reached an even broader social spectrum and thus democratized patriotic imagery on a wider scale. All these genres of visual art, however, spread the image of the wicked

---

[10] A comprehensive study of Segodniashnii lubok has not yet been done; many of the pictures have not even been attributed. See Kowtun, *Die Wiedergeburt*, 74–79; Miasoedov, "Russkii lubok," 248–50; E. F. Kovtun, *Russkaia futuristicheskaia kniga* (Moscow: Kniga, 1989), 150, 155, 167–68; and V. Botsianovskii, "Novyi lubok," *Teatr i iskusstvo*, no. 18 (1914): 810–12. Mashkov's picture has no title; it is signed with the pseudonym I. Gorskin and, like all Segodniashnii lubok works, was printed by S. M. Mukharskii in Moscow, 1914. The size is 71 x 53 cm, and the caption reads: "U Vil'gel'ma Gogentsolerno / Razmaliuem rozhu kolerno. / Nasha pika—ta-zhe kist', / Esli smazhem—nuka schist'!" ("As for Wilhelm Hohenzollern / We'll paint up his mug quite colorfully. / Our lance is that good old brush, / If we mess it up, we can clean it!") Moor's raek is reproduced in Shol'te, *Grimasy voiny*, 49. Lebedev's picture was printed by A. A. Strel'tsov (Moscow, n.d., 44 x 60 cm) and is kept in the Slavonic Library of the University of Helsinki.

[11] Nikolai Spiridonovich Tagrin, *Mir v otkrytke* (Moscow: Izobrazitel'noe iskusstvo, 1978), 50–51; R. Lebeck and M. Schütte, eds., *Propagandapostkarten* (Dortmund: Harenberg, 1980), 21; Denisov, *Voina i lubok*, 33.

[12] Nevskii, *Vozdushnyi flot Germanii* (Iskusstvo, Kiev, no. 221, 1914, 14 x 9 cm); P. N. Troianskii, *Vas'ka Berlinskii* (Bussel, Petrograd, n.d., 9 x 14 cm); Gar[ ], *Zoologicheskii sad* (Gramakov, Moscow, n.d., 14 x 8.5 cm); G. K., *Vot tebe babushka i "Iur'ev den'"!* (Sheibel', Moscow, n.d., 9 x 14 cm).

kaiser, his whiskers, and his spiked helmet, and thus achieved a personification of the enemy in high and popular culture alike.

In the performing arts, there was a similar thematic unity between genres of high and popular culture. One could follow the pernicious kaiser
from the stages of reputable metropolitan theaters to the makeshift plat-
forms of theaters improvised by soldiers at the front. Pieces like Mamont
Dal'sky's *Pozor Germanii* (The Shame of Germany) achieved great success in Aleksei Suvorin's Malyi teatr (Little Theater) in Petrograd, where
it was produced in September 1914. It featured N. N. Rybnikov as Wilhelm, with oversized whiskers and a stern face. Wilhelm was also the
target of numerous estrada artists and circus clowns; Anatolii Leonido-
vich Durov, one of the most famous Russian clowns ever, even produced
a film with a monkey playing the kaiser. Respected academicians like
Vladimir Mikhailovich Bekhterev gave lectures about "Wilhelm II—from
the Psychiatric Point of View" in the Petrograd City Duma, while nightclubs treated their visitors to "Wilhelm's Bloody Tango." Madness and
bloodthirstiness were the kaiser's major traits in a number of films that
featured him as "Antichrist" or in similar villainous roles. The list was
long.[13]

Other patriotic motifs were also widespread, which showed that the
war evoked a similar set of images on all levels of Russian culture. Belgium as a country suffering from German aggression and deserving of
Russian help and compassion was one of these motifs. As in the other
Allied countries, Belgium became a symbol of heroism and was treated
with sentimental sympathy and melodramatic verve in Russian patriotic
culture. As with the kaiser, Belgium appeared in all sorts of visual material. Lubki showed German soldiers drowning after the Belgians opened
the dikes; Georgii Narbut illustrated a book about Brussels lace makers;

---

[13] A photograph of a soldier with whiskers and a feather in his hair who played Wilhelm
as the devil is in Gosudarstvennyi muzei politicheskoi istorii Rossii (hereafter GMPIR; formerly GMVOSR), f. 9, no. OF 228. On Dal'sky's piece, see Grigorii Markovich Iaron, *O
liubimom zhanre* (Moscow: Iskusstvo, 1960), 73; and the review and photos of the production in *Teatr i iskusstvo*, no. 18 (1914): 788–89. The kaiser as the target of clowns and
estrada artists is discussed in Evgenii Mikhailovich Kuznetsov, *Iz proshlogo russkoi estrady:
Istoricheskie ocherki* (Moscow: Iskusstvo, 1958), 324–28, 336; see also the manuscripts of
Ernani [V. F. Bil'iani], Kol'petti, and Eduard Korrado in the Muzei tsirkovogo iskusstva, St.
Petersburg (hereafter MTsI). Durov's film, released by A. O. Drankov in Moscow, is described in *Sine-Fono*, no. 4–5 (1914): 58–59. For Bekhterev's and similar "kaiser lectures,"
see Tsentral'nyi gosudarstvennyi istoricheskii arkhiv Sankt-Peterburga (hereafter TsGIA
SPb; formerly LGIA), f. 569, op. 13, d. 1132, ll. 15–16ob. The "Bloody Tango" is mentioned in L. S. Volkov-Lannit, *Iskusstvo zapechatlennogo zvuka* (Moscow: Iskusstvo,
1964), 79. See the pages of journals such as *Sine-Fono*, *Vestnik kinematografii*, and *Proektor* for detailed descriptions of films featuring Wilhelm.

and the newly created patriotic journal *Voina* devoted one of its issues exclusively to Belgium, with pictures of King Albert and Belgian towns.[14] Belgium was also prominent on stage, on the screen, and in the circus ring.

By the turn of the century, the Russian circus had become a quite variegated art form. New genres like tango dancing, acting, and wrestling increasingly overshadowed the traditions of horse training and clown numbers and offered a broad spectrum of sensations to audiences from diverse social backgrounds. During World War I, so-called patriotic circus pantomimes reemerged as big attractions. An outgrowth of the post-Napoleonic French circus, they were reenactments of famous battles with a host of people and animals participating. In Russia they had been staged for a while in the late nineteenth century, but had soon been replaced by more easygoing show pieces.[15]

Technical wonders, the whole spectrum of patriotic imagery, and horseback acrobatics were the main ingredients of pantomimes during World War I. Belgium regularly appeared in the usually grandiose finales of these shows, where the unity of the Allied powers was conjured up by a host of flags and national anthems. Akim Nikitin, the founder of the first purely Russian circus—who had already proudly presented a Belgian artist in his show at the beginning of the war and who spent a good part of his income on war-related charity—even produced a pantomime devoted solely to Belgium. "The Great War of 1914, on Land, at Sea, and in the Air: The Deluge of Belgium" had three hundred performers and achieved great success in Moscow in January 1915. The audience in the sold-out circus could watch as Germans attacked, fighter planes and zeppelins battled in the cupola, locks were blown-up, and finally the water streamed in and caught the Germans by surprise. The show's finale was an exaltation of the Allied powers.[16]

The circus was also the setting for a number of charitable events. In the two Moscow circuses of Nikitin and A. Salamonsky, concerts were held in November 1915 by the association Artisty Moskvy—Russkoi armii i zhertvam voiny (Moscow Artists in Support of the Russian Army and War Victims). Among the participants were famous singers from the Bol-

[14] *Zatoplenie bel'giitsami nemtsev* (Konovalova, Moscow, n.d., 85 x 63 cm); Beletskii, *Narbut*, 119–21; *Voina*, no. 20 (1915).

[15] Jewgenii Kusnezow [Evgenii Mikhailovich Kuznetsov], *Der Zirkus der Welt* (Berlin: Henschelverlag, 1970), 53–59, 153, 191; Iurii Arsen'evich Dmitriev, *Tsirk v Rossii: Ot istokov do 1917 g.* (Moscow: Iskusstvo, 1977), 263. See also Boris Fedorovich Geier, "Tsirk," *Organ*, no. 126 (January 1915).

[16] Dmitriev, *Tsirk v Rossii*, 267, 281; Rudol'f Evgen'evich Slavskii, *Brat'ia Nikitiny* (Moscow: Iskusstvo, 1987), 267; *Organ*, no. 126 (January 1915).

shoi Theater and actors from the Moscow Art Theater. In Petrograd's Circus Ciniselli, the "Patriotic Concerts" organized by the Soloist of His Imperial Highness, the soprano Mariia Ivanovna Dolina, were regular attractions throughout the war. The substantial proceeds of these concerts (eight thousand rubles in the first two and almost sixty thousand rubles in the first sixteen concerts) went to all sorts of charitable organizations. Belgium was the sole beneficiary of at least one of the Patriotic Concerts and perhaps of other events.[17]

Dolina's concerts were attended by a rather mixed audience. Tickets for them were distributed in such different places as factories and the Petrograd Medical Institute for Women. Despite their pronounced conservative touch, with heavy use of national symbols and the frequent participation of army bands, the concerts had some support among Petrograd's artistic intelligentsia. People like Vsevolod Meierkhol'd, Nikolai Evreinov, and Leonid Andreev met with Dolina in late 1914 to discuss patriotic repertoire, and some famous artists appeared in her shows. In her "Belgian Patriotic Matinée" (Bel'giiskoe Patrioticheskoe Utro) on October 19, 1914, for example, the well-known theater critic, actor, and director Anatolii Kremlev declaimed his own "To the Heroes of Belgium" and A. Matveev's "Belgium" as part of a program that featured Belgian violinists, a cantata about Belgium, several other declamations by less well known artists, and the premiere of the famous "Poem about Belgium" (Poeza o Bel'gii) by Igor Severianin, read by the author himself.[18]

Severianin was a salon poet and founder of the Ego-Futurist group, a circle of authors espousing decadence and a snobbish urban life-style. During the war, he was known for his "Poetry Evenings" on the estrada stage. His "Poem about Belgium" was repeated at such occasions, and was even set to music by the eccentric pianist of the Petrograd cabaret Brodiachaia sobaka (Stray Dog), Nikolai Karlovich Tsybul'sky, whose epithet was Graf Okontrer (Count Au Contraire). In that form it was performed at the Stray Dog at least three times in November 1914, once at an evening devoted exclusively to Belgian music and poetry. (Mayakovsky, who also appeared at the Stray Dog from time to time, viciously

[17] See the programs of the two Moscow performances on the inside cover of *Stsena i arena*, no. 20–21 (1915). On Dolina's concerts, see Kuznetsov, *Iz proshlogo*, 342–43. The figures on proceeds are from *Teatr i iskusstvo*, no. 18 (1914): 726; and from the program of Dolina's concert in support of Belgium, which is located in the Fond plakatov of the Gosudarstvennyi muzei istorii goroda (hereafter GMIG; formerly GMIL).

[18] On the distribution of tickets to Dolina's concerts, see TsGIA SPb, f. 1458, op. 2, d. 1043; f. 1365, op. 1, d. 62, ll. 331–44ob.; f. 436, op. 1, d. 14967, l. 35. Voina i iskusstvo (The War and the Arts), the meeting about patriotic repertoire and related issues, took place on October 31, 1914, in Petrograd. TsGIA SPb, f. 569, op. 13, d. 1144, ll. 134–40ob.

attacked Severianin's piece for its culinary metaphors. He found it wide of the mark to praise Ostend for its oysters while the city had suffered so much in the war.)[19]

Belgium was a common theme not only in refined metropolitan cabarets, but also in the increasingly popular theaters of the miniature across the country. Estrada artists, who performed in these places as *kupletisty* (performers of couplets) or *zlobisty* (people commenting on the talk of the day, or *zloba dnia*), usually had at least one piece about Belgium in their repertoire. V. F. Bil'iani, for example, who appeared under the name Ernani in the Circus Truzzi, in restaurants, and in theaters of the miniature in and around Moscow, declaimed his "Song of a Belgian Soldier" in the fall of 1914, a story about the Belgian spirit of resistance. Sergei Sokol'sky, lauded by contemporaries as the "most talented and most popular Russian humorist"—who had great success with his war couplets at the Nizhnii Novgorod fair in late 1914 and later on in the Moscow vaudeville theater Ermitazh (Hermitage) and in Petrograd's Teatr Lin—praised Belgium's beauty and culture, as well as its heroic king. At the end of his "Fair Belgium" (O Bel'gii prekrasnoi), the artist invoked history to judge this beautiful and heroic country.[20]

Belgian heroism, the flooding of the country, and the amicable cooperation between the brave King Albert and the great national poet Maurice Maeterlinck were the subjects of the most serious patriotic piece on Belgium in Russian wartime dramatic art. Written by one of the most famous playwrights of the time, Leonid Andreev, and titled *Korol', zakon i svoboda* (King, Law, and Freedom) after a line from the Belgian national anthem, the play had its first performance in October 1914 in the Moskovskii dramaticheskii teatr (Moscow Drama Theater) and its Petrograd premiere in December at the Aleksandrinskii teatr. The public dress rehearsal was a great success, as was the premiere. The critics, however,

---

[19] For more about Severianin, see Anna Lawton, ed., *Russian Futurism through Its Manifestoes, 1912–1928* (Ithaca, N.Y.: Cornell University Press, 1988), 20–25; and Johannes Holthusen, *Russische Literatur im 20. Jahrhundert* (Munich: Francke, 1978), 93–94. On his evenings at the Stray Dog and Mayakovsky's reaction, see A. E. Parnis and R. D. Timenchik, "Programmy 'Brodiachei sobaki'," in *Pamiatniki kul'tury: Novye otkrytiia: Pis'mennost, iskusstvo, arkheologiia: Ezhegodnik 1983* (Leningrad: Nauka, 1985), 236–38; and Vladimir Maiakovskii, "Poezovecher Igoria Severianina," in *Polnoe sobranie sochinenii v trinadtsati tomakh* (Moscow: Khudozhestvennaia literatura, 1955–61), 1:338–39.

[20] Kuznetsov, *Iz proshlogo*, 336–37; Ernani, "Pesn' bel'giiskogo voina, 1914," and "Otzyvy o spektakliakh V. Ernani, 1906 ff.," a collection of newspaper clippings (both in MTsI); Sergei Sokol'skii, *Pliashushchaia lirika: Stikhotvoreniia i pesni* (Petrograd: Zhdarskii, 1916), 10–12 ("O Bel'gii prekrasnoi"). On Sokol'sky's performances and successes, see *Teatr i iskusstvo*, no. 19 (1915): 542; *Stsena i arena*, no. 5 (1914): 16; *Var'ete i tsirk*, no. 6 (1916): 7; and *Sine-Fono*, no. 6–7 (1915): 53.

received the piece with polite distance. Nikolai Efros, for example, found it too trivial and full of pathos and felt that it played too much on contemporary relevance. No wonder, he wrote, that every time the king (played by the film star Ivan Mozzhukhin) appeared on stage, the audience interrupted the play with applause.[21]

The Russian theater audience had by that time lost its purely elitist character; it had become democratized to some extent, including intellectuals, officials, urban merchants and middle-class citizens, and even some workers who could afford to pay for a place in the gallery. In addition, wealthy refugees from the western regions of the country began to frequent the theaters and cabarets of the two capitals. The social background of cinemagoers was even broader. According to a contemporary observer, everyone went to the movies. And Belgium as a symbol of patriotic spirit probably found its widest dissemination there.[22]

Andreev's play *Korol', zakon i svoboda* was made into one of the artistically most ambitious patriotic films. Directed by Petr Chardynin and released by Aleksandr Khanzhonkov, the film was praised by critics especially for avoiding the horror scenes that were the main ingredients of most patriotic movies. The film *Germanskie varvary v Bel'gii* (The German Barbarians in Belgium), for example, showed a young boy forced by a German officer to shoot his father in front of his mother and the attempted assault on the mother by three German soldiers. The film was a production of the semiofficial Skobelev Committee, an organization in charge of war propaganda. That committee also released yet another film with the Belgium motif—*Liliia Bel'gii* (The Lily of Belgium), a "contemporary allegory" aimed at children and adults alike. It featured a girl who finds a broken lily in a forest. She takes the flower to her grandfather, who then tells her the story of heroic Belgium, which has been "broken" by the Germans like the lily in the forest.[23]

---

[21] "Moskovskie vesti," *Teatr i iskusstvo*, no. 18 (1914): 833; Nikolai Efros, "Moskovskie pis'ma," *Teatr i iskusstvo*, no. 18 (1914): 851–52; M. S. Berlina, "P'esy Leonida Andreeva na Aleksandrinskoi stsene," in *Russkii teatr i dramaturgiia, 1907–1917 godov: Sbornik nauchnykh trudov* (Leningrad: Leningradskii gosudarstvennyi institut teatra, muzyki i kinematografii, 1988), 79–82 (includes a short description of the play).

[22] See the editorial in *Teatr i iskusstvo*, no. 19 (1915): 73–74; Ira Fedorovna Petrovskaia, *Teatr i zritel' rossiiskikh stolits, 1895–1917* (Leningrad: Iskusstvo, 1990), 10–11; Konechnyi et al., "'Prival komediantov'," 98; and Neia Markovna Zorkaia, "Vokrug pervykh russkikh kinoseansov," *Voprosy kino-iskusstva* 15 (1974): 189.

[23] On Andreev's film, see *Vestnik kinematografii*, no. 105 (January 1915): 30–31 and the photos on pp. 25, 27–29, 33–35; and *Sine-Fono*, no. 8 (1915): 68, 70. The two films by the Skobelev Committee are described in *Proektor*, no. 4 (1915): 25; and in *Ekran Rossii*, no. 1 (1916): 20. See also *Silent Witnesses: Russian Films, 1908–1919* (London: British Film Institute, 1989), 224, 272–74.

Belgium was thus available as a patriotic motif for every taste and every intellectual level, in the circus ring and the cinema, in metropolitan theaters and cabarets. Its widespread use, as with the kaiser theme, suggested a far-reaching unity of patriotic imagery within Russian society and, implicitly, a common level of communication among diverse social strata, between high and popular culture. But if workers, business owners, state officials, and intellectuals saw the same patriotic images and thus had the same patriotic "keywords" on their minds, how then was it possible that by 1917 Russian society was split over the war issue? How was it possible that by 1917 almost nobody supported the monarchy anymore, the traditional focus of patriotic feelings?

The two patriotic motifs described so far were "external" motifs and thus acceptable to all Russians. Neither required a definition of one's patriotism. Was it rooted in the tsar, in Russia, neither, or both? A look at only a few "internal" patriotic motifs shows that it was virtually impossible to find common ground on this question. Except for the national anthem and the flag, symbols that can have different meanings for different people, there were apparently no motifs that could have reflected the patriotic convictions of all parts of Russian society. And not even the flag or the anthem were part of all genres of cultural life. In cabarets and in satirical journals, for example, they were absent altogether.[24]

Slavophile ideas or Russian history and traditions might have provided common patriotic values and themes, but they either were restricted to a segment of the intelligentsia and its following or were too broad and open to varying interpretations. Historical motifs, for example, could range from direct references to military heroes like Mikhail Kutuzov and Aleksandr Suvorov in lubki or as *tableaux vivants* in Dolina's concerts to the revival of old Russian aesthetic forms and folklore. The latter was an important trend—particularly among the artistic intelligentsia—as evidenced by enterprises like Segodniashnii lubok or the wave of old Russian songs, tales, and *byliny* (epic folk songs) in estrada performances. This trend had begun long before the war, especially in the fine arts, handicrafts, and music; but during the war it gained momentum, because it offered the possibility of identifying with Russian cultural traditions without having to side with the existing state or ruler. Russian culture thus became the main focal point of patriotism among the artistic intelligentsia. Obviously, there was an important qualitative difference between this understanding of tradition and the eulogizing of former military heroes in the service of the empire.[25]

[24] Raymond Firth, *Symbols: Public and Private* (Ithaca, N.Y.: Cornell University Press, 1973), 75, 427; Leonard W. Doob, *Patriotism and Nationalism: Their Psychological Foundations* (New Haven, Conn.: Yale University Press, 1964), 6, 10.

[25] On Slavophile ideas during the war, see Ben Hellman, "Kogda vremia slavianofil'stvovalo: Russkie filosofy i pervaia mirovaia voina," in *Studia Russica Helsingiensia et*

Military heroes, allegorical figures of medieval knights, St. George, or the tsar and his family—all these motifs that symbolized a strong Russian monarchy and a powerful military were restricted to certain segments of wartime cultural life. Propagated by the radical right, they were present in official propaganda efforts, such as films and postcards from the Skobelev Committee, and in posters promoting war loans in 1916. They were also widely used in patriotic publications and shows aimed specifically at lower-class or mass audiences. Lubki, for example, had a long tradition of allegorical depictions or portraits of military heroes; that tradition was taken up again during World War I, particularly by big publishing houses like Sytin and Chelnokov. Other publishers put out calendars and postcards with portraits of Nicholas II and his family. In the circus, in patriotic events in parks, and on the estrada stages, strong knights appeared and grandiose finales featured historical figures and national symbols like the flag and the anthem in *tableaux vivants*—a traditional way to express patriotism in plays of the nineteenth-century *balagan* (fair booth) and a component part of the patriotic manifestations of the radical right. Among the latter, the portrait of the tsar enjoyed particular reverence as a patriotic icon.[26]

It is impossible to measure the impact that these motifs of monarchy and traditional symbolism had on a lower-class audience. The popularity, however, of heroes like Kuz'ma Kriuchkov, the brave pilot P. N. Nesterov, and a host of other clever cossacks who appeared in countless

---

Tartuensia: Problemy istorii russkoi literatury nachala XX veka, ed. Liisa Byckling and Pekka Pesonen (Helsinki: Helsinki University Press, 1989), 211–39. The lubok titled *Suvorov i Slava* (E. F. Chelnokov, Moscow, n.d., 74 x 55.5 cm) showed Suvorov standing on a cloud and watching the Russian army. Dolina's shows and the revival of *byliny* in estrada shows are discussed in Kuznetsov, *Iz proshlogo*, 339–43; see also the program of a reading of old Russian tales by M. D. Krivopolenova, the star of this sort of entertainment, in TsGIA SPb, f. 569, op. 13, d. 1360, ll. 118–118ob. On the revival of folklore in general see Alison Hilton, "Russian Folk Art and 'High' Art in the Early Nineteenth Century," in *Art and Culture in Nineteenth-Century Russia*, ed. Theofanis George Stavrou (Bloomington: Indiana University Press, 1983), 237–38; and Eric Hobsbawm, "Inventing Traditions," introduction to *The Invention of Tradition*, ed. Eric Hobsbawm and Terence Ranger (Cambridge: Cambridge University Press, 1983), 1–2, 8.

[26] For a discussion of rightist propaganda, see Heinz-Dietrich Löwe, "Political Symbols and Rituals of the Russian Radical Right, 1900–1917," ms., 12–17. On films, see Aleksandr Andreevich Levitskii, *Rasskazy o kinematografe* (Moscow: Iskusstvo, 1964), 113. Reproductions of war-loan posters showing the St. George motif or the double-headed eagle are in *Affiches et imageries russes, 1914–1920* (Paris: Musée des deux guerres mondiales, 1982), 3–5. For examples of lubki, see E. P. Ivanov, *Russkii narodnyi lubok* (Moscow: Gos. izd. izobrazitel'nykh iskusstv, 1937), 63. Calendars for 1917 by Moskovskaia khudozhestvennaia pechatnia and for 1915 by Gosudarstvennaia tipografiia may be seen in GMIG. See also postcards by the Riga publisher Gempel', and *Organ*, no. 120 (1914). On popular fairs, see Evgenii Mikhailovich Kuznetsov, comp., *Russkie narodnye gulian'ia po rasskazam A. Ia. Alekseeva-Iakovleva* (Moscow and Leningrad: Iskusstvo, 1948), 54.

lubki, circus pantomimes, and films suggests that it was easier for many to relate patriotic feelings to more realistic personifications of Russian military prowess, comparable in a way to the kaiser as the handy embodiment of all evil. The tsar, the monarchy, and its symbols were, obviously, only one theme among many others. They were used extensively as props for an unimaginative official propaganda or simply relegated to the role of ritualized ornament, something that belonged in a grandiose finale as a matter of course. They appeared in a similarly ritualized form in places of high culture like the imperial operas, where the anthem might be played at the beginning of performances and where traditionally the season began with Glinka's *A Life for the Tsar*.[27]

"Internal" patriotic motifs (of which only some have been mentioned here) did not have the broad and unanimous acceptance that "external" ones had in Russian society. While the figure of Wilhelm II personified the enemy for everyone, the tsar certainly did not embody Russia for everyone. Some preferred either Russian culture and folklore or the wit and bravery of the cossacks as points of patriotic identification. The absence of a unified and generally valid, positive patriotic symbol, of a common "keyword," thus indicated a rift within society that eludes classification along lines of elite and popular culture—a rift that finally came to the fore in 1917.

Russian patriotic culture as described here was a phenomenon predominantly of the year 1914 and the first months of 1915. Most of the shows and performances mentioned took place within this period; almost all patriotic lubki and most postcards and caricatures were published in that time. The interest in patriotic culture declined rapidly after this initial outburst; social criticism began to replace attacks on the kaiser in estrada shows and in caricatures. Theaters returned to their standard repertoires of international high culture. The thematic unity between elite and popular culture with regard to the kaiser and Belgium did not break up; rather, it withered away with the decrease of interest in patriotic topics altogether. The social unity against a foreign enemy and in favor of an ally turned out to be only temporary, a fiction covering up for a while the general disunity of patriotic convictions among Russians with respect to their own country.

Patriotic culture, however, was divided not only over motifs; there were also driving forces behind it that were at odds with one another. For

---

[27] For an idea of the popularity of the Kriuchkov motif, see the collection of lubki devoted to it in GMPIR, f. 5, nos. 11756–11782. See also Dmitriev, *Tsirk v Rossii*, 280–81; V. E. Vishnevskii, *Khudozhestvennye filmy dorevoliutsionnoi Rossii: Fil'mograficheskoe opisanie* (Moscow: Goskinoizdat, 1945), 36, 45, 152; N. Fatov, "Opernyi sezon 1914–15 g. v Moskve," *Russkaia muzykal'naia gazeta*, no. 21–22 (1915): 380; and *Teatr i iskusstvo*, no. 19 (1915): 706.

example, business interests and social consciousness, mixed with political goals, competed for the attention of audiences. Charitable performances and publications tried to raise funds for war victims, whereas film companies, theaters, the circus, and so forth had to make money with their products. The war as a commodity—as entertainment—was their contribution to patriotic culture. Meanwhile, members of the artistic intelligentsia, especially in the two capitals, played and sang free of charge in hospitals and in metropolitan cafés and collected money and warm clothing in the streets. Differences between high and popular culture vanished on such occasions; circus and estrada artists mixed with ballerinas from the operas and theater stars like Ol'ga Knipper.[28]

The opposite of socially responsible attitudes and activities was the vicarious pleasure of cultural consumption: experiencing the war from a cinema seat or before a lubok. Unlike with charity, the attraction of this consumption soon gave way to an escapist trend—to lighter plays, films, and shows that allowed one to forget the war. This was not a trend of only one part of society. As theater and circus programs and the output of film companies show, popular and high culture alike turned away from patriotic repertoire by mid-1915, after the shocking defeats suffered in the Austro-German offensive under August von Mackensen.[29]

Patriotism in Russia during World War I was, obviously, understood in a variety of ways. This investigation of the motifs of patriotic culture reveals a broad initial reaction to the war, to the foreign enemy, and to its atrocities in an Allied country. The unanimous condemnation of the kaiser and the support for Belgium, however, were not matched by a unanimous outlook on other aspects of the war or even of nationhood. The variety of motifs shows that there was not just one loyalty—to the tsar; rather, patriotic feelings were attached to Russian culture and tradition, to popular heroes, and only to a small extent to the ruler.[30] When the war became more burdensome, these differences blurred in the face of the human aspects of the war, which were reflected in widespread charity and in the wish to forget and to escape.

---

[28] Nadezhda Aleksandrovna Smirnova, *Vospominaniia* (Moscow: Vserossiiskoe teatral'noe obshchestvo, 1947), 280–84. See also the photos of a charitable performance by a mixed group of Moscow artists (Russkoi armii—artisty Moskvy) in *Rampa i zhizn'*, February 21, 1916, 10; and the files of the Petrograd group Artist—soldatu (Artist for the Soldier) in TsGIA SPb, f. 287, op. 1, d. 332, ll. 15–122.

[29] *Istoriia russkogo dramaticheskogo teatra*, vol. 7, *1898–1917* (Moscow: Iskusstvo, 1987), 445–560; Moisei Osipovich Iankovskii, *Operetta: Vozniknovenie i razvitie zhanra na zapade i v SSSR* (Moscow and Leningrad: Iskusstvo, 1937), 359–61; Dmitriev, *Tsirk v Rossii*, 281–82; Vishnevskii, *Khudozhestvennye filmy*, 35–123.

[30] The decline of popular loyalty to the tsar has also been noted by Brooks, *When Russia Learned to Read*, 217.

World War I, consequently, intensified the process of the breakup of Russian society. As Stephen Carter recently pointed out, empires in decline usually undergo a crisis of identity. This was certainly the case with the Russian Empire before the revolution. The diversity in patriotic motifs indicates a deep crisis in national identity. Most Russians did not see themselves as loyal subjects of the empire. There existed no functioning integrative ideology of a common nation, no "deliberate political option" for it—which, according to Eric Hobsbawm constitutes a nation and distinguishes free citizens from mere subjects of a state.[31] The explosion of February 1917 raised this issue of civil society and put the question of national identity back on the agenda. But despite the elimination of the tsar, a unanimous solution could not be found.

[31] Stephen K. Carter, *Russian Nationalism: Yesterday, Today, Tomorrow* (London: Pinter Publishers, 1990), 3; Eric Hobsbawm, *Nations and Nationalism since 1780: Programme, Myth, Reality* (Cambridge: Cambridge University Press, 1990), 88.

8

THE PENNY PRESS AND ITS READERS

Daniel R. Brower

IN THE LAST decades of the nineteenth century, the Russian penny press became a cultural bridge between writers and the urban population. It was a far more visible presence than the chapbooks, which until then had been the sole print medium to reach large numbers of readers. The penny press was an innovation both because it threw out a daily barrage of images, stories, and news reports, and because it cast an inquisitive, at times accusatory light on public and private behavior in the capitals and in provincial cities. The message was often sensationalist, invariably personalized and localized, and usually as ephemeral as the events of daily life that inspired the news items. The penny press created a new arena of communication, persuasion, and censure in the cultural life of the country. For the first time, a large reading public had access to stories intentionally written to draw attention to matters that would entertain, arouse curiosity, and occasionally even inspire indignation. A peculiar sort of muckraking appeared in the Russian daily press, whose contents bore little or no resemblance to those of the sober thick journals and dignified national newspapers.

The penny press operated under conditions of official censorship that, in theory, still applied strict controls on the content of newspapers. In the decades following the introduction of the 1865 temporary statute on censorship, supervision eased somewhat. Newspapers in the capitals enjoyed the right to publish without "preliminary censorship," though punitive measures invariably followed the publication of articles judged by the censorship committees to be unacceptable. As the number of papers increased, censors were forced to give considerable leeway to editors eager for more autonomy in their struggle to keep their newspapers alive. In the provinces, regulations maintained the censor's right to approve news copy in advance; but there, too, controls over local news and human-interest stories had relaxed considerably by the 1890s.[1]

---

[1] See Charles Ruud, *Fighting Words: Imperial Censorship and the Russian Press, 1804–1906* (Toronto, 1982), chaps. 9–12.

This flourishing penny press of the late tsarist period opens up to historians of Russian popular culture a multitude of images of the daily life, beliefs, social practices, and prejudices of the Russian urban population, and those of villagers as viewed through an urban lens. Labeled at the time the "boulevard newspapers," these publications are a window onto a social landscape in rapid transformation. They constitute a source of primary importance in assessing the impact in Russia of mass print culture—a term that in its broadest sense refers to the sharing of information, cultural symbols, and modes of understanding between a large reading public and the print media.[2] An expanding urban population, a rising standard of living, and the spread of literacy created a mass market in which these boulevard newspapers grew and flourished.[3]

But we have few records of the impact of these publications. Reading was as much a public as a private affair, and the stories were read aloud in family circles and in public meeting places such as taverns. These audiences turned newspaper articles into subjects of discussion and debate, revising the information to fit their own expectations and preconceptions. Recent studies of Russia's new print culture have examined its output primarily in terms of the authors' messages.[4] Yet the very nature of this cultural product made it dependent on the reader/consumer. How did the editors and reporters seek to involve potential readers in their daily fare of stories and information, and what aroused the interest of the average reader? These questions are the focus of this essay. The first generation of Russian mass readers had limited opportunities to give voice to its concerns. Uncovering this scarcely visible new cultural actor is a key to understanding the new directions that mass print gave to Russian popular culture. The sources that I have used are of necessity selective, but they strongly suggest the important new cultural role of the penny press.

The study of its daily outpouring of articles and stories directs our attention to that moment of encounter between printed word and popular mind, between cultural producer and consumer. The French philoso-

---

[2] The concept is discussed in Roger Chartier, "Print Culture," in *The Culture of Print: Power and the Uses of Print in Early Modern Europe*, trans. Lydia Cochrane, ed. Roger Chartier (Cambridge, 1989), 1–3.

[3] The new urban context that nurtured these papers is discussed in Daniel Brower, *The Russian City between Tradition and Modernity, 1850–1900* (Berkeley, 1990), chap. 4.

[4] Jeffrey Brooks discusses education and the expanding reading public in addressing the topic of Russian popular literature, but he does not explore the process of reader-author interaction. *When Russia Learned to Read: Literacy and Popular Literature, 1861–1917* (Princeton, 1985), chaps. 1, 2. The recent study of Russian newspapers in the tsarist period by Louise McReynolds touches briefly on the subject of the reader and the penny press but does not consider the mediating factor of the implied reader in the production and impact of the press's output. *The News under Russia's Old Regime: The Development of a Mass-Circulation Press* (Princeton, 1991), 53–63.

pher Paul Ricoeur suggests that we consider reading to be a "truly vital experience" in which the reader uses texts to make the unfamiliar familiar, filters the information found there to avoid an "excess of meaning," and expects the author to be the guide in a "search for coherence."[5] Many readers implies many different readings. The notion of the implied reader, developed by Wolfgang Iser, suggests an important clue to uncovering the reader-author link. Iser argues that the text has a "potential meaning," which is "actualized" by the "reading process."[6] I propose to carry the argument one step further by looking for the implied or imagined reader not only in the text itself, but also in the process of the creation of the text. This perspective points to the direct connection between the penny press's daily output and the reader to whom the newspaper editors and journalists directed their texts.

To use the Russian boulevard newspaper in this way to interpret popular culture, we must look closely for the explicit and implicit signs of the presence of the reader in the newspaper texts themselves. We also need to examine the records that the writers left of their imagined and real encounters with their reader-consumers. Our reading cannot duplicate that of the contemporary Russian, but it can hope to locate the symbols and messages by which authors identified their readers.

My approach rests on several key assumptions regarding modes of popular discourse in Russian culture. Though the term *popular culture* has acquired considerable vogue, Roger Chartier urges historians to employ the concept with great care. Studying prerevolutionary French culture, he proposes broadening the term's meaning to refer to a multitude of coexisting and competing cultural domains, for "different media and multiple practices almost always mingled in complex ways." In the period of emergent print culture, folk beliefs remain dynamic and vigorous, creating models for and responding to the "innovative impact of the written word." Furthermore, the study of a "popular" stratum of society should take account of competing perceptions, interests, values and cultural identities in that stratum. Finally, Chartier warns against the assumption that authoritative texts or dominant classes determine the evolution of popular culture. In his view, popular practices and beliefs evolve in complex patterns of "discipline and invention, reutilizations and innovations, models imposed (by the state, the church, or the market), and freedoms preserved."[7]

His warning is particularly pertinent to the study of historical moments when the practices and attitudes of the population are being

[5] *Time and Narrative*, trans. K. Blamey and D. Pellauer (Chicago, 1988), 3:169.

[6] *The Implied Reader: Patterns of Communication in Prose Fiction* (Baltimore, 1974), xii.

[7] *The Cultural Uses of Print in Early Modern France*, trans. Lydia Cochrane (Princeton, 1987), 3–6.

sharply contested and rapidly altered. From this perspective, the emergence of popular newspapers in late-nineteenth-century Russia is an important sign of cultural innovation. They enjoyed great popularity among the new reading public; at the same time, they had to pay close attention to the views, concerns, and interests of that public, which represented their mass market.

The primacy of the marketplace was a central feature of the new press in Russia, as in the West. The fact that this penny press was first and foremost a commercial enterprise is an advantage, not a handicap, for the historian of popular culture. Financial need forces editors and reporters to search widely for their customers. What to Russian intellectuals at the time constituted blatant vulgarity represented commercial survival to the publishers of the penny press, who had to sustain the daily interest of their readers. An editor of the first boulevard newspaper, *Peterburgskii listok* (The Petersburg Sheet), pointed out that the readers' "passive attitude . . . can reduce all our activity to nothing."[8] Simply put, the public's lack of interest would lead straight to bankruptcy. The few archival records of newspaper circulation in those years make clear why this was so.

The commercial success of a penny-press newspaper hung on its ability to cajole a few kopeks every day from a fickle reader of modest means, who was reached most easily through street sales. The national papers that emerged in the same years had a regular (and fairly well-to-do) readership of subscribers whose advance payments gave these papers substantial financial security. In the early 1870s, for example, one of them, *Birzhevye vedomosti* (Stock Exchange News), sold over half of its daily printings by subscription outside St. Petersburg, its city of publication. By contrast, the circulation of *Peterburgskii listok*, begun in the mid-1860s, was mainly local and depended on daily street sales.[9] Censors often forbade these sales as punishment for infractions of the censorship rules. As the St. Petersburg censorship committee well knew, this simple measure was "very painful" for boulevard newspapers and a lengthy prohibition created a "heavy burden."[10] Editors had to keep the censor away from the door while attracting the maximum number of readers (most of whom were newcomers to newspaper reading) with the type of news they wished to find.

[8] N. A. Skrobotov, in an 1889 speech, quoted in Frolov, *Za 50 let sushchestvovaniia Peterburgskogo listka* (Petrograd, 1916), 40.

[9] "Otchet o deiatel'nosti Peterburgskogo tsenzurnogo komiteta za 1873," Rossiiskii gosudarstvennyi istoricheskii arkhiv (hereafter RGIA; formerly TsGIA), f. 777, op. 11, d. 120, ll. 4–6.

[10] "Zhurnal soveta Glavnogo upravleniia po delam pechati za 1869," RGIA, f. 776, op. 2, d. 6, l. 164.

To survive in these conditions, editors required a wide array of skills, not least of which was responsiveness to prevalent public interests and concerns. By the standards of high culture, such editing was not a worthy cause, but it did bring fame and wealth to the successful editor. The rise of Moscow's most popular boulevard newspaper of the 1880s and 1890s, *Moskovskii listok* (The Moscow Sheet), was due largely to the talents of its owner and editor, Nikolai Pastukhov. He had first worked as a newspaper reporter before founding his own paper in 1881. He lacked the graces and classical learning of educated Russians, but he possessed a remarkable ability to attract a wide array of readers while appeasing and conciliating the Moscow authorities. Archival records for the paper do not reveal a single official reprimand to the editor in its first ten years of existence.[11]

Pastukhov was an object of mockery, even by his journalists. Vladimir Giliarovsky, who worked for him in the first years, described him later as an "illiterate editor who in the midst of illiterate readers . . . knew how to speak their language."[12] Giliarovsky's backhanded compliment turned illiteracy into a mark of the common touch, implying that an editor had to be no more sophisticated culturally and socially than the mass reading public. This condescending opinion of Pastukhov was typical; critics often mocked his earlier occupation of tavernkeeper, for example. Even his goal of commercial success was an object of scorn. A story that circulated in Moscow told of his first visit to Moscow's governor-general, who asked him to characterize the political tendency of the new newspaper. He was reported to have replied: "Feeding ourselves, Your Honor."[13]

Tsarist surveillance of the penny press paid critical attention to any supposed pandering to the sordid tastes of lower-class readers. In the discussions of the St. Petersburg censorship authorities in the 1860s and 1870s, a newspaper's accuracy in reporting appeared less a concern than its standards of public morality and propriety. One censor, surveying the first five years of publishing under the new censorship statute of 1865, pointed to *Peterburgskii listok* as an exemplary case of the new public vulgarity. In his opinion, its pages formed in his opinion "a sort of junkyard of all sorts of rumors, gossip, and news," and the whole paper

---

[11] This conclusion is drawn from a search through the two archival files on *Moskovskii listok* of the Moscow Censorship Committee, in Tsentral'nyi gosudarstvennyi istoricheskii arkhiv goroda Moskvy (TsGIAgM), f. 31 (Moskovskoe glavnoe upravlenie po delam pechati), op. 2, d. 156 and d. 288.

[12] "Moskva gazetnaia," in *Sochineniia* (Moscow, 1963), 3:84.

[13] The anecdote is reported in B. P. Koz'min, *Russkaia zhurnalistika 70–80kh godov XIX veka* (Moscow, 1948), 51.

had a "defamatory [*oblichitel'nyi*] character."[14] His reading of the paper had uncovered a reprehensible degree of disrespect for authority. To staunch conservatives and defenders of public order, its readiness to highlight the drama of everyday life at the expense of social deference was a mark of muckraking. The Russian penny press, like Western popular newspapers of that period, was creating a new genre of writing by dramatizing the world of the ordinary Russian townsperson. The formula proved a commercial success, despite the censors' disapproval.

This irreverent tone remained a notable trait of Russian popular newspapers and gave them a style substantially different from that of the socially respectful and intellectually demanding articles of the national press. Pastukhov, whose journalistic entrepreneurship made him one of the pioneers of the penny press, appeared to be particularly well aware of the commercial benefits of adopting a style implicitly and explicitly critical of social privilege, though within the narrow limits permitted by the censors. His somewhat exaggerated qualities—and defects—should not obscure the traits that he shared with other self-made editors. Censorship remained a constant concern, but the pressure eased as its focus shifted to signs of suspected political disloyalty. In the daily affairs of the penny press, editors enjoyed considerable latitude to inspire and instill in their writers a provocative approach in the selection and presentation of information and social commentary. The boulevard newspapers all shared a common interest in attracting the popular reader, to whom they addressed their message and for whom they hoped to become a necessary daily commodity.

One of their most effective stylistic techniques to this end was the ubiquitous feuilleton, or human-interest story, which could appear in either a factual or a fictionalized version. They adapted this device from the Russian national newspapers, which contained a rubric (usually at the bottom of the front page) for serialized novels or tales drawn from real life. The popular newspapers added the "small feuilleton," which encompassed a wide variety of short human-interest stories scattered among the local news items. They received titles such as "Little Scenes" (Stsenki) and "Trivia" (Melochi dnia). These stories, often a dramatized retelling of what was purportedly a real event, sought to entertain the reader. Often it shifted to a mildly muckraking mode. Similar types of stories had appeared earlier in the penny press in Western countries, where they took the form of "chatty little reports of tragic or comic incidents in the lives of the people."[15]

[14] "Opyt kratkoi istoricheskoi otsenki napravlenii razlichnykh sovremennykh izdanii," January 13, 1871, RGIA, f. 776, op. 5, d. 38, l. 28.

[15] Helen Hughes, *News and the Human Interest Story* (New York, 1940), 7.

The key to a feuilleton author's success was the ability to capture the popular mood, both in content and form. These stories spoke in a language that intentionally imitated popular speech, recounting events as if in a conversation with the readers. In other words, they created the illusion of reflecting the everyday world of ordinary townspeople (the much-maligned *obyvateli*) and thus made everyday occurrences newsworthy. At times, the event chosen was one of the injustices that filled daily life. The search for the meaningful happening turned the story itself into an event. In this way, the market was shaping the newspaper.

Writing such stories was usually a humdrum occupation; there was room here for invention and dramatization, but only on a very modest scale. But journalists with higher cultural and political ambitions were aware of the logic expressed by the editor N. A. Leikin, who reassured a reluctant feuilleton writer—young Anton Chekhov—that "we'll grab the readers with stupidities and then instruct them with learned articles."[16] Leikin himself was drawn into journalism in the 1860s after the appearance of his first collection of semiautobiographical stories, which described the life of St. Petersburg merchants (his father was a struggling trader in the Apraksin market). Leikin's new editor proclaimed that "this [type of story] is the sort of daily life [*byt*] about which one must write now . . . to acquaint the reader with the people and with those who are emerging from the people. After all, the whole future of Russia is in their hands. . . . So give us as many everyday events [*zloby*] as possible. That's how it is now!"[17]

The boundary separating the journalists and readers of the penny press was thus very porous. The events recounted on the pages of these papers focused on situations and characters familiar to the mass public that the editors sought to attract. Rather than assuming the tone characteristic of the national papers—that of a learned monologue on complex topics of politics and economics—this press sought to give the reader the impression of being on an equal footing with the authors of the articles. The short human-interest stories of the feuilleton created an effect of immediate, tangible reality. *Peterburgskii listok* set the precedent: its first columnist proclaimed his intent to present the reader with a "chronicle" of "scandals, disorders, amusing and sad events" of St. Petersburg life, on the condition it be "something new—topical, so to speak."[18]

The effort to capture the lively and unusual events in the life of the city was largely contrived. The credibility of these stories depended more on

[16] Letter of September 8, 1883, in N. A. Leikin, *Vospominaniia i perepiski* (St. Petersburg, 1907), 236.
[17] Ibid., 186.
[18] *Peterburgskii listok*, March 15, 1864.

plausibility than veracity, for they were directed to an imagined mass reader for whom the fairy tale, not fiction, marked the limits of reality. Both the content and style of the stories reflected conscious choices of the editors and writers. Their act of creation extended to the readers as well, for they had to create a social profile of readers whose tastes and interests they could only dimly discern.

For good or ill, the reader was a vital presence in the ephemeral existence of the newspaper, an existence renewed every day. One editor of *Peterburgskii listok*, speaking at its twenty-fifth anniversary celebration, explained his side of the newspaper-reader dialogue by remarking that "one must know not the subscriber and reader, but his needs and wishes. If you become aware of what questions interest him and if you treat him honestly, then you will have done all that is required to expand the paper's circle of readers."[19] This idealized characterization of editorial guidance demanded a remarkable power to discern the Russian vox populi. From a more cynical perspective, Pastukhov's reputed manipulation of news gave him pride of place among editors of boulevard papers in finding the vulgar tone suitable to lower-class townspeople. He reportedly turned down newspaper copy if he believed that it would not interest "janitors and shopkeepers."[20]

A careful reading of *Moskovskii listok* reveals how extensively Pastukhov used the folksy style of the feuilleton to enliven his local news stories. The distinction between news and sensationalism was blurred, particularly in the headlines that broadcast these noteworthy happenings. Telegraphic, snap judgments characterized news items—such as an attack on an old man whose vicious assailant was proclaimed "An Animal, Not a Man" (January 6, 1883) or the death of a Moscow visitor, labeled "From Guest to Graveyard" (January 1, 1883). Each account had the topicality and tone of daily gossip that ordinary Muscovites themselves would wish to pass on to their family and neighbors.

The constant presence of the imagined reader required that the penny press work with images, symbols, and views understandable to that reader. It also encouraged the selection of events that would arouse popular concern, even indignation. The critical attention that was focused on abuses and wrongs made the immediacy of the event particularly plausible to those Russians who brought to their newspaper reading a strong resentment of social injustice and abuses of power. It might appear vulgar, naive, or petty to intellectuals, whose scale of values differed greatly from that of the popular reader. But journalists could turn the pages of the penny press into an arena where daily dramas were acted out between

---

[19] Quoted in Frolov, *Za 50 let*, 11.
[20] Quoted in Brooks, *When Russia Learned to Read*, 128.

good and evil, kindness and cruelty. Their work gave the boulevard papers an irreverent, critical tone, offensive to officials and vulgar to intellectuals but nonetheless highly successful among their readers.

Human-interest stories of the penny press turned often to criticizing abusive treatment of less fortunate residents of the city. It was an innovative and ambitious undertaking, and it attracted from the start an attentive audience—some approving and others deeply hostile. A few readers wrote to laud their paper's defense of their interests. One letter that caught the attention of the editors of *Peterburgskii listok* early in the paper's existence approved strongly of articles on "vital facts of our daily life" and "the inquiry into questions concerning this life."[21] That reader's immediate concern was the high prices charged by the city's pharmacists, but the potential spectrum of "vital facts" extended to more controversial and troubling issues, such as poverty and crime.

The readiness of *Peterburgskii listok* to criticize social ills aroused the ire of the St. Petersburg censorship committee, which in 1869 condemned it for publishing "news of abuses, disorders, and scandals encountered in various ranks of St. Petersburg society." The committee was especially offended by what it claimed to be the paper's use of events "from everyday life to paint in the most somber tones the helpless situation of the most humble and poorest classes of the population." By comparison with later boulevard newspapers, *Peterburgskii listok* appears a model of decorum, but the committee's conservative members were convinced that its articles "produce among its readers a very painful [*tiazheloe*] impression."[22] The conservatives' loyalty to estate rank, privilege, and deference made them highly suspicious of any published reports of the difficulties and hardships confronting ordinary townspeople. The result of their hostility to this alleged muckraking was repeated and prolonged banning of street sales of the newspaper in the 1860s and 1870s.

One ought not exaggerate either the zeal of the penny press in pursuing injustice or the moral commitment of its readers to the downtrodden. Pastukhov is an exemplary case of a profit-minded, self-made newspaper titan who simply fell into the role of defender of the weak. His *Moskovskii listok* contained from its early years a wide array of local news and human-interest articles, focusing primarily on events in and around the city under headings such as "Moscow Life," "Along the Streets and Alleys," and "Near Moscow." The January 18, 1883, issue, for example, featured excerpts from the diary of a bookkeeper on trial for embezzlement. The column "Moscow Life" told of a mother's appear-

---

[21] *Peterburgskii listok*, July 19, 1865.

[22] "Otchet o deiatel'nosti Sanktpeterburgskogo tsenzurnogo komiteta," RGIA, f. 777, op. 2 (1870), d. 28, l. 21.

ance in a police station and her demand that her two grown sons be arrested for stealing her money. "Tale of a Merchant" recounted a merchant's abortive effort to arrange the marriage of his son, whom the bride's family rejected because they had read in the same newspaper of another merchant's bankruptcy. "I should never have subscribed to the newspaper," concludes the frustrated father. But the implicit moral of this petty tale was really that the paper was a pervasive presence in the daily life of Moscow's townspeople.

The paper's appeal quickly spread to provincial readers. We know from Maksim Gorky's memoirs that while he was a young apprentice to relatives in Nizhnii Novgorod in 1882, he read *Moskovskii listok* aloud in the evenings to his family. That provincial family, which to him typified everything that was bigoted and materialistic about the Russian petty bourgeoisie, took great pleasure in Moscow's new boulevard newspaper. If we can believe Gorky, they were readers without compassion or concern for others who turned to the paper for want of anything better to do. He characterized their reading as "bromide [Gorky uses *pishchevarenie*, or, roughly, 'cud'] for people bored to death."[23] This critical judgment, made a quarter century later, comes from a mature, politically committed writer. A younger and less critical Gorky's first writing job in 1892 was composing human-interest stories for a provincial newspaper. At that time, he was prepared to assume that his readership included people less complacent and more responsive to accounts of hardship and injustice than his relatives.

Both Pastukhov and his journalists were pleased by the attention that the paper had attracted. A story in the spring of 1882 portrayed merchants gathered in a tavern reading a newspaper (clearly *Moskovskii listok*) and asking, "Are they talking about us [in the paper] again?" One of the merchants, finding his drunken adventures described there, complains that "now everyone has read about me and condemned me." His clerk comments quietly in an aside that concludes the story: "Say what you will, but the paper really stuck it to the boss [*lovka osadila khoziaina*]."[24] The lowly, sober clerk becomes in this story the voice of the reader.

The paper used its journalistic authority to judge real-life conflicts and problems encountered by its readers. One month after the paper began publishing, its editorial board published a statement welcoming letters on "all possible abuses, on the sole condition that these letters are signed."[25] The response must have been enthusiastic, for several days later the pub-

[23] Maksim Gorkii, *Detstvo, B liudakh, Moi universitety* (Leningrad, 1974), 275.
[24] Shapka Nevidimka, "Prodernuli," *Moskovskii listok* (hereafter *ML*), May 1, 1882.
[25] *ML*, October 4, 1881.

lic discovered a daily column entitled "Advice and Answers" that recounted the objectionable public behavior of Muscovites and invariably
ended with a brief admonitory comment from the editorial board. The
tone remained folksy and the situations were the same type of everyday
experiences that appeared in the human-interest stories. But these were
not simple descriptions, nor were they "tales." The column took the form
of brief, conversational messages addressed to people of scarcely camou-
flaged identity, telling of their misdeeds and calling for redress. The liveli-
ness of the column came from its very personalized and judgmental approach to everyday personal encounters among Muscovites and later, as
we will see, among people from distant parts of the empire.

The array of social types castigated in "Advice and Answers" ranged
from abusive master craftsmen and negligent landlords to disrespectful
clerks and wayward sons (censorship regulations forbade criticism of the
nobility). The individual misdeeds were usually trivial, but the publicity
broadened their significance greatly. When the column held up for public
censure the guard on the Mozhaisk road (leading to Moscow) who
"seizes the hammers and axes of passing peasants who haven't the money
to pay," it could count on its readers to recognize the presence of *proizvol*
(arbitrariness). Anyone in favor of honest business practices had to agree
that brewer Gorshanov ought to "wash [his] bottles better and then fill
them with beer, not half with beer and half with kerosene, dregs, and
other garbage."[26] Plain talk and the use of real, commonplace encounters
gave the editorial judgments the authority of social consensus.

In the main, "Advice and Answers" relied on what could be called a
sense of communitarian equity in judging people in its informal court of
popular justice. The column spoke for an implied reader who was an
ordinary townsperson with compassion for the weak and a belief in simple human values. More than half of the over thirteen hundred incidents
described before the column suddenly ended in June 1882 involved commercial or business affairs. The everyday public life of urban Russia was
above all a place of intensive, small-scale economic exchange, where fairness and personal dignity suffered when greed or insensitivity gained the
upper hand. Each scene was a minor drama that could easily evoke a
sympathetic response from readers for whom such events were daily occurrences. The paper's judgments thus appeared to emerge out of the natural reactions of ordinary Russians. A baker in the Rogozhka district
learned late in 1881 that his customers "thank [him] for the first roll ever
to come from [his] oven that doesn't contain cockroaches and wood
chips. Might it be possible to bake like this in the future?"[27]

[26] Ibid., November 8, 1881.
[27] Ibid., September 23, 1881.

Servants as well as customers had a right to have their grievances heard. In fall 1881, the owner of the Peterhof Hotel was asked to give his servants better quarters. If his "humane spirit" did not inspire him to act, the newspaper warned, there would be a "visit from the [municipal] health commission."[28] The reader might have been sitting in a neighborhood tearoom or tavern listening to complaints from the hotel employees. On the pages of *Moskovskii listok*, personal unpleasantness became public knowledge. The point of each story was the redress of a wrong, to which the newspaper was witness and judge.

Shady, unruly, and cruel business practices dotted the urban landscape re-created in "Advice and Answers." It found particular fault with the behavior of Russian traders and manufacturers. In some cases, the transgression was the verbal abuse or importunities of store owners or clerks lacking proper respect for their customers. The column passed on a "proper warning" to the manager of a store on Tverskoi Boulevard from a customer who accused him of "insults to his customers." The editors added their own admonition to "stop this disgrace [*bezobrazie*] and not forget that the store where you work exists for the public and not the other way around."[29]

The newspaper appeared equally concerned to stand up for abused employees and workers. It was prepared to concede that "a penny saved is a penny earned" (literally, "a kopek gives birth to a ruble")—but not at the expense, as it warned Zakhar Stepanovich of Neglinsky Passage, of "starving your workers and assessing fines for the pettiest matter undeserving of punishment."[30] A factory owner in Ovchinikov received the summons to "fear God," for "you throw away thousands of rubles on gambling and begrudge three rubles to a family whose breadwinner cannot work because of you. You may end up in court and will pay a lawyer a lot of money."[31] On a folksy note, they queried "Grandma Borisova" on Tverskoi Boulevard: "Aren't you ashamed, little mother, to give your workers soup made from filthy old bones. One ought not work twelve hours and for that get a bowl of soup smelling like a heap of garbage."[32] With these short, colloquial tales and judgments, the column claimed the right to speak for the weak and the downtrodden of Russia's growing urban economy. It created an authentic outraged reader, recognizable to the public and visible every day in the pages of the newspaper.

Several points deserve to be emphasized in assessing the significance of these calls to communitarian equity. First, the column came close to being

[28] Ibid., November 2, 1881.
[29] Ibid., April 21, 1882.
[30] Ibid., May 25, 1882.
[31] Ibid., April 2, 1882.
[32] Ibid., December 6, 1881.

the "voice of the people," since it depended for its subject matter upon letters from readers (though the editors claimed the final word in passing judgment). Second, the editors were prepared to summon, without hesitation, higher authorities to support their calls for justice. The police, the courts, and even God appeared in their columns to enforce their daily advice. In effect, they had taken on the role of defender of the public, present wherever the paper was read—in the homes, tearooms, and taverns of Moscow and in the provinces. Third, their pronouncements did not rely on the liberal procedures of judicial process, nor did they invoke principles of equality and collective interests in the populist spirit. It is no wonder that the other claimants to moral leadership in the public arena scorned the voice of the penny press.

The column struck a responsive chord among readers outside Moscow as well. Its attention to public misdeeds soon widened—presumably as a result of letters from provincial readers—to encompass a much larger territory. Censorious comments appeared on events in places as far away as Smolensk, Kostroma, Khar'kov, and even Orenburg. Readers from provincial Russia judged the newspaper a proper forum to air their grievances, and they joined with Muscovites to help the editors create a discourse of public grievance. Nothing like this had ever existed before. *Moskovskii listok* turned daily events into a source of daily entertainment—the attraction that made readers out of Gorky's repugnant relatives—but it also constructed, with the help of its readers, a self-styled public court, where an audience that reached far beyond Moscow could find a sympathetic hearing.

The tenor of journalistic admonition and judgment in "Advice and Answers" used popular forms of speech and relied on a basic set of moral values in condemning misdeeds and demanding rectification. The column employed a language understandable to its readers, who saw reflected in the pages of the newspaper a moral order with which they were familiar. It repeatedly extolled "conscience," "morality," "honor," "proprieties," and "courtesy," urging people to treat one another in a manner that was "humane" (*po-chelovecheski*) and "in the Christian spirit." Conversely, it identified reprehensible moral behavior with "crudeness" (*grubost'*), "insults," "scandal," "disorder" (*buistvo*), "insolence," "debauch," "greed," "cheating," and "arrogance" (*samodurstvo*). The accumulated daily admonitions, applied to a wide variety of events, added up to an unstated moral code of social behavior.

This vocabulary was not complex, yet it was sufficiently coherent to transcend the limits of the ephemeral daily news item and become what contemporary literary theory characterizes as a meaningful text. It escaped, as Paul Ricoeur put it, "the momentary character of the event" and the limits of a face-to-face encounter by bringing the incidents to the attention of "an unknown, invisible reader," who is "the unprivileged addressee of the discourse."[33] In transcending daily life while still situating the event in an immediate, known social context, "Advice and Answers" created, in J. G. A. Pocock's words, "both a conceptual world and the authority structures, or social worlds, related to it," and was directly engaged with and interacted with the surrounding society.[34] Both Ricoeur and Pocock are proposing theories of language by which to extract meaning from ordinary discourse. Their approach seems to fit the explicit moralizing advice of "Advice and Answers," and in broader terms it is applicable as well to the penny press's serious human-interest stories. If so, it suggests that this press, by giving voice to a critical view of daily life, added in its own modest way to public perceptions of injustice in urban Russia.

This moralizing journalistic language seems to have been highly eclectic in drawing its inspiration from Russian culture. Somewhat "bourgeois," it avoided the authoritarian vocabulary of nobles and bureaucrats. It relied vaguely on Orthodox Christian teaching, but added a concern for human dignity that in those years was echoed frequently in worker protests against employers. It is tempting to find its powers of ethical persuasion in the social universe of the village commune; yet it contained a more sophisticated set of moral strictures, which were needed to deal with the increasingly complex social relations of Russian urban society. This language was a peculiarly Russian innovation—as unique as the message from the American penny press, which "expressed and built the culture of a democratic market society, a culture which had no place for social and intellectual deference."[35] The Russian penny press endowed the urban community with a personalized ethical code. The "Advice and Answers" column is a fascinating condensation of new public discourse created by both the popular press and its readers.

The incidents described in the penny press emerged from conflicts originating in the daily practices and attitudes of a rapidly changing urban world. The editors of *Moskovskii listok* welcomed the passing of that "blessed, undisturbed past when all was quiet in Moscow and when for months nothing happened."[36] This perspective was self-serving, of course, since the paper relied upon daily dramas mixing old and new settings, familiar and unfamiliar behavior, to capture and hold its readers' attention. The success of "Advice and Answers" would suggest that

[33] "The Model of the Text: Meaningful Action Considered as Text," in *Interpretive Social Science*, ed. Paul Rabinow and William Sullivan (Berkeley, 1982), 80.

[34] *Politics, Language, and Time* (New York, 1971), 15.

[35] Michael Schudson, *Discovering the News: A Social History of American Newspapers* (New York, 1978), 60.

[36] "Obozrenie dnia," *ML*, June 11, 1882.

the readers were aware of the social changes under way and that they welcomed a forum to share their grievances, generated by the tumult of the new urban life.

In its first years of publication, *Moskovskii listok* was prepared, in "Advice and Answers" and elsewhere, to confront the new world of capitalists and industrialists. Pastukhov's famous serialized novel, *The Bandit Churkin*, constituted on one level a conscious effort to appeal to the rapidly growing working population. Vasilii Churkin, in real life and in the novel, was a worker from the Moscow region who had chosen the life of a bandit. In his reports of factory life, Pastukhov took the side of the workers. He was delighted at Vladimir Giliarovsky's vivid articles on a destructive fire in June 1882 at the barracks of the Morozov textile workers in Orekhovo-Zuevo. According to Giliarovsky, he exclaimed, "The workers will read the paper from front to back page and then deluge us with letters about disorders."[37] Pastukhov's own editorial used the tragedy to attack factory policies, summoning Morozov "more seriously to take care of his workers" and "to think of preventive measures in case of [another] fire."[38] Among his readers were an indignant Moscow business community and an irate Moscow governor-general, who called in the editor to make clear his displeasure. Pastukhov managed to avoid an official reprimand, but one week later "Advice and Answers" vanished from the newspaper—probably sacrificed to the high priests of official Russia.

In the end, Pastukhov was true to his commercial interest of managing a profitable newspaper. He was prepared to abandon "Advice and Answers," just as he later sacrificed *The Bandit Churkin*, to remain in the good graces of the tsarist authorities in those years of political reaction. He was conservative in his political convictions. The communitarian ethic defended in the column was compatible with his paternalistic views, which called on the fortunate and powerful to follow in good conscience the dictates of morality and justice and on inferiors to accept gratefully the protection—or admonition—of their superiors.

Still, Pastukhov had been prepared for a time to open the pages of his newspaper to public protest against social abuses. By allowing readers to share authorial power with the editors, the newspaper contributed—far more forcefully than had its predecessor, *Peterburgskii listok*—to the appearance of a public discourse of civic morality in the journalistic world of Russian print culture. Word of mouth had once given individuals their only opportunity to damn the powerful and the greedy; the penny press created a new public forum for such protest. Editors and reporters in turn created a new sort of implied reader. "Advice and Answers" was a public

[37] Giliarovskii, "Moskva gazetnaia," 107.
[38] *ML*, June 4, 1882; June 8, 1882.

court and popular conscience combined, and its powerful resonance among the urban public was a guarantee that its moralizing tone (though not its claim to epistolary truth) would remain a part of the penny press.

The spread of popular newspapers into the provinces, soon after their appearance in the capitals, multiplied many times over the opportunities to write daily human-interest stories. The capitals' papers, sold in many provincial towns, introduced the feuilleton into the lives of townspeople throughout the country. As a result, the editors and reporters of the new provincial newspapers, which resembled the penny press in their dependence on daily street sales, were encouraged to appeal to an imagined public attracted by a modest degree of muckraking. The capitals were the center of cultural diffusion in this as in other ways. In the last decades of the nineteenth century, provincial towns became a new arena for the reading public's encounters with morality tales in human-interest form.

The process appeared so likely—and desirable—to journalists such as A. Pazukhin, one of the leading feuilleton writers of *Moskovskii listok*, that he made it the subject of one of his early articles. Called "They're Publishing a Newspaper," the story mocks the crudeness and ignorance of provincial townspeople who hear rumors that a "literary" newspaper (as opposed to an official provincial newsletter, the *vedomosti*) will be published in their town. One shopkeeper is afraid that "a newspaper like a metropolitan one will print all the inside dope and will preach morality and will criticize everything [*vyvodit kritiky*]. It'll be like a cholera epidemic." A building contractor foresees "trouble," thinking that if he keeps on beating his workers, the newspaper "will embarrass me about this and will preach a sermon [*moral' pustit'*]." A lowly servant, clearly the voice of Pazukhin's imagined reader, observes at the end of the story that "maybe it's a good thing. People here are rough, kind of wild. They commit all kinds of abuses, and now they'll quiet down."[39] Pazukhin implies that a boulevard newspaper will become the cultural catalyst in the provinces for a sort of everyday civic consciousness. Beneath the satirical style, his tale suggests also that he welcomed this responsibility.

Though a sense of moral mission may also have driven this muckraking, commercial considerations—stimulating public interest in buying the newspapers—were certainly uppermost in the minds of the editors. Publishing conditions in the provincial capitals, though rougher, resembled those of the metropolitan centers of the empire. Censorship lay in the hands of administrative officials and hence was more arbitrary, yet censors had to allow considerable latitude to their local papers in daily affairs. The vox populi of the provinces spoke less forcefully, but its demands and expectations seem to have been as diverse as those of the Moscow public.

---

[39] A. Pazukhin, "Gazetu izdaiut (Ocherki iz zhizni provintsii)," *ML*, January 21, 1882.

We possess a substantial amount of information on the emergence of mass print culture in the Volga town of Samara in the 1890s, thanks to the presence on one of the two local papers there of a young writer beginning to call himself Maksim Gorky. The newspapers had been in existence for several years when Gorky arrived in early 1895 at the age of twenty-six to work for *Samarskaia gazeta* (Samara Gazette). He remained for over a year, writing extensively and even serving briefly as editor. He specialized in human-interest stories, choosing, as was customary, to write under an imaginative pseudonym (Iegudiil Khlamyda). Despite his later scorn for the profession, he quickly took on the role of muckraking reporter, denouncing minor abuses and misdeeds and appealing to a communitarian ethic identified with his reading public.

In Samara, as elsewhere, journalists and editors had by inclination and by necessity to arouse the interest of the weak and unprivileged. Despite censorship and the pressure from influential local townspeople, they were tempted to become witness and judge to everyday conflicts. Some were clearly driven by a moral commitment to justice; others simply responded to the readers' interest. Their dramatization of daily life, usually in the form of the human-interest story, followed the model of papers such as *Moskovskii listok*, mingling fact and fiction but adhering closely to the folksy style of popular speech. The events were situated in familiar local settings. Sometimes they involved thoughtless, abusive, or cruel action, which under the newspapers' public scrutiny became reprehensible behavior. In Samara's other paper, *Samarskii vestnik* (Samara Herald), the writer of human-interest stories (under the name "Sphinx") wrote a column entitled "Trivia of a Townsperson's Life." Often his stories were simple entertainment, but at times they assumed an admonitory tone similar to that of "Advice and Answers." On one occasion he pilloried a pretentious merchant on the town council; on another he criticized a doctor for failing to aid a needy patient; and yet another time he called for the punishment of a well-to-do townsman whose horse had run over a small boy.

Gorky's own articles carried on the work of his predecessor as feuilleton writer, S. S. Gusev, who wrote under the pseudonym "The Verb" (Slovo glagol'). Gusev had written a large number of admonitory stories appealing to the conscience of his readers to judge local events. One story described a husband's public beating of his wife, to the amusement of an audience of townspeople. These "daily practices," Gusev observes, "confirm the teaching that 'you can do anything with a wife.'" The story concludes with the simple question "Is it just?"[40]

Gorky fit well into the garb of moral crusader as well as publicist and reporter, all of which came with the job of helping a struggling provincial

[40] *Samarskaia gazeta*, July 5, 1895.

newspaper. His journalistic personage of Iegudiil Khlamyda, public censor of provincial daily life, appeared several months after his arrival. His stories told of poor residents whose shanties were to be torn down by the "millionaires" of the municipal council, of students beaten by a gang of toughs, or of poor street traders without protection against the weather. His articles followed closely the model of the serious human-interest story in both style and content; and in their own small way, they helped to sustain in this provincial newspaper a level of moral discourse reminiscent of the popular Moscow and St. Petersburg newspapers.

Gorky himself created in Samara the journalistic "trouble" anticipated in 1882 by Pazukhin's fictitious provincial townspeople. In a well-documented incident, he aroused the ire of a town manufacturer whom Iegudiil Khlamyda had denounced for the injury of a worker. The outraged manufacturer accused him in a public letter of a "vile lie" and appealed to the provincial authorities for support. The paper subsequently received a formal reprimand from the censor.[41] Gorky had carried muckraking beyond the limits tolerated by tsarist officials. This quarrel, like other incidents that led to costly official reprimands of popular newspapers, personalized the issues around the action of the journalist. Yet on the fringes of this conflict lurked the implied reader—to whom Gorky, as much as any other feuilleton writer of the penny press, attributed a civic morality and a communitarian moral code.

If one were to judge solely by the comments Gorky made then and later on newspaper work, one might easily conclude that his writing in Samara was little better than the "literary bromide" of *Moskovskii listok* that he recalled having served as a boy to his philistine relatives. Occasionally he explicitly created imaginary newspaper readers, who appear in various guises to give voice to his views of culture and the mission of the writer. After a stint as editor of his paper, he wrote a satirical story about the experience entitled "A Few Days in the Role of Editor of a Provincial Newspaper (Translated from the American)." Confronted by an array of readers—all distinctly provincial Russian types—who present wild or absurd demands, the fictitious American editor concludes that "each town resident [*obyvatel'*] has a definite opinion of the press," which is expected to meet his or her personal needs and interests.[42] Samara readers found in his story a reflection of themselves as a provincial public unable to rise above its petty concerns to appreciate the public role of the press. But the

---

[41] The story and the relevant documents are included in M. Gork'ii (Iegudil Khlamida), *Mezhdu prochim: Fel'etony, 1895–1896* (Kuibyshev, 1941), 308–9.

[42] "Neskol'ko dnei v roli redaktora provintsial'noi gazety: Prekrasnaia tema dlia ostroumnykh liudei (Perevod s amerikanskogo)," in *Gor'kii v Samare*, ed. M. O. Chechanovskii (Moscow, 1938), 174. This volume contains a selection of Gorky's articles from his Samara days.

satire was incomplete, for it made no provision for those readers to whom Gorky addressed his human-interest stories and from whom he anticipated sympathetic understanding of civic issues.

If the boulevard press did indeed promote (albeit intermittently) a low-key moral discourse of communitarian equity, one may well ask why such newspapers were held in low esteem by intellectuals and writers, even some who had at one time worked for these papers. Part of the answer must lie in the material constraints that forced these papers to produce pages of ephemeral news in a constant struggle to stay alive. A second reason lies in the very close contact between the penny press and a diverse public, which could not be reduced to any one implied reader. This ordinary public, usually identified by the demeaning term *obyvateli* (residents), was not a welcome presence by the side (or looking over the shoulder) of the lofty writer. From the point of view of the defenders of Russian literary culture, the public and the journalist represented an unholy pair. The alliance of the two demeaned the true calling of writer and debased the cultural life of the country.

Gorky, summing up his impressions of a year in Samara, concluded that the local residents "treat the newspaper suspiciously and capriciously," demanding at times entertainment and at other times "something useful and good—but it is very difficult to define their views on the good and useful." It seemed to him that, as a result of this confusion, the newspaper took a "defensive stance toward the readers, always expecting to be attacked from all sides by a whole fusillade of objections, corrections, and [letters beginning] 'a few words in regard to. . . .'"[43] Gorky, like so many other writers aspiring to a voice in Russian high culture, preferred to control the message. Monologue was their model of writing.

A third reason for Russian intellectuals' hostility toward the message of the penny press—perhaps the most important—lies in the deep disdain they felt toward popular culture. In the late 1890s Gorky himself, newly converted to high culture, damned the penny press for exercising, as did other mass cultural products, a deplorable moral influence. He dedicated a lengthy essay to "The Reader," idealizing this personage whom he wishfully imagined to be in search of writings "to create in [man] a longing for truth; to combat what is evil in man and discover what is good in him." To do so, the writer had the obligation to avoid "encumbering people's memory with the trash of photographic images of their lives."[44] Where else but in boulevard newspapers were "trashy photographic images" to be found? The sacred mission of the true writer was incompatible with the vocation of journalist.

[43] "Samara vo vsekh otnosheniiakh (Pis'mo odnogo stranstvuiushchego rytsaria)," *Samarskaia gazeta*, March 13, 1896.

[44] "Chitatel'," in *Sobranie sochinenii* (Moscow, 1949), 2:195, 202.

A few years later, the noted writer Kornei Chukovsky delivered an even stronger condemnation of cultural profit making. Referring to the new industry of cinematography but in words that applied equally well to the penny press, he attacked the "mass, vulgar [*stadnyi*] taste" that, he claimed, characterized "any market product" obliged to "adopt the tastes of its consumer." He deplored particularly the fact that the author lost control over the creative process. The cultural product, to be salable, had to become merely "the creation of the public."[45] Whether in the form of image or text, popular culture in its marketed form was antithetical, in Chukovsky's opinion, to both the autonomous role of the writer-cum-critic and the writer's fidelity to meaningful ethical standards. In a real sense, his criticism supposed that authentic cultural creativity required that the audience (reader) be controlled by the author.

In this context, the Russian penny press symbolized all that was abhorrent and threatening to the defenders of high culture. Their enemy was the newspaper editor as capitalist, and their hero was the writer-intellectual defending morality against vulgarity. The terms by which the intellectuals defined the issues and the history of the confrontation tell us a great deal about the intelligentsia's cultural models in late tsarist Russia. They reveal nothing at all about the dynamic impact of the popular press as a medium of communication and a locus of cultural change. We need to be prepared, as most educated Russians were not, to distinguish between civilization and culture, and to recognize that the appearance of a mass reading public in Russian cities was, in its own way, as important a phenomenon in Russian cultural history as the rise of the intelligentsia.

This study of the creation of a public language of communitarian ethics in the pages of the Russian boulevard newspapers is a part of the larger story of the evolution of those patterns of symbolic knowledge, perception, and representation that we term Russian popular culture. The evidence offered here suggests that the reader occupied a prominent place in the work of journalists and editors. Their attention to the literary genre of human-interest story is understandable if we view their writing as a dialogue with their reading public, whose presence emerged most clearly in these stories. Roger Chartier's observations on the "multiple practices" of popular culture are relevant here.[46] The entrepreneurial editor like Pastukhov found his own interests well served by highlighting popular grievances and speaking in the voice of popular, communitarian justice.

The mild muckraking in the Russian penny press is particularly noteworthy when we recall the political tenor of those times. This press emerged in a period of political reaction and authoritarian control of the

---

[45] K. Chukovskii, *Sobranie sochinenii* (Moscow, 1966), 6:126–27.
[46] See n. 7 above.

press. Nonetheless, it was able to carve out an important place for itself in the print culture of the time. It did so through its ability to establish its own links with its readers and to define, in many different forms, the public interest of everyday events. The human-interest stories created one of those bonds and gave new publicity to a moral language by which to judge persons and events. In the process, the public sphere in Russia encompassed a much larger audience than previously. These stories relied on a set of moral values, never clearly defined and constantly revised. This ethical code did not possess the logical rigor of radical ideology or the punitive force of the authoritarian culture of the tsarist state. Between these two powerful voices, however, the ephemeral words of the penny press constituted both a reflection of and an influential force in the creation of urban culture in the turbulent years of late tsarist Russia.

9

WORKER-AUTHORS AND THE

CULT OF THE PERSON

Mark D. Steinberg

ONCEPTIONS OF the person are often central to the ways people reason about ethics, rights, and justice. These conceptions are not the same everywhere. In various cultures individuals are defined as people mainly by their status or social role, by their age or gender, or by the particular relationships into which they enter. This relativist image of the person has been opposed, most strongly in cultures that have been heir to the Western classical and Judeo-Christian cultural tradition, by a view of the individual as a particular incarnation of a generalized category of personhood—the notion of "man" as both individual and collectivity—without regard to status or situation.[1]

These differing conceptions of the person are deeply intertwined with social ethics. In particular, the idea that all people share a common nature, with which they are endowed simply by virtue of their being human,

I wish to thank Tony Anemone, Daniel Brower, Stephen Frank, Jane Hedges, Richard Miller, Bernice Glatzer Rosenthal, Robert Rothstein, Richard Stites, and William Todd for their comments on earlier drafts of this essay. I am also grateful for financial assistance from the International Research and Exchanges Board, the Social Science Research Council, and Yale University.

[1] For a discussion of the development of anthropological and sociological studies of the category of the person and its relationship to morality, see Michael Carrithers, Steven Collins, and Steven Lukes, eds., *The Category of the Person: Anthropology, Philosophy, History* (Cambridge, 1985); Clifford Geertz, " 'From the Native's Point of View': On the Nature of Anthropological Understanding," in *Local Knowledge* (New York, 1983), 55–70; and Richard A. Shweder, *Thinking through Cultures: Expeditions in Cultural Psychology* (Cambridge, 1991), 113–85. For influential studies by a psychologist arguing for the importance of ideas about the self in moral reasoning, see the writings of Lawrence Kohlberg, especially *Essays in Moral Development*, 2 vols. (New York, 1981, 1983). A rare social-historical study using the concept of the person is David Warren Sabean, *Power in the Blood: Popular Culture and Village Discourse in Early Modern Germany* (Cambridge, 1984), esp. 30–36. Michel Foucault, during his last years, also began to explore the historical importance of ideas about the self in the "genealogy of ethics." See his interview in Hubert L. Dreyfus and Paul Rabinow, *Michel Foucault: Beyond Structuralism and Hermeneutics*, 2d ed. (Chicago, 1983), 229–52.

defines the person as a moral category, a value in and of itself against which social structures and relationships can be judged. In reality, there has been great tension in Western societies between universalistic and particularistic ethics—especially socially situated, racial, and gender-bound ethics.[2] Still, and precisely because it has been so imperfectly realized, the universalized notion of the person has played a vital role in making conflicts over social and political arrangements into moral battles.

This essay describes and examines the place of such a universalized category of the person in the discourse of Russian workers in the early twentieth century. I focus on a particular group of workers: those who wrote, especially for other workers, whether as essayists, story writers, or poets. Historians of Russian labor have frequently mentioned workers' demands for "polite address" and, more generally, to be treated as befit their worth as "human beings."[3] These challenges to "humiliation and insult" (unizhenie i oskorblenie), however, were very often not merely points on a list of demands, but were at the heart of an ethical vision by which many workers judged the entirety of social and political life. At the core of this ethics, though often stated indirectly, was the liberal belief in the natural and equal worth and hence rights of the individual person as a human being. The natural dignity and rights of the individual, not the particularistic interests of a class, became the foundation of social judgment and their realization the measure of a just society. Indeed, in the view of one observer of working-class attitudes, a full-blown "cult of the person" (kul't lichnosti or kul't cheloveka) existed in the discourse of Russian workers.[4]

---

[2] This tension is minimized in many of the works cited above, which often disregard the ways in which the universalistic conception of personhood in the West has been compromised by distinctions based on class, gender, and race. Some aspects of this tension are examined, from a philosophical perspective, in Richard Eldridge, On Moral Personhood: Philosophy, Literature, Criticism, and Self-Understanding (Chicago, 1989).

[3] V. F. Shishkin, Tak skladyvalas' revoliutsionnaia moral': Istoricheskii ocherk (Moscow, 1967); Reginald E. Zelnik, "Russian Bebels," Russian Review 35, no. 3 (July 1976): 265, 272–77; Victoria E. Bonnell, Roots of Rebellion: Workers' Politics and Organizations in St. Petersburg and Moscow, 1900–1914 (Berkeley, 1983), 43–72, 90, 102, 170–71, 183–84, 191, 264, 449, 452; Tim McDaniel, Autocracy, Capitalism, and Revolution in Russia (Berkeley, 1988), 161, 169–74, 194–95; Leopold H. Haimson, "The Problem of Social Identities in Early Twentieth Century Russia," Slavic Review, Spring 1988, esp. 2–8; Mark D. Steinberg, Moral Communities: The Culture of Class Relations in the Russian Printing Industry, 1867–1907 (Berkeley, 1992), 235–36, 242–45.

[4] L. M. Kleinbort, "Ocherki rabochei demokratii," parts 1, 5, Sovremennyi mir, March, November 1913, 32–44, 178–85 (for use of the term, see 182, 185). This term was earlier used by Emile Durkheim. See "L'Individualisme et les intellectuels" (1898), trans. Steven Lukes, Political Studies 17, no. 1 (March 1969): 19–30. Although Kleinbort employs kul't cheloveka in quotation marks, he mentions no source.

The pervasiveness in workers' writings of universalistic notions of the natural dignity and rights of the worker as a human being is only half the story, however. Equally important is how workers interpreted and used these ideas. For it is clear that as they tried to give public voice to their experiences, anger, and ideals, to make sense of their own lives, and to communicate this to others, they made distinctive uses of the various ideas, metaphors, and images that came to hand, including the ethical idealization of human personhood. Paradoxically, viewed through the prism of their own and other workers' lives, the universalized ideal of the individual person often encouraged class identity and commitment to class action. Heightened feelings of self-awareness and self-worth very often stimulated workers to feel more intensely their *class* oppression. They generalized in reverse, as it were, from the dignity of all people to their own particular class humiliation. Still, this identification of the individual with the collective was ultimately ambivalent. Sacralization of the self was a powerful stimulus to individual action in collective movements, but it also subverted the idea of class with an erosive "cult" of the individual person.

Impressive numbers of Russian workers took to the pen for self-expression in the early years of the twentieth century. Well before the official promotion by the Bolshevik state of "proletarian literature," workers began writing poetry, stories, and essays and getting them published in socialist and trade-union papers, commercial newspapers and popular weeklies, and pamphlets and anthologies of workers' writings.[5] In social origins and occupation, and even in education, worker-writers were not exceptional members of their class. Although they had usually attended a rural or urban primary school for two years (a few finished four-year schools), this level of schooling was no longer exceptional among Russian workers and certainly did not propel most to become writers. Worker-writers differed from the average mainly in more personal ways—in the passion they brought to reading and in their drive to write. Before 1917, very few were able to quit their shops and survive off their literary or journalistic work. But even though they continued to labor side by side with other workers, they created a subculture in the interstices of working-class existence—reading, pondering, and writing after hours and in

---

[5] For discussion and references, see M. Gorkii, "O pisateliakh-samouchkakh" (1911), in *Sobranie sochinenii* (Moscow, 1953), 24:99–101; L. M. Kleinbort, *Ocherki narodnoi literatury (1880–1923 gg.)* (Leningrad, 1924); V. L. L'vov-Rogachevskii, *Ocherki proletarskoi literatury* (Moscow and Leningrad, 1927); and N. V. Os'makov, *Russkaia proletarskaia poeziia, 1890–1917* (Moscow, 1968).

stolen moments on the job. Not surprisingly, they often felt alienated from their less cultured fellows.[6]

The cultural marginality of worker-writers within their class, however, could also be a profound stimulus to collective identification with other workers and involvement in the class struggle. Class consciousness was often intimately bound up with workers' heightened awareness of themselves. In Jacques Rancière's words, to become class-conscious, a worker needed not to be told that he was poor and exploited—which he already knew—but to acquire "a knowledge of self that reveals to him a being dedicated to something else besides exploitation."[7] This subversive knowledge of self was most likely to be nurtured not in the depths of working-class life but at its margins, where everyday experiences of proletarian existence encountered ideas shaped in different settings, and where aspiring and questioning workers were daily reminded of the social and political barriers around them. Historians have tended to neglect the influence of such marginal types in the formation of a class. But it was precisely the ambiguous location of such workers within their own social class that made them an important conduit of ideas, vocabularies, and images across the boundary between the educated and the masses. Indeed, many believed that it was their duty to spread enlightenment and "consciousness" among other workers—echoing in a popular key the moral debt to the people felt by educated, upper-class *intelligenty*.

Literate and inquiring workers encountered the ethical ideal of universal personhood in the cultural world they shared with other social groups. Since the end of the eighteenth century, in Russia as in western Europe, public discussions of ethics and social order—in journals, newspapers, and literature—focused increasingly on the innate worth, freedom, and rights of the individual person, on *lichnost'* and its moral significance.[8] It was an article of faith among Russia's intelligentsia, from liberals even to many Marxists, that social change ought above all to promote the freedom and worth of the human person by removing the social, cultural, and political constraints that hindered the full development of the individual personality. The writings of such influential critics

---

[6] This sense of alienation is testified to in numerous memoirs. For some published examples, see P. Ia. Zavolokin, ed., *Sovremennye raboche-krest'ianskie poety* (Ivanovo-Voznesensk, 1925); and S. A. Rodov, ed., *Proletarskie pisateli* (Moscow, 1925).

[7] *The Night of the Proletarians: The Workers' Dream in Nineteenth-Century France* (Philadelphia, 1989), 20.

[8] For some examples, see George L. Kline, "Changing Attitudes Toward the Individual," in *The Transformation of Russian Society*, ed. Cyril E. Black (Cambridge, 1960), 606–25. See also Vladimir Solov'ev's entry on *lichnost'* in *Entsiklopedicheskii slovar'*, ed. F. A. Brokgaus and I. A. Efron (St. Petersburg, 1890–1907), 17:868.

of the status quo as Vissarion Belinsky, Aleksandr Herzen, Dmitrii Pisarev, Nikolai Dobroliubov, Nikolai Chernyshevsky, and Petr Lavrov resounded with this credo of personal emancipation.

But these Russian *intelligenty* insisted also on the social nature of their individualism. Most of Russia's influential social thinkers in the nineteenth century shared Lavrov's conviction that "individual dignity is maintained only by upholding the dignity of all."[9] The ideal of the "critically thinking individual," one of the central tropes of Russian radicalism, embodied this socialized individualism. Critically thinking individuals were expected, as Pisarev wrote, to assert their "originality and autonomy" against both the conventional moralities of the established state and "the mob." But the purpose of their self-assertion was to fight for social changes that would emancipate all.[10] In the 1890s and after, Nikolai Mikhailovsky and others linked this tradition explicitly to Nietzsche's ideal, increasingly influential in Russia, of the sacred and morally autonomous self reaching out beyond narrow individualism.[11] In this same vein, some Marxists, especially Anatolii Lunacharsky and Aleksandr Bogdanov, advocated what Lunacharsky called a "macropsychic individualism" in which the personal "I" is "identified with some broad and enduring 'we,'" and the vital and autonomous revolutionary hero strives not for wolfish private gain but for the progress of all humanity.[12]

Although most literate workers were likely to have been at best only faintly aware of these discussions among the educated, they encountered similar ideas about the person in more accessible and popular settings and texts. Among the more literate common readers, popular belles lettres—especially the writings of Nekrasov, Korolenko, Dostoevsky, Tolstoy, Chekhov, and Gorky—offered various presentations of the ideal of the person as a moral and sacred category. Starting in the 1890s, echoes of Nietzsche's idealization of the proud, striving, exuberant, and rebellious individual became influential among writers—including many whom workers read, notably Maksim Gorky and Leonid Andreev.[13]

[9] *Historical Letters* (1868–69), trans. and ed. James P. Scanlan (Berkeley, 1967), 113.

[10] Quoted in Kline, "Changing Attitudes," 609.

[11] See the discussions in Bernice Glatzer Rosenthal, ed., *Nietzsche in Russia* (Princeton, 1986). On Mikhailovsky, see Ann Lane, "Nietzsche Comes to Russia: Popularization and Protest in the 1890s," ibid., 63–65.

[12] A. V. Lunacharskii, "Voprosy morali i M. Meterlink" (1904), quoted in Kline, "Changing Attitudes," 619. See also A. V. Lunacharskii, "Meshchanstvo i individualizm" (1909), in *Meshchanstvo i individualizm: Sbornik statei* (Moscow and Petrograd, 1923), 5–136.

[13] See especially Lane, "Nietzsche Comes to Russia"; Mary Louise Loe, "Gorky and Nietzsche: The Quest for the Russian Superman"; and Edith Clowes, "Literary Reception as Vulgarization: Nietzsche's Idea of the Superman in Neo-Realist Fiction," all in Rosenthal, *Nietzsche in Russia*. Of course, Nietzsche was not the only source of "Nietzschean" ideas.

Gorky's stories, in particular, were filled with vital, restless, freedom-seeking individuals—plebeian supermen—living and wandering on the fringes of society, challenging established moralities and authorities, and condemning the slavish submissiveness of the masses.[14]

Workers did not need to have read Pisarev, Mikhailovsky, or Gorky, however, to be encouraged to think about the worth and importance of the human individual. As Jeffrey Brooks has described, the popular commercial print media increasingly set before common readers images of the degradation and humiliation that individuals so often suffered in Russia and models of autonomous moral choice and individual achievement. Tales of bandits and adventurers, especially, had popularized among a wide Russian audience positive images of "self-assertive and superior individuals," of rebellious outsiders challenging authority.[15] Even if we question Brooks's view that commercial publishers and writers accurately reflected popular values in order to sell their books and newspapers—popular readers were perfectly capable of disregarding the message when the medium was sufficiently appealing, so the message need not necessarily have coincided with their actual views—it is clear that commercial literature exposed lower-class readers to a popularized version of the same cult of the person that so preoccupied educated readers and writers.

Most telling, some workers themselves interpreted Russia's literary and intellectual heritage as devoted to elevating and defending the human person. Nikolai Liashko, one of Russia's best-known worker-writers, portrayed the entire corpus of Russian literature as fighting a heroic struggle "for the oppressed and humiliated, for truth and the dignity of the person."[16] Ivan Kubikov, a compositor turned literary critic and union activist, writing in the paper of the St. Petersburg printers' union in 1909, likewise found the most important "teaching" in Gogol's writings to be that "one must not forget one's human dignity."[17] Kubikov similarly viewed Belinsky as having taught chiefly "the dignity and social worth of man" and having shown how social conditions in Russia "hinder the development of the human person [*lichnost'*]."[18] It was not only

---

Dostoevsky, in particular, voiced many similar ideas. See Mihajlo Mihajlov, "The Great Catalyzer," ibid.

[14] For a discussion of Gorky's attitude toward the individual in the light of Nietzsche's ideas, see Loe, "Gorky and Nietzsche."

[15] Jeffrey Brooks, *When Russia Learned to Read: Literacy and Popular Literature, 1861–1917* (Princeton, 1985); idem, "Competing Modes of Popular Discourse: Individualism and Class Consciousness in the Russian Print Media," in *Culture et révolution*, ed. M. Ferro and S. Fitzpatrick (Paris, 1989), 71–81.

[16] *Ogni*, no. 3 (January 1913): 27.

[17] I. Dement'ev [Kubikov], "N. V. Gogol'," *Pechatnoe delo*, no. 5 (March 21, 1909): 9

[18] Kvadrat [Kubikov], "V. G. Belinskii," *Novoe pechatnoe delo*, no. 1 (June 16, 1911): 3–6.

readers of Gogol and Belinsky who were considered equipped to understand this ideal. It was seen as pervading Russia's public printed discourse: "The recognition of the human personality [*lichnost'*]," a type compositor observed in 1903, is a principle about which "we read and set type every day."[19]

Awareness of degrading social discrimination pervaded the poetry, stories, and essays that workers wrote. Indeed, authorship itself served as an act of personal and social self-assertion. The very practice of workers writing implicitly challenged their ascription as lower class, violating the conventional divisions between manual and intellectual labor and between popular culture and the literary high culture. Thus, it was appropriate that worker-writers almost invariably adopted an established literary style rather than a folk or plebeian style. Instead of echoing the rhythms and vocabulary of peasant songs and rhymes, worker-poets typically imitated popular established writers, especially Pushkin, Nekrasov, Nikitin, and Nadson; foreign writers like Whitman and Verhaeren; and occasionally, though rarely, contemporary poets like Blok and Briusov. And instead of telling stories in the manner of the folktale—a style often adopted by radical intellectuals who sought to appeal to the common people—worker prose writers were more likely to emulate Turgenev, Korolenko, or Chekhov.

Writing in the language of one's betters was, if only half-consciously, a subversive gesture. High literary style was an emblem of the culture from which workers were excluded. Thus, in Russia as elsewhere, "workers' poetry was not at first an echo of popular speech but an initiation into the sacred language, the forbidden and fascinating language of others."[20] Its fascination derived precisely from its sanctified position in the established culture. Its otherness made it a symbol of workers' subordination and exclusion and made cultural imitation also appropriation, a half-conscious act of self-assertion and social rebellion. The reverence with which workers often regarded the printed word reflected this function of challenging boundaries.

The content of workers' writings also challenged the social divide that set workers apart as different. Workers spoke explicitly of the egalitarian idea of "all-human dignity" (*obshchechelovecheskoe dostoinstvo*).[21] This was a pervading theme, for example, in *Naborshchik* (The Compositor), the first legal workers' paper in Russia and the only one before 1905. The compositors who contributed essays and poems to this widely read

---

[19] *Naborshchik* 1, no. 52 (October 26, 1903): 796. See also no. 19 (March 9, 1903): 313.

[20] Jacques Rancière, "Ronds de fumée (Les poètes ouvriers dans la France de Louis-Philippe)," *Revue des sciences humaines*, no. 190 (April–June 1983): 33.

[21] For example, in the tavern workers' paper *Chelovek*, no. 1 (February 13, 1911): 1.

weekly endlessly repeated variations on this leitmotif: "We are people like any other"; we are "men and not machines;" those in authority must "respect the human dignity in each of us;" "the rights of the worker, as a human being, must not be trampled upon."[22] Workers who wrote before 1905 invariably dwelled on their sufferings: exhaustion, hunger, illness, and death. Egor Nechaev, for example, a worker in a provincial glass factory, penned dozens of poems describing the physical and psychic torments he experienced: painful weariness from work and from lack of sleep, harsh treatment, cruel beatings. Thoughts of suicide, mentioned in many workers' autobiographies and creative writings, were emblematic. In a poem Nechaev first drafted in 1881, a group of young apprentices discuss throwing themselves into the river: "That would be the thing—to die, to sleep."[23] Death was symbolic sometimes of escape, as here, but often of suffering. Many workers' writings contained images of death, especially of the young, reflecting the realities of disease and physical harm in workers' lives as well as the ready understandability of death as a symbol of personal injury. Many workers' poems were literally dirges. At a literary evening for printers in St. Petersburg in the summer of 1903, several workers read aloud mournful and fatalistic verses portraying workers dying of work-induced tuberculosis.[24] Nechaev repeatedly returned in his writings to the memory of the beating death of a boy, a fellow apprentice and a friend, by a factory foreman.[25]

Such a melancholy view of working-class life, in the view of Soviet literary critics, was not truly "proletarian," though they admitted it was widespread among worker-writers (especially, they claimed, before the 1905 revolution and among workers of recent peasant background). Soviet critics purged this grim aesthetic from the orthodox canon by defining "true" proletarian poetry ideologically, as expressing a certain worldview—positive, confident, militant, and collectivist—rather than sociologically, as poetry written by workers.[26]

---

[22] *Naborshchik* 1, no. 5 (December 1, 1902): 89; no. 8 (December 22, 1902): 134; no. 15 (February 9, 1903): 251; no. 19 (March 9, 1903): 313; no. 46 (September 14, 1903): 694. Many such examples could be cited.

[23] "Na raboty" (1881; first published 1919), in *U istokov russkoi proletarskoi poezii* (Moscow, 1965), 43. See also "Na rabote" (1880; revised for its first publication in 1920), ibid., 40.

[24] *Naborshchik* 1, no. 45 (September 7, 1903): 682. See also no. 49 (October 5, 1903): 745.

[25] See especially "Pered shabashom" (1880) in *U istokov*, 40–41; and "Bublik," in Egor Nechaev, *Gutari: Izbrannaia proza* (Moscow, 1938), 7–12.

[26] See, for example, Valerian Polianskii [P. I. Lebedev], "Motivy rabochei poezii" (1918), in his *Na literaturnom fronte* (Moscow, 1924), 23–28; L'vov-Rogachevskii, *Ocherki proletarskoi literatury* 14; Os'makov, *Russkaia proletarskaia poeziia*, 50–51, 69–70, 100; and "Proletarskaia poeziia," in *Istoriia russkoi literatury* (Leningrad, 1983), 4:396–97.

This political manipulation of the definition of proletarian perception, however, mistook attention to the sorrowing self as a passive response to life. In the face of censorship, simply chronicling workers' sufferings could imply a challenge and a protest. To be sure, there was plenty of self-pity, sublimation of anger into fantasies of escape, and even explicit pleas for sympathy and help from above.[27] But undertones of anger were already clearly visible before 1905, and frequent allusions to dreams of "freedom" and "justice" and denunciations of pervading "evil" partly belied the humble tone of most poems.

Class identity and social protest certainly became more evident in workers' writings in 1905 and after. But consciousness of class and consciousness of self were perceptions that were not necessarily in conflict. On the contrary, articulate workers persistently interpreted class oppression and class struggle as concerned above all with human worth and dignity. Worker-publicists and worker-poets typically directed their critical voices not against the class structure per se, but rather against the harm it inflicted on people's lives and spirits—the damage it caused to workers' personalities, to *lichnost'*. "One must stand at all the crossroads," wrote the compositor-publicist Stepan Tsorn in July 1905, "and shout that the strong are suffocating the weak. Let everyone know that . . . force still rules over the human person [*lichnost' cheloveka*]."[28] The worker's right to be treated as a human being was seen as fundamental. Repeatedly during the struggles of 1905 and after, workers reiterated that they were "human beings," not "cattle," "machines," or "slaves." This identity was treated as the essential and legitimating source of their rights. The universal right to "live as human beings" was viewed as necessitated by historical progress: "We live in the twentieth century," wrote the worker-publicist Savelii Degterev in August 1905, "when the human person [*lichnost' cheloveka*] is completely free and when every manifestation of a person's autonomy ought to be welcomed by every thinking person." This right was also seen as grounded in Western culture, especially in the ethical teachings of Christianity: Christ, Degterev insisted, "preached His whole life the freedom of the person [*svoboda lichnosti*]."[29] Variations on these themes pervaded workers' writings in 1905 and after.[30]

[27] See, for example, *Naborshchik* 1, no. 45 (September 7, 1903): 682. Such pleas appear at times to have been ironic, however.

[28] *Pechatnyi vestnik*, 1905, no. 4 (July 24): 5.

[29] *Pechatnyi vestnik*, 1905, no. 9 (August 28): 8.

[30] For some typical examples, see *Pechatnyi vestnik*, 1905, no. 3 (June 23): 21–23; no. 11 (September 11): 3, 7; *Vestnik pechatnikov*, 1906, no. 3 (May 9): 4; no. 5 (May 20): 3, 5; no. 6 (May 28): 2–3; *Pechatnik*, 1906, no. 3 (May 14): 12–13; no. 8 (July 23): 6–7; Egor Nechaev, "Golos dushi," *Zhurnal dlia vsekh*, 1906, no. 2:66, reprinted in *U istokov*, 88; *Bulochnik*, no. 3 (March 12, 1906): 39–40; and *Metallist*, 1912, no. 8 (January 13): 8

The 1905 revolution itself, as many saw it, was the moment not only when Russian workers first came together as a class, but when they were reborn as people. "Baker!" read an essay in their trade-union paper in 1906—appropriately, on the anniversary of the abolition of serfdom in Russia—"You are a Human Being [Chelovek]. From now on you will be a Human Being. Consider 1905 the year of your creation [tvorenie]."[31] The leaders of the Moscow tavern workers' union emphasized the same point by naming their union paper "Man" (Chelovek), ironically appropriating the customer's conventional term of address for waiters in order to remind people that the tavern worker is not simply a " 'man' in quotation marks" but a "living human person" (zhivaia chelovecheskaia lichnost') whose "human dignity" (obshchechelovecheskoe dostoinstvo) must be respected.[32] The seemingly simple identification of the worker as a human being was, in Russia as elsewhere, a universalizing image of the individual person that implicitly questioned the natural justice of social subordination.

Exploitation, in this light, was treated in workers' poems, essays, and other writings not simply as an unequal economic relationship, but also as an insult to workers' personality (lichnost')—as "moral oppression," in the words of the printer Ivan Kubikov.[33] Illustrations of the suffering personality were plentiful: lost childhoods;[34] dreams "tortured by exhaustion";[35] the anguish of a mother watching her children starve;[36] the sexual abuse of working women—"white slaves" whose "feelings of human dignity were trampled in the dirt";[37] the suicide of a young woman raped by her employer;[38] the frustrated sexuality of male workers from the village who could not afford to keep their wives with them in the city;[39] the pervasive violence as well as maimings and death that often occurred in factories.[40] Premature death continued to be both a real and literary expression of the denial of workers' "right to live as a human being."[41] So was suicide. The "epidemic" of suicides around 1910 among

[31] *Bulochnik*, no. 1 (February 19, 1906): 8.

[32] *Chelovek*, no. 1 (February 13, 1911): 1.

[33] *Pechatnoe delo*, no. 24 (September 11, 1910): 2.

[34] Egor Nechaev, "Bezrabotnyi" (published in 1909 and again in 1922) and "Moia pesnia" (1906), both in *U istokov*, 48, 92.

[35] F. Gavrilov, "Son," in *Proletarskie poety*, vol. 1, ed. A. Dymshchits (Leningrad, 1935), 197–201.

[36] Stepan Bruskov, in *Rodnye vesti*, 1911, no. 3 (4): 5–6.

[37] *Golos portnogo*, no. 1–2 (May 10, 1910): 10.

[38] N. Ivanov, in *Pervyi sbornik proletarskikh pisatelei* (St. Petersburg, 1914), 56–61.

[39] *Bulochnik*, no. 2 (February 26, 1906): 20–22.

[40] *Metallist*, 1911, no. 4 (November 10): 7–8; *Pechatnoe delo*, no. 24 (September 11, 1910): 3–4.

[41] *Pechatnyi vestnik*, 1906, no. 1 (February 12): 2; *Pechatnik*, 1906, no. 1 (April 23): 12; *Vestnik pechatnikov*, 1906, no. 6 (May 28): 3.

tailoring workers, for example, was explained not by poverty and unemployment—since conditions were in fact relatively good—but by workers' feelings that life had become a "big, dark, empty and cold barn" in
which there was "no one whom they may tell of their insults."[42]

The suffering self, which remained a prominent image in workers'
writings and which drew variously upon Christian, radical, and romantic
traditions, was increasingly a matter of pride. Especially after 1905,
many worker-poets considered "singing of suffering" to be an expression
not of passive resignation, as Soviet critics would later suggest, but of
honor and defiance. "Don't expect happy tunes from me / Friend, I cannot comfort you / I learned to sing in menacing times / With sorrow in my
mind and soul."[43] "I am a bard of the working masses / My song is not to
be envied / I sing of neither flowers nor the sun."[44] Personal injury was
portrayed as the essence of the worker's class experience. Suffering both
defined and ennobled a worker, and it cast reproach on the established
social order.

Although most workers' writings were solemn in tone, a number of
worker-writers perceived the subversive and transgressive power of satire
and humor. Laughter, by its nature, can be life-affirming and self-confi-
dent;[45] but it can also be a weapon of criticism targeting especially personal indignities and social boundaries.[46] Thus, it is not surprising that
satire and humor were regular and popular features of trade-union papers in Russia between 1905 and 1917.[47] In 1907, printing workers established a short-lived journal devoted entirely to humor.[48] From 1909

[42] *Golos portnogo*, no. 3 (July 10, 1910): 3–4, 8. See also Petr Zaitsev (a shoemaker who
briefly published and did most of the writing for this magazine for the common reader), in
Kolotushka, 1911, no. 1: 3; no. 2: 4; and M. Chernysheva (a seamstress and salesclerk who
wrote under the name "Baba Mar'ia"), in *Dumy narodnye*, no. 7 (March 13, 1910): 5.

[43] Egor Nechaev, "Mne khotelos' by pesniu svobodnuiu pet'" (1906), in *U istokov*, 89.

[44] A. Pomorskii, "Pesnia," *Metallist*, 1913, no. 4 (28) (July 3): 4.

[45] In 1895, Dmitrii Merezhkovsky predicted that a "reign of godlike men, eternally laughing, like the sun, will exist on earth." D. Merezhkovskii, "Otverzhenyi," *Severnyi vestnik*,
1895, no. 6: 53–54, quoted in Bernice Glatzer Rosenthal, "Stages of Nietzscheanism:
Merezhkovsky's Intellectual Evolution," in Rosenthal, *Nietzsche in Russia*, 73.

[46] A. V. Lunacharskii, "O smekhe" (1931), in *Sobranie sochinenii* (Moscow, 1963–67),
8:531–38 (first printed in *Literaturnyi kritik*, 1935, no. 4 [April]); Mikhail Bakhtin, *Rabelais and His World* (Cambridge, Mass., 1965). Incidentally, during the last days of Soviet
communism, citizens frequently took their well-developed, iconoclastic political laughter
into the streets—as when crowds gathered around an empty pedestal in front of the Com-
munist party headquarters in Tallinn, from which a large bronze statue of Lenin had just
been toppled, and laughed raucously. *New York Times*, August 24, 1991, 1.

[47] L. Kleinbort, "Ocherki rabochei demokratii," *Sovremennyi mir*, August 1913, 190–91.

[48] Called at first *Balda*, the journal was renamed *Topor* when it reregistered after being
closed by the government. The titles were terms in printers' jargon referring to drinking
customs. *Balda* was also the name of a figure in Russian folklore, a worker whose mocking
punishment of an avaricious priest-employer was retold in a famous poem by Pushkin.

until the war, a number of satirical periodicals appeared, directed at a wide popular audience and edited by self-described *samorodki*—a term used to describe uneducated but gifted common people who had become authors or artists.[49]

In satirical writings, as in more earnest pieces, worker-humorists sought to shame the institutions, classes, and individuals that humiliated them as people. Worker-satirists laughed most heartily at those who used their power to degrade workers, who treated workers as if they were less than human. For example, in a feuilleton that extended over two issues of the printers' journal *Balda*, a female teacher was lampooned for befriending a compositor when she did not know he was a worker, but rudely acting as if she had never even met him when she discovered him at work in a shop where she had come to place an order for calling cards.[50] Worker-writers were determined to respond to the "insults of the bourgeois," as one worker-poet put it, with a "free proletarian laugh."[51]

The assertion and defense of workers' human worth was not simply *class* criticism in a moral key. Self-criticism was no less pervasive, for it was the condition of the self that was most essential. Drunkenness was particularly targeted. In the words of one worker—who in 1905 would be killed during the march to the Winter Palace on Bloody Sunday— drunkenness was "a great and powerful evil, tongs, which disfigure [*uroduiut*] a man once they grab hold of him."[52] Sobriety was linked to the larger pursuit of "culture." Worker-writers continually called for more "culture," "knowledge," and "personal development" among workers, and condemned drunkenness, obscenity, swearing, card playing, and other "unseemly behavior."[53]

This critique of workers' morality became especially forceful in the difficult years between 1907 and 1912. Satirical writings often shamed

---

[49] For example, *Balagur* (Moscow, 1910–14), *Dolina* (Moscow, 1910–12), *Balalaika* (Moscow, 1910–11), *Boi-rozhok* (Moscow, 1911–14), *Ostriak: Kopeika-zlodeika* (Moscow, 1909–14), *Rodnoi gusliar* (Moscow, 1910–11), and *Veselyi skomorokh* (Moscow, 1911–13). Satire was also used frequently in other journals edited and authored by *samorodki* (in some cases identifiable as former workers) and directed at common readers, such as the worker M. A. Loginov's *Dumy narodnye* (Moscow, 1910–12).

[50] *Balda*, no. 2 (January 9, 1907): 5–6; no. 3 (January 16, 1907): 4–5.

[51] *Balda*, no. 1 (January 7, 1907): 2. This intent was also expressed in the journal's motto, "In laughter there is strength [*smekh-sila*]"—a wry but respectful echo of the ubiquitous workers' slogan "In unity there is strength."

[52] *Naborshchik* 1, no. 34 (June 22, 1903): 534.

[53] See, for example, *Naborshchik i pechatnyi mir*, 1905, no. 109 (May 10): 203; *Pechatnyi vestnik*, 1905, no. 6 (August 7): 4; 1906, no. 2 (February 19): 2–3; *Pechatnik*, 1906, no. 4 (May 21): 6–7; no. 8 (July 23): 16; *Pechatnoe delo* (Moscow), no. 15 (February 9, 1907): 7; *Edinstvo*, no. 15 (March 12, 1910): 11–12; *Chelovek*, no. 3 (March 27, 1911): 12; *Pechatnoe delo*, 1917, no. 3 (June 17): 7; *Pechatnik*, 1917, no. 2–3 (August 6): 5–7, 15; and no. 6 (October 28): 8.

workers for their obsessive love of vodka,[54] for lying to their wives about wages squandered on drink, for treating women as sexual objects, and for the constant profanity in their speech.[55] An essay in the paper of the St. Petersburg metalworkers' union in 1908 gloomily noted the irony that just at the moment when employers' assaults on labor were reaching the most "crude and inhuman forms," one saw among workers themselves a "growing shallowness [izmel'chanie] of proletarian thinking [and] the manifestation of base instincts."[56] Two years later, the prominent worker-leader of the metalworkers' union, Fedor Bulkin, wrote a stinging indictment of workers' "moral nonchalance" (nravstvennyi khalatnost'), dishonesty, crass literary tastes (Pinkertonovshchina), and generally the "flourishing of low instincts" among workers. Like other Marxists, Bulkin blamed society and especially the autocratic state for "dehumanizing" workers, but also insisted that workers and especially their leaders must take responsibility for these effects.[57] Similarly, August Tens, a compositor well known for his many writings in trade-union papers and for his years of leadership in the St. Petersburg printers' union, insisted that drunkenness could not be dismissed as simply a product of social conditions: "Drunkenness is a disease of the will, and the will depends on reason. It is necessary to develop reason. It is all about culture."[58] And, one might add—for this was implicit—the self.

Drunkenness, undiscipline, ignorance, and a general lack of culture were condemned partly as practical obstacles hindering workers' collective struggle, as factors making workers "passive," "apathetic," "undisciplined," and unable to "stand up for their interests."[59] Taking a longer but still largely practical view, some worker-authors, like Ivan Kubikov—writing in 1909, when he was chair of the St. Petersburg printers' union—insisted that workers needed to be culturally and morally prepared for their future historical role. Quoting Ferdinand Lassalle, Kubikov maintained that since workers were the "stone upon which the church of the future will be built," that foundation needed to be strong *and polished*.

---

[54] *Balda*, no. 1 (January 7, 1907): 8; no. 2 (January 9, 1907): 4, 5–6; no. 3 (January 16, 1907): 2, 4–6. At one shop it was noted that a new athletic record had been set: workers could now run out to buy vodka and *zakuski* and be back in only four minutes (the old record was ten). Ibid., no. 2 (January 9, 1907): 7.

[55] *Balda*, no. 2 (January 9, 1907): 1, 5–7.

[56] Metallist, "Ko karakteristike nastroenii v rabochei srede," *Nadezhda*, no. 2 (September 26, 1908): 10.

[57] "Bol'noi vopros (upadok nravov v rabochei srede)," *Nash Put'*, no. 11 (December 20, 1910): 7–8.

[58] *Pechatnoe delo*, no. 13 (November 24, 1909): 10–11.

[59] *Pechatnik*, 1906, no. 1 (April 23): 11–12; *Pechatnoe delo* (Moscow), no. 15 (February 9, 1907): 7; *Protokoly pervoi vserossiiskoi konferentsii soiuzov rabochikh pechatnogo dela* (St. Petersburg, 1907), 80, 82, 109.

More immediately, Kubikov argued, echoing a view held by many activists, workers' "class consciousness" was closely connected with their "cultural consciousness": every lecture on science and every reading of a classic work of literature led workers to "understand the order of things."[60]

Moral and cultural backwardness, however, were denounced not only on the pragmatic grounds of the needs of the class struggle, but also as inherent evils, for the harm they inflicted on the individual self. No boundary was seen separating the individual and the collective. Just as personal culture was believed to aid the class struggle, so was class struggle seen as serving the development of the individual self. Each depended on the other. Indeed, the purpose of the labor movement, many thought, was precisely to emancipate the workers' human self. Even in the midst of the 1917 revolution, workers were still to be heard blaming drunkenness not only for hindering collective action but also for "defacing the image of man" (*obezlichivaiushchee obraz cheloveka*).[61]

Activist worker-writers made every effort to link the individual and the collective. In their minds, the linkage was partly epistemological: by recognizing the equal worth of every person, they sought to highlight all the more strongly the discrimination against workers as a class. The linkage was also partly practical: they viewed class struggle as emancipating individuals from social and political constraints on their development, and viewed developed individuals as best serving the common cause. However, the tidy logic of this identification of the individual with the collective did not remove the uncertainties and tensions in the self-identities of these worker-writers themselves. This was clearly evident in the ways they wrote about themselves and especially about their will to write.

Almost invariably, workers portrayed their drive to write as reflecting a deep personal need and marking them as special individuals. The glass-worker Egor Nechaev, for example, described responding to a semimystical call that came to him when he was seventeen years old. His mother, a domestic, brought home leftovers from her employer's dinner wrapped in an old magazine that happened to contain the autobiography, portrait, and verses of the self-taught shopkeeper-poet Ivan Surikov. After feverishly reading these texts, Nechaev reported, he heard an "inner voice" advising him that he, too, could become a writer.[62] Nikolai Kuznetsov, whose parents were textile workers near Moscow, recalls that as a child left to wander the streets, he found himself uncontrollably drawn to book

[60] Kvadrat [Kubikov], "Alkogolizm i usloviia bor'by s nim," *Professional'nyi vestnik*, no. 26 (October 31, 1909): 6–8.

[61] *Pechatnik*, 1917, no. 2–3 (August 6): 6. See also *Pechatnoe delo*, 1917, no. 2 (June 4): 8.

[62] Rodov, *Proletarskie pisateli*, 434.

kiosks, where he would stand and stare at the books behind the windows—even before he had learned to read.[63] Maksim Gorky, who corresponded with hundreds of beginning writers before and after 1917, reported that many of the workers and peasants who wrote to him similarly described some higher or inner force driving them to read and write. One worker, a turner, told Gorky that he could not sleep nights because he was so tortured by the thoughts that were inside of him trying to get out. Another, who died soon after writing to Gorky, portrayed himself as "burning" to communicate his ideas. A metalworker claimed—and Gorky reported that such expressions were typical—that a "mysterious force" (*nevedomaia sila*) drove him to write.[64]

Workers typically viewed themselves as not only inspired to write, but also sanctified as individuals by their sufferings in service to this calling. Many recalled being beaten when they were caught reading or writing at work or even by their parents at home. Il'ia Sadof'ev, for example, wrote that at the age of ten he was told by his father that "scribbling was shameful" and was beaten so severely that he was confined to bed for two weeks. Sergei Obradovich, a stereotyper in a print shop, was repeatedly tormented by his foreman for writing poems on scraps of paper. Some workers even claimed to torture themselves out of devotion—denying themselves food, for example, in order to save money to buy books.[65]

These autobiographical representations of assertive and suffering selves were mixtures of memory and conscious mythmaking. But the myth they presented is a telling one. Although insisting on their devotion to the common good, these worker-writers voiced self-identities as striving individuals, as heroes and outsiders—not as common members of the popular community or even rank-and-file soldiers in the class struggle. We can recognize here images refracted from literature: the self-assertive, superior, and rebellious individuals of bandit tales and adventure sagas,[66] or Nietzschean rebels against convention and slavishness. There are even echoes of the lives of saints (often the first literature that workers encountered), with their inspiring accounts of exceptional individual suffering in the pursuit and in the service of truth.

Like Nietzsche's supermen, but also in the Russian radical tradition, these worker-writers were individualists who realized their selves by looking beyond themselves. The worker-poet Aleksei Solov'ev, for example, recalled that after reading stories as a youth about bandits, heroes,

---

[63] Zavolokin, *Sovremennye raboche-krest'ianskie poety*, 128. See also 15, 62.

[64] Gorkii, "O pisateliakh-samouchkakh," 105–8. See also Arkhiv A. M. Gor'kogo, shifr KG-NP/A 22-4-1–2.

[65] Zavolokin, *Sovremennye raboche-krest'ianskie poety*, 53–54, 76, 107; Gorkii, "O pisatelei-samouchkakh," 106, 108.

[66] Brooks, *When Russia Learned to Read*, esp. chap. 5.

and adventurers, he dreamed of himself "becoming one of the most daring of heroes . . . ruthlessly wreaking vengeance against the powerful and especially against their lackey-parasites for squeezing the juices out of the working folk."[67] Solov'ev joined the Bolsheviks partly to realize this self-ideal in militant class struggle. But his self-image remained individualistic and heroic. Indeed, he chose as his revolutionary pseudonym "Neliudim," which may be loosely translated as "one who is not one of the ordinary people." Similarly, the Bolshevik metalworker-poet Aleksei Mashirov renamed himself "Samobytnik," expressing his own self-image as unique and original.

Worker-poets repeatedly envisioned themselves in flight, typically as eagles or falcons[68]—but not for themselves alone. In the tradition of the Russian intelligentsia, individualistic self-realization was linked to an identity and a purpose that went beyond self. Sergei Ganshin, a frequent contributor to *Pravda* in 1913–14, described himself as "an eagle from the skies . . . from which my mighty voice / like a tocsin" rings out for victory "in the great and sacred struggle."[69] Mashirov portrayed himself coming to the people in sacrificial but inspiring flight as a "meteor falling into the deep abyss."[70] Similarly, Ivan Kubikov was attracted by Gleb Uspensky's self-fantasy (apparently stimulated by his mental illness) that he could fly and that the sight of him soaring above the world would shame the oppressors and inspire the oppressed.[71] Individual exaltation and devotion to the collective were assumed to be intertwined.

But ambivalence remained. "Flight" above the common and harsh world often seemed to be for its own pleasure; idealization and assertion of the self often seemed an end in itself. Most important, at the level of ethics, the moral primacy given to workers' identity as human beings acted to undermine class identity. The purpose of the workers' movement, as voiced by these outspoken and influential workers, was not to build a "proletarian" social and cultural order, but to demolish the barriers that kept workers separate. Class struggle, in their conception, was aimed less against a different and dominant class than against class differ-

---

[67] Zavolokin, *Sovremennye raboche-krest'ianskie poety*, 115, 214.

[68] For Nietzsche's use of the symbol of human flight, see *Thus Spoke Zarathustra*, trans. R. J. Hollingdale (Hammondsworth, Eng., 1961), esp. 68–69, 89, 166, 185. Maksim Gorky used the image of flight with consciously Nietzschean intent in his well-known and influential *Pesnia o sokole* (1895).

[69] "Orel," a manuscript poem sent to Maxim Gorky, in Arkhiv A. M. Gor'kogo, shifr RAV-PG 37-13-1.

[70] See especially "Moim sobrat'iam," in "Prosnuvshaiasia zhizn'" (manuscript journal, 1913); and "Zarnitsy," *Proletarskaia pravda*, September 18, 1913, both reprinted in *Proletarskie poety*, vol. 2, ed. G. D. Vladimirskii (Leningrad, 1936), 89–90. See also "Grebtsy" (1912), ibid., 87.

[71] *Pechatnoe delo*, 1912, no. 5 (May 11): 9.

ence and domination itself. At least implicitly, this view echoed the Marxist dialectic that saw the particularistic class outlook of the proletariat as negating the very idea of class, thereby giving to the working class a messianic historical role as a "universal class" destined not only to save itself but to deliver all humanity. The neat logic of this dialectic, however, did not erase the ambivalence in the self-identity of many workers. At the heart of workers' self-ideal remained the desire to be treated respectfully, as human beings, and thus as individuals rather than as workers. There may have been more "bourgeois individualism" here than these workers cared to admit. But this ambivalence did not weaken the inspirational power of the cult of the person to explain, legitimize, and mobilize. This was an image to engrave on one's banners and fight by.

10

CULTURE BESIEGED: HOOLIGANISM
AND FUTURISM

Joan Neuberger

IN THE 1900s and 1910s, young, male, lower-class street toughs and
elite avant-garde artists in Russia both used shocking behavior and
offensive public pranks for similar reasons: to attack old authorities,
advertise an alternative set of values, and assert their own power. The
rough concurrence of hooliganism and futurism—that is, the appearance,
across class lines, of similar behaviors with similar goals, both of which
highlighted cultural conflict—illumines a number of issues critical to understanding popular culture in Russia, the relationship between what we
think of as popular and elite culture, and the role culture in general played
in the social and political world.[1]

   The hooligans' and futurists' public mockery of bourgeois propriety
and philistinism represented a deep and widespread hostility toward the
values of the traditional cultural authority of the nineteenth-century intelligentsia and toward what has been called "culturalism": the old intelligentsia's commitment to the "cultural development" of the people and
the cultural unity of the nation.[2] The futurists' attack was articulate and
explicit: they claimed that culturalist aesthetics were outdated, and they
provided their own alternatives. They called for the recognition of a new
aesthetics that more accurately reflected both the increasing complexity
of social and cultural life and new ideas about what constituted "civilization" in the modern industrial age. The hooligans' challenge to cultural-

   With the permission of the University of California Press, this essay uses in revised form
portions of chapter 3 of Joan Neuberger, *Hooliganism: Crime, Culture, and Power in St.
Petersburg, 1900–1914* (Berkeley, 1993).

   [1] I use the term *culture* in two ways in this essay: first, in the turn-of-the-century sense to
mean possessing the education, manners, awareness, and refinement necessary to be part of
civilized society; and second, in the broader, generally anthropological sense to mean the
values, beliefs, conventions, and behavior that define a group of people and provide them
with an identity.

   [2] On culturalism, see Jeffrey Brooks, *When Russia Learned to Read: Literacy and Popular
Literature, 1861–1917* (Princeton, 1985), 317–33.

ism was implicit in their attack on the respectable bourgeoisie. Their defiant assertion of "uncultured" behavior provided evidence of the failure of culturalism to civilize the common folk or assimilate them into society. Hooligans openly refused to accept the role of cultureless objects who could be transformed with a simple infusion of what the intelligentsia, playing Pygmalion, considered culture. Both futurism and hooliganism demonstrated (though not necessarily consciously) the breakdown of an apparent consensus on culture into a fragmented world of multiple cultures, a process that was beginning to take place throughout Europe at the turn of the century. The fin-de-siècle movements have been viewed almost exclusively in intellectual terms, but both hooliganism and futurism make it clear that the transformation of public behavior and public interaction among social groups was integral in the intellectual challenge to enlightenment rationalism and bourgeois respectability.

The hooligans' and futurists' outrageous behavior attracted attention specifically because their exhibitions were *public* phenomena and because they used public space in new ways. They adopted street theater as a medium because they understood (though again not necessarily consciously) the ways in which public performance (like style, clothing, and manners) defined people and identified them with a set of values. Hooligans found behavior a useful weapon in part because they lacked a sophisticated political language; futurists used dramatic public displays to fill the gap left by a stagnant literary language that inadequately captured their modern, fragmented, urban vision. The growing cities and bustling streets of the early twentieth century provided both hooligans and futurists with a new stage and a new audience. Their public antics, in turn, reveal for us some of the ways in which public social life was changing.

The similarities between the hooligans' and the futurists' public performance force us to reconsider the practice of designating any particular cultural artifact as a product solely of class. The use of "unculture" to attack the "cultured" and challenge the authority of the cultural hierarchy suggests that we miss an important dimension of the revolutionary conflict heating up in urban Russia in the 1910s if we concentrate exclusively on the sociopolitical aspects of the conflict between classes or between state and a society of classes. Culture also offers a battlefield for repression and rebellion, and the lines it draws supersede class distinctions and create their own social topography. So we have to make sure, when discussing any product of popular or elite culture, that the issues being expressed are not part of a larger phenomenon—like the challenge to culturalism or the new uses of public space—whose values or ideas cross class lines. This is not to say that hooliganism and futurism were devoid of class issues, or that hooliganism in particular was not a class conflict; but I am arguing that class was only one component of the conflicts in question. Hooliganism and futurism were each parts of a broad cultural conflict, which contained a class component, a gender component, and, for futurists, an aesthetic component as well.

Hooliganism and futurism were first and foremost struggles for power, but the weapons were cultural and they were fighting for power over cultural expression. Viewing them each as part of a broader cultural movement helps explain why a rash of petty crimes and a series of silly public displays gained extraordinary prominence. In part, they both attracted attention because their street performances were unavoidable, because they were public exhibitions in a newly awakening public age. But more important, they both dramatized cultural issues that concerned all of Russian society. They spoke to a wide dissatisfaction with the old intelligentsia's answers to the new problems of urban life. Their appearance and assertiveness demonstrated the breakdown of a consensus on the nature and purpose of culture or civilization. And they convinced a significant portion of society—including a host of prominent intellectuals and political leaders, as well as local social reformers, commercial press journalists, and reactionary defenders of the regime—that Russia's capacity to assimilate its poor into cultured society and become a civilized and politically unified nation was diminishing with each passing day.[3]

This article presents little new material on either hooliganism or futurism. I have written elsewhere about hooliganism,[4] and literary and art historians have long known that avant-garde artists, futurists in particular, used iconoclastic behavior to advertise their innovative ideas about art. However, futurist public behavior has never been presented in its full social or historical context. Juxtaposing futurism and hooliganism reveals unexpected cultural cross-class symmetries within an increasingly fragmented society; it shows the role public space played in shaping the discourses and alignments of the prerevolutionary city; and it demonstrates the importance of iconoclasm in defining popular ideologies.

---

[3] My focus on the cultural content of hooliganism and futurism draws attention away from the genuine dangers they posed. Hooligan violence and pranks were, of course, truly frightening; and while hooligans asserted their right to "act as they pleased," they obviously denied that right to their victims. Futurists, too, were only slightly less exclusionary than the institutionalized aesthetic they attacked. Before the 1917 revolution, when art remained more or less peripheral to politics, the futurists' attacks on tradition had primarily abstract ramifications. But after 1917, the futurists' aggressive and exclusionary tactics, as well as their valorization of confrontation (of course, they were not alone in any of this), contributed to the repressive art policies of the Soviet government.

[4] The discussion in this article is a much-condensed version of the arguments presented in Joan Neuberger, *Hooliganism: Crime, Culture, and Power in St. Petersburg, 1900–1914* (Berkeley, 1993); and idem, "Stories of the Street: Hooliganism in the St. Petersburg Popular Press," *Slavic Review* 48, no. 2 (Summer 1989).

Hooliganism

At the turn of the century, St. Petersburg, Moscow, and other major Russian cities witnessed a massive influx of population from the countryside. The demographic shift was accompanied by, among other things, a marked increase in the visibility of the poor, a transformation of inter-class attitudes, and a dramatic rise in the incidence of crime.[5] By 1903 at the latest, there was a widespread perception that crime was out of control.[6] Crimes of all kinds had increased, but the category that received the lion's share of attention during this period—in the press, from the police, and in the courts—was a set of crimes with exceptional social and cultural implications. Hooliganism included a wide variety of public street crimes in which young, poor, mostly male street toughs threatened, harassed, and assaulted respectable pedestrians on the streets. Their crimes ranged from shocking and offensive but basically harmless activities such as whistling and shouting or careening about in a drunken stupor, to more aggressive acts such as bumping into passersby or yelling obscenities in ladies' ears, to genuinely dangerous, even life-threatening crimes such as the back-alley stabbings and muggings that seemed to demonstrate contempt for human life. Violent hooliganism proliferated in cities and spread to the countryside, especially during and after the 1905–07 revolution; but it was the deliberately shocking forms of hooliganism that received the most attention in the press and from government officials. And it was the hooligans' extraordinary ability to irritate, shock, and offend respectable society that defined the phenomenon in the public discourse on hooliganism.

It is difficult to say precisely what hooligans were doing and why, since they rarely used words to speak for themselves. But the patterns of their actions make some points clear, so that we can read their public behavior like a text. Hooligans obviously did not invent public drunkenness, disturbing the peace, or assault and battery. But these and the other disparate offenses became noteworthy and were lumped together as hooligan-

---

[5] "Real" crime rates are notoriously difficult to pin down because crime statistics reflect only the level of official attention to crime, and public perceptions of crime fluctuations are often no more than reflections of changing attitudes. However, a variety of sources corroborate the public perception of the increase in crime, especially petty crime and, after 1907, violent street crime as well. And while popular perceptions may be inaccurate indicators of crime rates, they are exceptionally revealing of interclass relations.

[6] *Peterburgskii listok* (hereafter *PL*), November 10, 1903; *Sudebnaia gazeta*, December 14, 1903; *Iurist*, 1904, no. 8; *Otchet o deiatel'nosti S-Peterburgskoi sysknoi politsii za 1903* (St. Petersburg, 1904), 7; *S.Peterburgskie stolichnye sudebnye mirovye ustanovleniia i arestnyi dom za 1903: Otchet* (St. Petersburg, 1904), 148.

ism because they were performed in a new setting and with a new demeanor. What made hooliganism stand out was the hooligans' conspicuous lack of deference to respectable society and their eagerness to exhibit their defiance openly and theatrically. In part, their defiance consisted of dramatic and exaggerated behavior specifically associated with the lower classes: rowdy, exuberant, crude behavior that stood in sharp contrast to bourgeois public propriety. And in part their defiance consisted of ignoring the cultural geography of the city. While rich and poor had inhabited together all but the most exclusive neighborhoods in St. Petersburg,[7] in the past the poor had accepted the cultural dominance of respectable society and had behaved "properly" and submissively in public. Then, at the beginning of the twentieth century, hooligans appeared with their mockery and their threats on streets where the poor had previously acted more or less humbly or inconspicuously. The commercial press and the police department portrayed hooligans as "invaders" of the previously tranquil neighborhoods where they blocked sidewalks, sang bawdy songs, swore at the top of their lungs, and "took over whole streets." Certain of attracting and shocking an audience, hooligans drank on the streets, whistled and sang, beat one another up, and threatened to harm spectators on the main streets of the capital. Sometimes they launched surprise attacks: a group of hooligans let loose a wasp's nest in a train carriage departing the Nikolaevskii Station, while others threw cups of tea at pedestrians passing by a tea shop on Sadovaia Street.[8] The more theatrical incidents combined challenge and threat with humiliation, and occasionally hooligans invented elaborate pranks designed especially to humble respectable passersby. In the spring of 1906, for example, a couple of hooligans loosened the bolts on park benches and hid in the bushes nearby so that when unsuspecting victims tumbled to the ground, the hooligans were close enough to add to their embarrassment with loud hoots of "ecstatic" laughter.[9]

In all these incidents, it seems clear that the hooligans were well aware of the effect they had on their audience and victims and that they reveled in the shock, embarrassment, and disgust they provoked. The respectable bourgeoisie, a relatively new and insecure presence in the urban social drama, was especially sensitive to hooligan behavior and the hooligan challenge to civilized conventions because they had only recently acquired the right to number themselves among the cultured. Outward,

[7] James H. Bater, *St. Petersburg: Industrialization and Change* (Montreal, 1976), 196–201, 373–80.

[8] "Dnevnik prikliuchenii: Khuliganskaia prodelka," *PL*, July 14, 1905; "Dnevnik prikliuchenii: Dikie detskie nravy," *PL*, August 24, 1904.

[9] E. M., "Iz kipy zaiavlenii: Bezobraziia v Tavricheskom sadu," *PL*, July 27, 1906.

public signs of culture, such as the mastery of proper behavior, were equally meaningful indications of cultured status as the mastery of the certifiable classics of Russian literature.[10] Thus, the street provided a stage both for those who wished to display their civilized status and for those who wished to challenge it. No street provided a better stage than Nevsky Prospect. Although prostitutes, beggars, and criminals had long appeared on Nevsky, the outcry against improper behavior reverberated louder still when hooligans began aggressively displaying their defiance on that last bastion of respectability.

In some ways, the most characteristic form of hooliganism was the harassment of women. Hooligans shouted obscenities at them, needlessly bumped into them, pulled ribbons from their hair, whistled in their ears. In 1906, hooligans selling pornographic pictures shoved their offensive wares under the noses of respectable young girls and women on Nevsky Prospect.[11] Here, as elsewhere, hooligans used defiant displays of crude culture to challenge respectability, but these were not daring criminals—they appeared in force only when power and authority were already weak. Just as hooligans chose to act when and where state power was weakest, they often chose the most vulnerable victims to torment. Whether or not women consciously upheld the values of respectability more tenaciously than men, women's respectability was considered more likely to be damaged by exposure to such "vices" as public drinking, verbal taunts, and pornographic displays. The victimization of women clearly shows that hooliganism was first and foremost a struggle over power: the power to define street behavior and to assert control over the streets. Not only was pestering women a relatively effortless display of hooligan power, it had the added benefit of threatening the ability of respectable men to protect their womenfolk from the dangers and vices of the street.

The hooligans' unruly and defiant behavior and the fact that it occurred on streets previously controlled by respectable conventions exaggerated their menace in the eyes of their audience and gave them a new kind of power. Hooliganism might be seen as an everyday, modern, urban version of the humorous and parodistic activities Mikhail Bakhtin detected in his famous study of the carnival in Rabelais, which European historians have found so useful for explaining early modern popular culture.[12] Because the carnival stood outside everyday life as an exceptional

---

[10] Jeffrey Brooks has described their preference for the classics in "Popular Philistinism and the Course of Russian Modernism," in *History and Literature: Theoretical Problems and Russian Case Studies*, ed. Gary Saul Morson (Stanford, 1986).

[11] G. B——n, "Bor'ba s pornografiei," *Peterburgskaia gazeta*, August 6, 1906.

[12] Mikhail Bakhtin, *Rabelais and His World*, trans. Helene Iswolsky (Bloomington, Ind., 1984). Among other historians who have mined Bakhtin's insights, see Natalie Zemon

occurrence and a temporary event, with its own circumscribed rituals, it provided a cover under which the powerless could use parody and bawdy humor to safely, symbolically, and temporarily reverse the hierarchy of power without threatening real social or political structures. Hooligans combined similar tactics—crude humor, mockery, street theater—with threats of violence (or real violence) to subvert the *actual* balance of power, on a small scale, on the streets. And they were successful. Their power to "control the streets," or at least create an illusion of control, transformed public behavior all over the capital and transformed inter-class attitudes as well.[13] Hooligans used obnoxious and "uncultured" behavior to make a mockery of respectable behavior and to challenge the "cultured" values underlying respectable conventions. Their victims felt that the capital was being inundated with "uncultured savages" and that Russia's hold on civilization was, as a result, slipping away.[14]

I certainly do not mean to romanticize hooligans as some kind of unsung heroes of the street—most of their behavior seems as simpleminded, destructive, dangerous, and unpleasant to me as it was to their turn-of-the-century audience. But, heroic or not, their unpalatable actions were a form of rebellion during the last years of imperial rule, and a significant form. Though genuinely dangerous and frightening, hooliganism was creative in its own way; but it was the creativity of people too inarticulate to produce poems, plays, or songs and too alienated to join in political protest. Hooliganism expressed the same anger over powerlessness that

---

Davis, "The Reasons of Misrule," in *Society and Culture in Early Modern France* (Stanford, 1975); and Carlo Ginzburg, *The Nightbattles* (London, 1983).

[13] Hooliganism was a serious threat rather than a humorous one because it occurred every day on the streets, rather than at the specified and limited time of carnival. It would be interesting to know the extent to which Bakhtin was cognizant of the parallels between his Rabelaisian carnival and contemporary hooliganism. It seems virtually impossible for him to have been oblivious to hooliganism and the outcry against it in both late imperial and early Soviet Moscow. Resonances of hooligan pranksterish inversion, hooliganlike combinations of violence, mockery, and humiliation, and intimidating hooligan misogyny occur throughout Bakhtin's vision of Rabelais. Bakhtin may also have been influenced by the futurist permutation of hooliganism: *Rabelais* is filled with echoes of Mayakovsky's costumes and grand gestures and Khlebnikov's "Zaklatie smekhom," both cousins of street hooligans. For example, Bakhtin writes that "all the scenes of thrashing in Rabelais' novel . . . are profoundly ambivalent; everything in them is done with laughter and for laughter's sake, et le tout en riant." *Rabelais and his World*, 208; see also 1–58, 196–217. For more on Bakhtin and hooliganism, see Neuberger, *Hooliganism*, 67, 152, 157.

[14] On the language depicting the tension between the savage and the civilized in the press reports of hooliganism, see Neuberger, *Hooliganism*, chaps. 1, 5. The recent literature on concepts of civilization and its antonyms is large and growing; relevant here are James Clifford, *The Predicament of Culture: Twentieth-Century Ethnography, Literature, and Art* (Cambridge, Mass., 1988); and Marianna Torgovnick, *Gone Primitive: Savage Intellects, Modern Lives* (Chicago, 1990).

motivated other forms of lower-class or working-class protest. But lacking discipline (among other things), hooligans manifested their anger in destructive and hostile forms. Their arsenal consisted of the most basic building blocks of identity. Spontaneous behavior rather than learned ideology or formulated grievances conveyed their message as powerfully as any strike or demonstration. Cultural weapons were especially potent in the 1910s because culture in general and the state of Russian culture in particular were central to the public discourse in Russian society at the turn of the century and into the 1910s—a point that historians have, curiously, overlooked.[15] The fact that the peculiar crimes of hooliganism became so deeply troubling and widely discussed is, I think, evidence of a sensitivity to cultural issues that permeated educated society at the time. Although some of the more hysterical observers exaggerated the hooligan threat and many of the traditional intelligentsia (especially jurists) dismissed it, other responsible commentators saw in hooliganlike manifestations of crime, violence, and amorality a sign of deepening hostility to cultured society as a whole and reason to fear for Russia's future.[16]

Futurism

Like hooligans, futurist poets, painters, musicians, and dramatists were rebellious, confrontational, and self-consciously crude or "anticultured." And like hooliganism, futurism embedded serious issues in pranksterish behavior. The significant aesthetic message that futurists sent conveyed a belief that the great artists and artistic traditions of the past had no relevance for the present, and that their power to influence succeeding generations had become a stultifying straitjacket. They called for "Pushkin,

[15] Discussions of culture filled the journals and newspapers in the 1910s, the most famous being the symposium *Vekhi* (St. Petersburg, 1909) and the response it provoked. Jeffrey Brooks has explored some aspects of the discourse on culture in unpublished portions of his dissertation, "Liberalism, Literacy, and the Idea of Culture: Russia, 1905–1914" (Stanford, 1972)—as have a few others who have written about major figures in the discussions, such as Richard Pipes, *Struve: Liberal on the Right, 1905–1944* (Cambridge, Mass., 1980); and Avril Pyman, *The Life of Aleksandr Blok* (New York, 1979). Nevertheless, this important topic awaits systematic research.

[16] In one of his numerous essays on popular attitudes after 1905, Aleksandr Blok cited a hooligan song as evidence of the deep hostility between the people and cultured society. See "Stikhiia i kul'tura," originally published in part in *Nasha gazeta*, January 6, 1909, published in full in the literary anthology *Italia* (St. Petersburg, 1909). See also *Gorodskoe delo*, 1913, no. 4; I. V. Gessen, "Vnutrennaia zhizn'," *Ezhegodnik gazety Rech' na 1913 god* (St. Petersburg, 1913), 31–32; Petr Struve, "Velikaia Rossiia," *Russkaia mysl'*, 1908, no. 1; A. E. Riabchenko, *O bor'be s khuliganstvom, vorovstvom, i brodiazhnichestvom* (St. Petersburg, 1914).

Dostoevsky, Tolstoy, etc., etc., to be thrown overboard from the ship of modernity."[17] The futurists assailed (what they imagined to be) the bourgeoisie because they saw the fetters of traditional aesthetic authority symbolized in the philistine commercialization of culture, in the bourgeoisie's superficial, unreflective reverence for the great works of the past, and in the equally deadening restrictions on behavior embodied in bourgeois respectability. Benedikt Livshits, the astute if eccentric chronicler of prerevolutionary futurism, described his friends' disgust with bourgeois manners and commercialization: "We were choking in a sea of well-intentioned, legalized triviality, and the energy with which a handful of people were trying to clamber out of this putrid mess of necrotic conventions was already prompting the legitimate suspicions of the powers that be."[18] The futurists' attack on the Russian literary canon and its conventional readers originated in the same impulse as the hooligans' invasion of Nevsky Prospect. Livshits captured the invasion well in his depiction of the painters Aleksandra Ekster, Natalia Goncharova, and Ol'ga Rozanova: arriving from the provinces, these "Scythian riders" galloped into Moscow and St. Petersburg to challenge the refinement, pretension, and westernism that reigned there[19]—not unlike the hooligans who infiltrated the main streets of the capital from their outposts in the slums on the city's periphery.

The futurists were hardly the first artists to challenge or reject past models of artistic achievement or the conventional tastes of their contemporaries. But rebellion and iconoclasm take forms specific to time and place. In Russia in the 1910s, the most important form of artistic rebellion—futurism—was hooliganistic. The futurists' most famous public pranks were designed to "shock the philistine," as Livshits put it,[20] and thereby both symbolize and attract attention to their more serious aesthetic iconoclasm. Like hooligans, they used the streets in new ways to create and seize a new kind of authority. They freed art from institutional control by exhibiting paintings and reciting poetry right on the streets.[21]

---

[17] "Poshchechina obshchestvennomu vkusu" (A Slap in the Face of Public Taste). This notorious manifesto was first published in the futurist collection of the same name (Moscow, 1912); it has been translated and republished numerous times. See Vladimir Markov, *Russian Futurism: A History* (Berkeley, 1968), 45–46; and Carl Proffer et al., eds., *Russian Literature of the 1920s: An Anthology* (Ann Arbor, Mich., 1987), 542.

[18] *The One and a Half-Eyed Archer*, trans. John E. Bowlt (Newtonville, Mass., 1977), 149.

[19] Ibid., 128–29; M. N. Yablonskaya, *Women Artists of Russia's New Age, 1900–1935*, ed. and trans. Anthony Parton (London, 1990), 117.

[20] Livshits, *Archer*, 121. He was referring here to the futurists' manifesto, "A Slap in the Face of Public Taste," but a similar spirit was apparent in all futurist productions.

[21] Camilla Gray, *The Russian Experiment in Art: 1863–1922* (New York, 1962), 114.

Mikhail Larionov, Natalia Goncharova, Vladimir Mayakovsky, David Burliuk, and others strutted about Moscow in 1912 and 1913 (and later in provincial capitals) with painted faces and wooden spoons or radishes in their lapels. Their decorated faces and outrageous clothes drew crowds of speechless onlookers, whom they tried to shock and entertain by declaiming poetry, reciting nonsense, or advertising that evening's public reading or lecture.[22] They made it clear that they viewed style as a powerful agent of change and a serious medium for expressing important cultural messages. In one of the many manifestos futurists produced, Larionov and Ilya Zdanevich claimed, "We paint ourselves because a clean face is offensive, because we want to herald the unknown, to rearrange life."[23] For Livshits, one of the less exhibitionist of the futurists, face painting not only had dramatic shock effect, but also could be used to assert one's independence from bourgeois philistinism and rebel against the weight and pomposity of artistic tradition.[24]

In a more serious vein, futurists defied artistic convention and "shocked the philistine" by creating serious works of art that appropriated elements of the culture society considered "uncultured." They rejected the realism and social didacticism of the nineteenth century as well as the ethereal aestheticism of their symbolist contemporaries. Instead, the futurists invaded the territory of "proper art" with the coarse, the crude, the primitive, the childlike, the blasphemous, and the erotic, all previously considered unfit for the realms of high culture—and they relished the discomfort they provoked.[25] Goncharova painted saints like peasants. Larionov depicted ordinary barbers and soldiers in anything-but-heroic poses. Livshits portrayed Burliuk's creative method as the behavior of a wild animal, celebrating the primitivism and destructiveness he found, for example, in Burliuk's response to a reading of Rimbaud:

> In front of my very eyes Burliuk was devouring his own god, his momentary idol. That's a real carnivore! The way he licked his teeth, the aping triangle

[22] Markov, *Russian futurism*, 133–38; Livshits, *Archer*, 141–42; Gray, *The Russian Experiment*, 115, 186; Edward J. Brown, *Mayakovsky: A Poet in the Revolution* (Princeton, 1973), 43–44; Ilya Zdanevich and Mikhail Larionov, "Why We Paint Ourselves: A Futurist Manifesto," in *Russian Art of the Avant-Garde: Theory and Criticism, 1902–1934*, ed. and trans. John E. Bowlt (New York, 1976), 79–83.

[23] Zdanevich and Larionov, "Why We Paint Ourselves," 83.

[24] Livshits, *Archer*, 204.

[25] Gray, *The Russian Experiment*, 106–8, 137; John E. Bowlt, "David Burliuk, the Father of Russian Futurism," *Canadian-American Slavic Studies* (hereafter *CASS*) 20, nos. 1–2 (Spring–Summer 1986): 17, 29; Markov, *Russian Futurism*, 33–35, 42; Patricia Carden, "The Aesthetic of Performance in the Russian Avant-Garde," *CASS* 19, no. 4 (Winter 1985); 375.

on his knee: 'The whole world belongs to me!' Could the Makovskys and Gumilevs withstand a folk-giant like this! . . . And how tempting is this pred-atoriness! Wherever you look, the world lies before you in utter nakedness, around her tower beskinned mountains, like bloody chunks of smoking meat. Seize it, tear it, get your teeth into it, crush it, create it anew—it's all yours, yours![26]

Primitivism in modern art had numerous sources, but among them—at least in Russia—one cannot help seeing the hooligan's impudent grin (or the real knife in his hand). Such futurist gestures perfectly adapted the dualism inherent in the boulevard-press discourse on hooliganism—its coarseness in the face of propriety and tradition, its seriousness and prankishness, its pettiness and its genuine challenge to cultural verities.

The futurists' most famous synthesis of serious artistic statement with dramatic attack on artistic tradition and assault on bourgeois culture was the manifesto with the distinctly hooligan title "A Slap in the Face of Public Taste."[27] Published in 1912 and signed by Burliuk, Aleksei Kru-chenykh, Mayakovsky, and Velemir Khlebnikov, the manifesto com-bined a challenge to the authority of past literary masters (this is where they threw "Pushkin, Dostoevsky, Tolstoy, etc., etc." overboard) with an attack on the superficial philistine standards of artistic merit that seemed to determine a work's success: "And if *for the first time* the filthy marks of your 'common sense' and 'good taste' remain in our lives, nevertheless, *for the first time* the lightning flashes of the New Future Beauty of the Self-Sufficient word are already on them."[28] The manifesto also promised the coming of a radical new art, but it was the futurists' rejection of the established masters that created a sensation.[29]

No one was more successful at fusing the playfulness and seriousness of futurism, at rejecting the authority of traditional aesthetics while re-taining a respect for its achievements, and at rejecting realism's social didacticism while addressing pressing social themes than Vladimir Maya-kovsky. His iconoclasm was meant to confront directly the prejudices and values of his audience, to provoke, offend, and display open contempt. In "We Also Want Meat," Mayakovsky welded lyricism and violence with brutal imagery rejecting poetic tradition:

[26] Livshits, *Archer*, 42; see also Markov, *Russian Futurism*, 33–34.

[27] See n. 16 above.

[28] Markov, *Russian Futurism*, 46.

[29] Elizabeth Kridl Valkenier disagrees, arguing that the futurists achieved public promi-nence only after Repin blamed the futurists' iconoclasm for indirectly inciting a mentally deranged icon painter to deface a Repin painting, an act widely deplored as hooliganism. "Il'ia Repin and David Burliuk," *CASS* 20, nos. 1–2 (Spring–Summer 1986): 55–57.

Soldiers I envy you!

You have it good!

Here on a shabby wall are the scraps of human brains, the imprint of
shrapnel's five fingers. How clever that hundreds of cut off human
heads have been affixed to a stupid field.

Yes, yes, yes it's more interesting for you!

You don't need to think that you owe Pushkin twenty kopecks and
why does Yablonovsky write articles.

. . . .

For us—the young poets—Futurism is the toreador's red cloak, it is
needed only for the bulls (poor bulls!—I compared them to the
critics).

. . . .

Today's poetry—is the poetry of strife.

Each word must, like a soldier in the army, be made of meat that is
healthy, of meat that is red!

Those who have it—join us!

Never mind that we used to be unjust.

When you tear along in a car through hundreds of persecuting enemies,
there's no point in sentimentalizing, "Oh a chicken was crushed under
the wheels."[30]

The futurists' various artistic experiments and public extravaganzas were
an attempt to create a new realism able to convey the fragmentation and
cultural complexity of the modern industrial city—an attempt in their
own words, "to join art to life."[31] The chaotic, violent, and materialistic
world ushered in by the process of urbanization and the trauma of the
1905–7 revolution required a new kind of social message—one that reflected an understanding of the complexity of society, a cynicism about
traditional culture and existing political methods for change, and yet a
continued faith in the possibility of transformation. Their message also
required a new language that could transcend the debasement of language
in the ubiquitous commercial press and that recognized the failure of traditional realism to capture the fragmentation of daily life and psyche.[32]

---

[30] Trans. Helen Segall, in *The Ardis Anthology of Russian Futurism*, ed. Carl Proffer and
Ellendea Proffer (Ann Arbor, Mich., 1980), 187–88 (originally published in *Nov'*, November 16, 1914.

[31] Larionov wrote, "We have joined art to life. After the long isolation of artists, we have
loudly summoned life and life has invaded art, it is time for art to invade life. The painting
of our faces is the beginning of the invasion. That is why our hearts are beating so."
Zdanevich and Larionov, "Why We Paint Ourselves," 81.

[32] On language in journalism after 1907, see Neuberger, *Hooliganism*, chap. 5.

With typical pragmatism, cynicism, and optimism, Larionov redefined the achievements of civilization: "We declare the genius of our day to be: trousers, jackets, shoes, tramways, buses, aeroplanes, railways, magnificent ships—what an enchantment—what a great epoch unrivalled in world history.[33] Larionov wanted to join art to life, but he meant a life unfettered by social conventions and free from philistine expectations. This dual goal was at the heart of the basic contradiction in futurism: on the one hand was its attraction to popular or mass culture and its belief that art has a genuine social purpose, and on the other hand was its arcane aestheticism. Camilla Gray condemned the futurists as "rude," "ludicrous," "twisted," and "naive," but she found in their "frantic desire for self-advertisement . . . the social conscience that has always been so active in the Russian artist."[34] Yet their rejection of their middlebrow audience and their search for pure forms in abstract painting, *zaum* (transrational) poetry, and dissonant music isolated them from a mass audience and from the street spirit that inspired them. And their aestheticism and modernist social sensibility differed radically from the "social conscience" of the old intelligentsia.

In practice, "joining art to life" often meant staging a theatrical confrontation between art and life. This is not the contradiction it seems. The dramatic affronts to bourgeois respectability served to illustrate the lifelessness of propriety in contrast to the genuine vitality the futurists possessed, with their crude manners and spontaneous nonsense. Futurist public performances always included a lively interaction with the audience, whether in a theater, lecture hall, or cabaret or on the street. In public readings and lectures, the futurists went beyond the theoretical attack of their manifestos and insulted their audience directly.[35] At a 1913 reading-performance ("The First Evening of the Speech Creators"), Mayakovsky offended and provoked the audience by addressing the military officers in the front rows as "folds of fat in the stalls." He singled out a young man, shouting at him (as a representative of all respectable society), "You men, you all have cabbage stuck in your mouths." And he condemned the artificiality of the respectable by pointing at a young girl and proclaiming, "You women, the powder is thick upon you. You look like oysters in shells of objects!" Soon, however, the whole audience, according to Livshits, "learn[ed] a rapid lesson in *budetlianin* [futurist]

[33] Gray, *The Russian Experiment*, 136.

[34] Ibid., 106–7, 116, 137.

[35] The manifestos also became more offensive. "Go to Hell," the manifesto that opens the 1914 anthology *Futurists: Roaring Parnassus*, consisted largely of personal insults without theory to justify them. The symbolists were "crawling little old men of Russian literature." Markov, *Russian Futurism*, 168.

good taste" and settled in for the fun of the repartee, trading insults with the speakers.[36]

Despite the generally good humor that greeted many of their performances, the futurists reveled in their role as outsiders, much as the hooligans seemed to take pleasure in theirs. At "The First Evening of the Speech Creators" and in his infamous libretto for the collaborative opera *Victory over the Sun*, Kruchenykh provoked audiences with maniacal and incomprehensible utterances. On other occasions, Kruchenykh declared that his poem "dyr-bul-shchyl" was "more Russian than all the poetry of Pushkin," and he often claimed he had "a sensual longing to be booed." It was Kruchenykh who initiated the futurist convention of throwing tea at the audience, adopted later by Mayakovsky, Burliuk, and Vasilii Kamensky on their seventeen-city provincial tour of futurist performances in 1913.[37]

The more sophisticated members of the futurists' audiences came to their performances for the fun of the scandal and participated with bemused detachment. Although the performances were well attended by the fashionable world of the capitals, at least some portion of the audience must have shared the futurists' distaste for bourgeois culture. And for the most part, it was understood that the attack on "Pushkin, Tolstoy, Dostoevsky, etc., etc." was an attack on philistine reading habits and the constrictions inherent in canonization, rather than an attack on the artists themselves. Even Livshits was incensed by the belligerent tone and style of "A Slap in the Face of Public Taste": "I slept with Pushkin under my pillow," he wrote, "and who didn't?"[38] This bemused appreciation was evident at the futurists' most ambitious undertaking: the tandem performances on alternating evenings of *Vladimir Mayakovsky: A Tragedy* and *Victory over the Sun* in December 1913. Mayakovsky later claimed that "they cat-called like hell"; and at one point during *Victory over the Sun* spectators shouted, "You're an ass yourself," and some "heavy fruit buzzed by [one actor's] ear." But for the most part, the audience responded to Kazimir Malevich's striking modernist sets and costumes, to

---

[36] Livshits, *Archer*, 150–51. Although it is hard to imagine a contingent of officers at a futurist reading (as spectators, not guards), officers and soldiers appear regularly in descriptions of such audiences. See K. Tomachevsky, "Vladimir Mayakovsky," in *Victory over the Sun*, trans. Ewa Bartos and Victoria Nes Kirby, *Drama Review* 15, no. 4 (Fall 1971): 99–100.

[37] Markov, *Russian Futurism*, 138; Livshits, *Archer*, 150–51; Brown, *Mayakovsky*, 44–46. Throwing tea became a regular event at futurist evenings and a symbol of the futurists' insolent challenge to their spectators.

[38] Livshits, *Archer*, 121.

Kruchenykh's nonsense libretto, and to Mikhail Matiushin's cacophonous music with good-natured, though vocal, amusement.[39]

For the futurists, the role of society's misfits was an important source of creativity. As outcasts, they could transcend conventional behavior and thought, which allowed them to challenge the standards that defined them as misfits. Just as hooligans challenged conventional behavior in order to "act as they pleased" in public, to quote one young hooligan,[40] the escape from convention freed the futurists to transcend traditional aesthetic conventions as well and exercise their creativity in new directions. The spontaneity of their street theater, their use of "inappropriate" elements of popular culture, their collaboration with one another and with their audiences—these unconventional elements were the building blocks of the futurists' imaginative achievements.

The freedom of the outcast was also explored by artists who were not futurists but who shared with them a fascination for hooliganlike behavior. Aleksei Remizov, for example, was intrigued by and identified with outsiders and socially marginal characters (such as minstrels [*skomorokhi*] and holy fools), and he was well known among his friends as an irreverent prankster. Pranks and imaginative play created for him a theater in which to cross the boundaries of socially acceptable behavior and free himself to imagine alternative worlds. Viktor Shklovsky, who participated in Remizov's "The Great Free Order of Monkeys" (a "theater without makeup and masks") and who parlayed the futurists' verbal experimentation into one of the basic tenets of Russian formalism, claimed about their group that "we play holy fools in order to be free."[41]

Fascination with some form of hooliganism was also a feature in the work of some of Russia's most prominent writers. Aleksandr Blok was unusual in his sensitivity to the conflict that divided the cultured from the uncultured in late imperial society, but he also believed that some hooligan characteristics—iconoclasm, blasphemy, vulgarity, drunkenness, and profligacy—were "an essential if contradictory part of the Russians' spiritual nature," that is, of Russia as a whole.[42] Blok viewed the intelligen-

---

[39] Ibid., 161; Markov, *Russian Futurism*, 146–47; Tomachevsky, "Vladimir Mayakovsky," 100.

[40] A. I. Svirskii, "Peterburgskie khuligany," in *Peterburg i ego zhizn'* (St. Petersburg, 1914), 252 and passim.

[41] This material on Remizov, including the quotations, is from Greta Nachtailer Slobin, "The Ethos of Performance in Remizov," *CASS* 19, no. 4 (Winter 1985): 419–25.

[42] Kornei Chukovsky, *Alexander Blok as Man and Poet*, trans. and ed. Diana Burgin and Katherine O'Connor (Ann Arbor, Mich., 1982), 136–37. The quotation is Chukovsky's characterization of Blok.

tsia's alienation, creativity, and political opposition as akin to hooligan alienation and defiance. But, of course, such a view meant recognizing that there had long been something to challenge: an entrenched conservatism, resistance to change, or the weight of tradition. Blok declared his identification with the iconoclasts rather than with the traditional or the philistine, commercial classes whom the hooligans and futurists assaulted. But he also understood that hooliganism represented an essentially destructive force and, because educated society (himself included) had virtually no understanding of the common people, an unpredictable one as well. The action in Blok's great poem of the revolution, "Dvenadtsat'" (The Twelve), revolves around the paradoxically creative potential (characteristic of hooliganism) in violence, death, and destruction. Stylistically, too, Blok provocatively juxtaposed a refined poetic sensibility with folk rhythms, *chastushki*, and the harsh, foul language of the streets. And he left the bourgeoisie stranded forlornly on a windswept corner with its tail between its legs.[43]

Sergei Esenin's attraction to hooliganism was less abstract than Blok's and more personally troubling, as well as more artistically stimulating. Esenin adopted a hooligan persona in his poems "Hooligan" and "A Hooligan's Confession," but he also engaged in public hooligan acts. He boasted about chopping up icons for firewood to heat tea, and in 1919 he painted obscene and blasphemous verse on the walls of the Novodevichi convent.[44] Adopting the pose of a brazen, vulgar hooligan allowed Esenin to reenact his own crossing of both cultural (especially religious) and class boundaries in his journey from peasant to poet. "A Hooligan's Confession" captivatingly alternates lyrical self-knowledge with vulgar self-assertion. Andrei Belyi's short poem "A Little Hooligan Song" depicts a jaded and ironic indifference in the face of death by joining the light singsong of a nursery rhyme with a violent hooligan's cynical disregard for the value of others' lives.[45]

Although these writers did not condone hooligan crimes, they saw hooliganism as indicative of an attitude that resonated throughout Russian culture in the 1910s. They recognized the hooligans' behavior as a

[43] "Dvenadtsat'" was originally published in *Znamia truda*, February 18, 1918.

[44] The painted lines included "Look at the fat thighs / Of this obscene wall. / Here the nuns at night / Remove Christ's trousers." Gordon McVay, *Esenin: A Life* (Ann Arbor, Mich., 1976), 119–20. "Khuligan" was published in *Znamia*, 1920, no. 5; and "Ispoved' khuligana" in *Poeziia revoliutsionnoi Moskvy*, November 1920.

[45] Andrei Belyi, "Khuliganskaia pesenka," in *Korabli* (Moscow, 1907), reprinted in *Vecherniaia zaria*, May 7, 1907. On the multiple hooligan motifs in Belyi's great novel *Petersburg*, see Neuberger, *Hooliganism*, chap. 3.

challenge to respectability and to the old intelligentsia's culturalism; but the artists embraced those challenges as a source of creativity—or as a purifying destruction necessary for some kind of rebirth.

Obviously, there is a world of difference between young thugs throwing tea out a doorway at unsuspecting pedestrians and artists throwing tea on spectators who come expecting scandal and pay for the privilege. However, the manifold differences in class, purpose, context, danger, and audience cannot efface the importance of the similarities between hooliganism and futurism. The two phenomena were responses to, and agents of, the same broad cultural changes taking place in Russian society. Despite differences in social background and motivation, the similarities between hooliganism and futurism show us how widespread and important cultural issues were in defining social identities, and they demonstrate the power of the public street as an arena for cultural conflict and public statement.

Geographic and social mobility had made urban society increasingly diverse by the early twentieth century, and it was also more diverse culturally. The huge influx of rural people made a clear imprint on popular awareness; growing literacy and wealth created new tastes and new markets for commercial culture. These changes challenged the established power of the highly educated to determine the course of cultural development. At the same time, of course, the city was the site of devastating poverty and disease, increasing crime, and disruptive revolutionary protest. In this environment of danger and excitement, cultural ferment and social tension, people learned to identify themselves and define social problems through public interaction of various kinds—whether right on the streets or in newspapers, songs, films, and cabaret and music-hall performances reflecting public confrontations on the streets of the city. Hooligans and futurists each dramatized some of the new cultural transactions occurring at the time and thus helped clarify social identities as well as cultural agendas, as responses to hooliganism and futurism show.

Both hooligans and futurists used public space in ways that precluded passive responses. Their direct confrontations and public performances forced everyone who participated in public street life to react in some way. Only those who were insulated from the streets could manage to transcend the fray and dismiss the phenomena as insignificant. Responses to hooliganism and futurism were similar in that the critics who attacked one attacked the other and those who dismissed one dismissed the other, often in the same terms. Significantly, those who paid these cultural rebels the least attention were also those who failed to appreciate the cultural challenge inherent in their ill-mannered public behavior. The middlebrow commercial press, read primarily (though not exclusively) by the kind of respectable philistines hooligans and futurists tried to offend, portrayed both hooligan ruffians and futurist artists as ill-mannered, uncultured savages out to destroy civilization. The "old" intelligentsia (liberal and socialist political activists, well-educated professionals in law and literature) tended to dismiss the importance of both hooliganism and futurism. Although local courts and police treated hooliganism as a serious crime problem, many jurists (often members of the most elite circles of the old intelligentsia) believed that the furor over hooliganism was exaggerated, that hooliganism was not a serious enough crime to demand such attention, and that those most frightened by it were themselves too antagonistic to the lower classes to see hooliganism for what they (the jurists) believed it really was: merely a rash of petty crimes. Although the futurists' publications and productions received some attention among artists, their public antics were long dismissed or ignored in serious literary circles and journals. Notably, the artists were often dismissed as "hooligans." Vasilii Kandinsky labeled "A Slap in the Face of Public Taste" a case of "hooliganism," and Burliuk was known as "a hooligan of the palette."[46] The implication was that, just as hooliganism was no real crime, Burliuk was no real innovator. Burliuk's wild, exhibitionist behavior was perceived as purposeless and unnecessary self-indulgence, just as hooliganism was seen as motiveless, petty self-assertion.

Time has proven the philistine boulevard press, despite its hysterical tone, to have been more perceptive (if less sympathetic) than the guardians of law and high culture. In retrospect, it is clear that the cultural conflicts embodied in the hooligans' and futurists' mockery of bourgeois respectability and their challenge to traditional cultural standards did indeed represent a deep-seated hostility toward elite culture—a hostility that erupted during and after the 1917 revolutions in a variety of forms of iconoclasm and that, in art, represented one of the waves of modernist innovation that changed the course of art in the twentieth century.[47] Ironically, the similarities in the hooligans' and the futurists' challenges revealed the fragmentation of the Russian educated elite and of Russian society as a whole, as hooligans and futurists dramatized difference and as members of educated society split over their responses to the public challenges to traditional cultural authority. For those who took the chal-

---

[46] Markov, *Russian Futurism*, 392 n. 26; Bowlt, "Burliuk," 25. For similar epithets applied to films and filmmakers, see Richard Taylor, "The Tenth Muse; Or, How Parnassus Learned to Stop Worrying and Love the Art of the Hottentots," in *Issues in Russian Literature before 1917: Selected Papers of the Third World Congress for Soviet and East European Studies*, ed. J. Douglas Clayton (Columbus, Ohio, 1989).

[47] Richard Stites, "Revolutionary Iconoclasm," in *Revolutionary Dreams* (Oxford, 1989), 59–78.

lenges seriously, hooligan and futurist defiance called into question Russia's place among civilized nations and the civilizing mission that had distinguished Russian educated society over the last century. As futurists forged new paths in artistic expression and as hooligans exhibited their resistance to the enlightenment efforts of the elite, many members of educated society were beginning to conclude that a large portion of the population was impervious to cultural development. The increasing fragmentation and complexity of Russian social and cultural life was more readily acknowledged (though not approvingly) in the boulevard press than among the country's political leaders, including opposition liberals and radicals, with their continued (though perhaps shaken) faith in the intelligentsia's mission to civilize the Russian people.

Neither hooliganism nor the hooligan behavior of the avant-garde were unique to Russia, but they took on special significance there because cultural issues enjoyed extraordinary importance in Russian society. In the absence of a developed commercial culture, education had long matched wealth as a mark of status, especially in urban Russia. Furthermore, for approximately a century, the educated elite had been motivated by a social commitment to an enlightenment vision of civilizing Russia and its people, the single-mindedness of which distinguished the Russian elite from its Western counterparts. The challenge to cultural dominance also took on special significance in Russia because it occurred in a politically charged period and thus fed political hostilities. Hooligans and futurists contributed to an environment in which old authorities were deemed obsolete and challenges to their power were increasingly virulent and uncompromising, as well as widely misunderstood. The perceptions of drift, divisiveness, and doom that permeated Russian culture in the last years before the outbreak of World War I were to a very large extent rooted in the threatening and iconoclastic displays that publicly, often physically challenged established aesthetic and behavioral values, dramatized cultural difference, and rejected cultural tutelage.

SELECT BIBLIOGRAPHY

RUSSIAN SOCIETY AND LOWER-CLASS CULTURE

Bater, James H. *St. Petersburg: Industrialization and Change.* Montreal, 1976.

Bonnell, Victoria E. *Roots of Rebellion: Workers' Politics and Organizations in St. Petersburg and Moscow, 1900–1914.* Berkeley, 1983.

———, ed. *The Russian Worker.* Berkeley, 1983.

Bradley, Joseph. " 'Once You've Eaten Khitrov Soup, You'll Never Leave!' Slum Renovation in Pre-revolutionary Moscow." *Russian History* 11, no. 1 (1984): 1–28.

———. *Muzhik and Muscovite: Urbanization in Late Imperial Russia.* Berkeley, 1985.

Brooks, Jeffrey. "Readers and Reading at the End of the Tsarist Era." In *Literature and Society in Imperial Russia, 1800–1914*, edited by William Mills Todd III. Stanford, 1978.

———. "The Kopeck Novels of Early Twentieth Century Russia," *Journal of Popular Culture* 13, no. 1 (Summer 1979): 85–97.

———. *When Russia Learned to Read: Literacy and Popular Literature, 1861–1917.* Princeton, 1985.

———. "Popular Philistinism and the Course of Russian Modernism." In *History and Literature: Theoretical Problems and Russian Case Studies*, edited by Gary Saul Morson. Stanford, 1986.

———. "Competing Modes of Popular Discourse: Individualism and Class Consciousness in the Russian Print Media." In *Culture et révolution*, edited by M. Ferro and S. Fitzpatrick. Paris, 1989.

Brower, Daniel. *The Russian City between Tradition and Modernity, 1850–1900.* Berkeley, 1990.

Bushnell, John. *Mutiny amid Repression: Russian Soldiers in the Revolution of 1905.* Bloomington, Ind., 1985.

Clay, Eugene. "The Theological Origins of the Christ-Faith [Khristovshchina]." *Russian History* 15, no. 1 (1988): 21–41.

Clements, Barbara Evans, Barbara Alpern Engel, and Christine D. Worobec, eds. *Russia's Women: Accommodation, Resistance, Transformation.* Berkeley, 1991.

Clowes, Edith W., Samuel D. Kassow, and James L. West, eds. *Between Tsar and People: Educated Society and the Quest for Identity in Late Imperial Russia.* Princeton, 1991.

Eklof, Ben. "Peasant Sloth Reconsidered: Strategies of Education and Learning in Rural Russia before the Revolution." *Journal of Social History* 14, no. 3 (1981): 355–85.

———. *Russian Peasant Schools: Officialdom, Village Culture, and Popular Pedagogy, 1861–1914.* Berkeley, 1986.

———. "Kindertempel or Shack? The School Building in Late Imperial Russia (A Case Study of Backwardness)." *Russian Review* 47, no. 2 (1988): 117–43.

Eklof, Ben, and Stephen P. Frank, eds. *The World of the Russian Peasant: Post-Emancipation Culture and Society.* Boston, 1990.

Engel, Barbara. "Peasant Morality and Pre-marital Relations in Late Nineteenth-Century Russia." *Journal of Social History* 23, no. 4 (1990): 695–714.

———. *Between the Fields and the City: Women, Work, and Family in Russia, 1861–1914.* New York, 1994.

Engelstein, Laura. *The Keys to Happiness: Sex and the Search for Modernity in Fin-de-Siècle Russia.* Ithaca, N.Y., 1992.

Farnsworth, Beatrice, and Lynne Viola. *Russian Peasant Women.* New York, 1992.

Farrell, Diane. "Laughter Transformed: The Shift from Medieval to Enlightenment Humor in Russian Popular Prints." In *Russia and the World of the Eighteenth Century*, edited by R. P. Bartlett, A. G. Cross, and Karen Rasmussen. Columbus, Ohio, 1986.

Field, Daniel. *Rebels in the Name of the Tsar.* Boston, 1976.

Frank, Stephen P. "Popular Justice, Community, and Culture among the Russian Peasantry, 1870–1900." *Russian Review* 46, no. 3 (1987): 239–65.

———. "'Simple Folk, Savage Customs?' Youth, Sociability, and the Dynamics of Culture in Rural Russia, 1856–1914." *Journal of Social History* 25, no. 4 (1992): 711–36.

Freeze, Gregory L. "The Soslovie (Estate) Paradigm and Russian Social History." *American Historical Review* 91, no. 1 (1986): 11–36.

———. "The Rechristianization of Russia: The Church and Popular Religion, 1750–1850." *Studia Slavica Finlandensia* 7 (1990): 101–36.

Frierson, Cathy A. *Peasant Icons: Representations of Rural People in Nineteenth-Century Russia.* New York, 1992.

Glickman, Rose L. *Russian Factory Women: Workplace and Society, 1880–1914.* Berkeley, 1984.

Gromyko, M. M. *Traditsionnye normy povedeniia i formy obshcheniia russkikh krest'ian XIX v.* Moscow, 1986.

———. *Mir russkoi derevni.* Moscow, 1991.

Gromyko, M. M., and T. A. Listova, eds. *Russkie: Semeinyi i obshchestvennyi byt.* Moscow, 1989.

Hamm, Michael F., ed. *The City in Late Imperial Russia.* Bloomington, Ind., 1986.

Herlihy, Patricia. "Joy of the Rus': Rites and Rituals of Russian Drinking." *Russian Review* 50, no. 2 (1991): 131–47.

Ivanits, Linda J. *Russian Folk Belief.* Armonk, N.Y., 1989.

Ivanov, L. M., et al., eds. *Rossiiskii proletariat: Oblik, bor'ba, gegemoniia.* Moscow, 1970.

Johnson, Robert E. *Peasant and Proletarian: The Working Class of Moscow in the Late Nineteenth Century.* New Brunswick, N.J., 1979.

Kingston-Mann, Esther, and Timothy Mixter, eds. *Peasant Economy, Culture, and Politics of European Russia, 1800–1921.* Princeton, 1991.

Kleinbort, L. M. *Ocherki rabochei intelligentsii.* Petrograd, 1923.

Lindenmeyer, Adele. "Charity and the Problem of Unemployment: Industrial Homes in Late Imperial Russia." *Russian Review* 45, no. 1 (1986): 1–22.

Lotman, Iurii M., Lidiia Ia. Ginsburg, and Boris A. Uspenskii. *The Semiotics of Russian Cultural History*. Edited by Alexander D. Nakhimovsky and Alice Stone Nakhimovsky. Ithaca, N.Y., 1985.

Lotman, Iu. M., and B. A. Uspenskii. *The Semiotics of Russian Culture*. Edited by Ann Shukman. Ann Arbor, Mich., 1984.

McDaniel, Tim. *Autocracy, Capitalism, and Revolution in Russia*. Berkeley, 1988.

McKean, Robert B. *St. Petersburg between the Revolutions: Workers and Revolutionaries, June 1907–February 1917*. New Haven, Conn., 1990.

McReynolds, Louise. *The News under Russia's Old Regime: The Development of a Mass-Circulation Press*. Princeton, 1991.

Nekrylova, A. F. *Russkie narodnye gorodskie prazdniki, uveseleniia i zrelishcha: Konets XVIII–nachalo XX veka*. Leningrad, 1988.

Neuberger, Joan. "Stories of the Street: Hooliganism in the St. Petersburg Popular Press." *Slavic Review* 48, no. 2 (1989): 177–94.

———. *Hooliganism: Crime, Culture, and Power in St. Petersburg, 1900–1914*. Berkeley, 1993.

Pearl, Deborah. "Educating Workers for Revolution." *Russian History* 14, no. 2–4 (1988): 255–84.

Perrie, Maureen. "Folklore as Evidence of Peasant Mentality." *Russian Review* 48, no. 2 (1989): 119–43.

Ransel, David, ed. *The Family in Imperial Russia*. Bloomington, Ind., 1978.

Semyonova Tian-Shanskaia, Olga. *Village Life in Late Tsarist Russia*. Edited by David L. Ransel. Bloomington, Ind., 1993.

Smith, R. E. F., and David Christian. *Bread and Salt: A Social and Economic History of Food and Drink in Russia*. Cambridge, 1984.

Stavrou, Theofanis G., ed. *Art and Culture in Nineteenth-Century Russia*. Bloomington, Ind., 1983.

Steinberg, Mark D. *Moral Communities: The Culture of Class Relations in the Russian Printing Industry, 1867–1907*. Berkeley, 1992.

———. "Workers on the Cross: Religious Imagination in the Writings of Russian Workers, 1910–1924." *Russian Review*, forthcoming.

Stites, Richard. *Russian Popular Culture: Entertainment and Society since 1900*. Cambridge, 1992.

Thurston, Gary. "The Impact of Russian Popular Theater, 1886–1915." *Journal of Modern History* 55 (June 1983): 237–67.

———. "Theater and Acculturation in Russia from the Peasant Emancipation to the First World War." *Journal of Popular Culture* 18, no. 2 (Fall 1984): 3–16.

Wada, Haruki. "The Inner World of Russian Peasants." *Annals of the Institute of Social Science* (Tokyo) 20 (1979): 61–94.

Ware, Richard. "Some Aspects of the Russian Reading Public in the 1880s." *Renaissance and Modern Studies* 24 (1980): 18–37.

Worobec, Christine D. *Peasant Russia: Family and Community in the Post-Emancipation Period*. Princeton, 1991.

Wynn, Charters. *Workers, Strikes, and Pogroms: The Donbass–Dnepr Bend in Late Imperial Russia, 1870–1905*. Princeton, 1992.

Zelnik, Reginald E. "Russian Bebels." Parts 1, 2. *Russian Review* 35, no. 3 (1976): 249–89; 36, no. 4 (October 1976): 417–47.

———, ed. *A Radical Worker in Tsarist Russia: The Autobiography of Semën Ivanovich Kanatchikov.* Stanford, 1986.

———. " 'To the Unaccustomed Eye': Religion and Irreligion in the Experience of St. Petersburg Workers in the 1870s." *Russian History* 16, no. 2–4 (1989): 313–26.

COMPARATIVE AND THEORETICAL WORKS

Bakhtin, Mikhail. *Rabelais and His World.* Translated by Helene Iswolsky. Bloomington, Ind., 1984.

Beauroy, Jacques, Marc Bertrand, and Edward T. Gargan, eds. *The Wolf and the Lamb: Popular Culture in France from the Old Regime to the Twentieth Century.* Saratoga, Calif., 1977.

Bell, Catherine. *Ritual Theory, Ritual Practice.* Oxford, 1992.

Boon, James A. *Other Tribes, Other Scribes: Symbolic Anthropology in the Comparative Study of Cultures, Histories, Religions, and Texts.* Cambridge, 1982.

Bourdieu, Pierre. *Outline of a Theory of Practice.* Translated by Richard Nice. Cambridge, 1977.

Browne, Ray B., ed. *Popular Culture and the Expanding Consciousness.* New York, 1973.

Burke, Peter. *Popular Culture in Early Modern Europe.* New York, 1978.

Burke, Peter, and Roy Porter, eds. *The Social History of Language.* Cambridge, 1987.

Certeau, Michel de. *The Practice of Everyday Life.* Translated by Steven Rendall. Berkeley, 1984.

Chartier, Roger. *The Cultural Uses of Print in Early Modern France.* Translated by Lydia Cochrane. Princeton, 1987.

———. *Cultural History: Between Practices and Representations.* Translated by Lydia G. Cochrane. Cambridge, 1988.

———, ed. *The Culture of Print: Power and the Uses of Print in Early Modern France.* Cambridge, 1989.

Clifford, James. *The Predicament of Culture: Twentieth-Century Ethnography, Literature, and Art.* Cambridge, Mass., 1988.

Clifford, James, and George Marcus, eds. *Writing Culture: The Poetics and Politics of Ethnography.* Berkeley, 1986.

Cohen, Stanley, and Andrew Scull, eds. *Social Control and the State.* New York, 1983.

Comaroff, Jean. *Body of Power, Spirit of Resistance: The Culture and History of a South African People.* Chicago, 1981.

Corbin, Alain. *The Village of Cannibals: Rage and Murder in France, 1870.* Cambridge, Mass., 1992.

Darnton, Robert. *The Great Cat Massacre.* New York, 1984.

Davis, Natalie Zemon. *Society and Culture in Early Modern France.* Stanford, 1975.

Dirks, Nicholas B., ed. *Colonialism and Culture*. Ann Arbor, Mich., 1992.

Falassi, Alessandro, ed. *Time Out of Time: Essays on the Festival*. Albuquerque, N.M., 1987.

Feierman, Steven. *Peasant Intellectuals: Anthropology and History in Tanzania*. Madison, Wis., 1990.

Gans, Herbert J. *Popular Culture and High Culture: An Analysis and Evaluation of Taste*. New York, 1974.

Geertz, Clifford. *The Interpretation of Cultures: Selected Essays*. New York, 1973.

———. *Local Knowledge*. New York, 1983.

Giddens, Anthony. *Central Problems in Social Theory*. Berkeley, 1979.

Golby, J. M., and A. W. Purdue. *The Civilization of the Crowd: Popular Culture in England, 1750–1900*. New York, 1984.

Grafton, Anthony, and Ann Blair, eds. *The Transmission of Culture in Early Modern Europe*. Philadelphia, 1990.

Grossberg, Lawrence, Cary Nelson, and Paula Teichler, eds. *Cultural Studies*. New York, 1992.

Gurevich, Aron. *Medieval Popular Culture: Problems of Belief and Perception*. Cambridge, 1988.

Hobsbawm, Eric, and Terence Ranger, eds. *The Invention of Tradition*. Cambridge, 1983.

Howkins, Alun, and C. Ian Dyck. "'The Time's Alteration': Popular Ballads, Rural Radicalism, and William Cobbett." *History Workshop* 23 (1987): 20–38.

Hunt, Lynn, ed. *The New Cultural History*. Berkeley, 1989.

Jones, Gareth Stedman. *Languages of Class: Studies in English Working Class History, 1832–1982*. Cambridge, 1983.

Kidd, A. J., and K. W. Roberts, eds. *City, Class and Culture: Studies of Cultural Production and Social Policy in Victorian Manchester*. Manchester, 1985.

Koven, Seth. "From Rough Lads to Hooligans: Boy Life, National Culture, and Social Reform." In *Nationalisms and Sexualities*, edited by Andrew Parker et al. New York, 1992.

McKay, Ian. "Historians, Anthropology, and the Concept of Culture." *Labour/ Le Travailleur* 8–9 (1981–82): 185–241.

MacKenzie, John M., ed. *Imperialism and Popular Culture*. Manchester, 1986.

Medick, Hans. "Plebian Culture in the Transition to Capitalism." In *Culture, Ideology, and Politics*, edited by Raphael Samuel and Gareth Stedman Jones. London, 1982.

———. "'Missionaries in the Row Boat?' Ethnological Ways of Knowing as a Challenge to Social History." *Comparative Studies in Society and History* 29, no. 1 (1987): 76–98.

Muir, Edward, and Guido Ruggiero, eds. *Microhistory and the Lost Peoples of Europe*. Baltimore, 1991.

Mukerji, Chandra and Michael Schudson, eds. *Rethinking Popular Culture*. Berkeley, 1991.

Ozouf, Mona. *Festivals and the French Revolution*. Cambridge, Mass., 1988.

Pearson, Geoffrey. *Hooligan: A History of Respectable Fears*. New York, 1983.

Rabinow, Paul, and William M. Sullivan, eds. *Interpretive Social Science: A Second Look*. Berkeley, 1987.

Rancière, Jacques. *The Night of the Proletarians: The Workers' Dream in Nineteenth-Century France*. Philadelphia, 1989.

Sabean, David Warren. *Power in the Blood: Popular Culture and Village Discourse in Early Modern Germany*. Cambridge, 1984.

Sackett, Robert Eben. *Popular Entertainment, Class, and Politics in Munich, 1900–1923*. Cambridge, Mass., 1982.

Sahlins, Marshall. *Islands of History*. Chicago, 1985.

Scott, James C. *Weapons of the Weak: Everyday Forms of Peasant Resistance*. New Haven, Conn., 1985.

———. *Domination and the Arts of Resistance: Hidden Transcripts*. New Haven, Conn., 1990.

Scott, Joan Wallach. *Gender and the Politics of History*. New York, 1988.

Sider, Gerald M. *Culture and Class in Anthropology and History: A Newfoundland Illustration*. Cambridge, 1986.

Thompson, E. P. *The Making of the English Working Class*. London, 1963.

———. *Customs in Common: Studies in Traditional Popular Culture*. New York, 1991.

Weber, Eugen. *Peasants into Frenchmen: The Modernization of Rural France, 1870–1914*. Stanford, 1976.

Wuthnow, Robert, James Davison Hunter, Albert Bergesen, and Edith Kurzweil. *Cultural Analysis: The Work of Peter L. Berger, Mary Douglas, Michel Foucault, and Jürgen Habermas*. London, 1984.

Yeo, Eileen and Stephen, eds. *Popular Culture and Class Conflict, 1590–1914: Explorations in the History of Labour and Leisure*. Sussex, Eng., 1981.

INDEX

RUSSIAN HISTORY

CULTURES IN FLUX
LOWER-CLASS VALUES, PRACTICES, AND
RESISTANCE IN LATE IMPERIAL RUSSIA

Edited by
Stephen P. Frank and Mark D. Steinberg

The popular culture of urban and rural tsarist Russia revealed a
dynamic and troubled world. Stephen Frank and Mark Steinberg have
gathered here a diverse collection of essays by Western and Russian
scholars who question conventional interpretations and recall neglected
stories about popular behavior, politics, and culture. What emerges is
a new picture of lower-class life, in which traditions and innovations
intermingled and social boundaries and identities were battered and
reconstructed.

The authors vividly convey the vitality as well as the contradictions
of social life in old regime Russia, while also confronting problems of
interpretation, methodology, and cultural theory. They tell of peasant
death rites and religious beliefs, family relationships and brutalities,
defiant peasant women, folk songs, urban amusement parks, expressions of popular patriotism, the penny press, workers' notions of the
self, street hooliganism, and attempts by educated Russians to transform popular festivities. Together, the authors portray popular culture
not as a static, separate world, but as the dynamic means through
which lower-class Russians engaged the world around them.

In addition to the editors, the contributors to this volume are Daniel
R. Brower, Barbara Alpern Engel, Hubertus F. Jahn, Al'bin M.
Konechnyi, Boris N. Mironov, Joan Neuberger, Robert A. Rothstein,
and Christine D. Worobec.

Stephen P. Frank is Assistant Professor of History at the University
of California, Los Angeles. Mark D. Steinberg is Assistant Professor of
History at Yale University.

Cover photograph: Popular storyteller,
St. Petersburg (Courtesy of the
Library of Congress)

Cover design by Donald Hatch

**PRINCETON
PAPERBACKS**

ISBN 0-691-00106-5

90000

9 780691 001067